RAISING HELL

RAISING HELL

How the Center
for Investigative Reporting
Gets the Story

by DAVID WEIR *and* DAN NOYES

Addison-Wesley Publishing Company
Reading, Massachusetts • Menlo Park, California
London • Amsterdam • Don Mills, Ontario • Sydney

"Nuclear Nightmare": Reprinted from *New West,* December 3, 1979, pp. 15–34. © 1979 by Michael Singer and David Weir. Cover reprinted with permission from New York Magazine Company, Inc.

"Citizen Scaife": Reprinted from *Columbia Journalism Review,* July/August 1981, pp. 41–50. © 1981 by Karen Rothmyer. Cover reprinted with permission from Julio Fernandez.

"Teamster Madness": Reprinted from *Mother Jones,* January 1982, pp. 28–34, 53. © 1981 by Douglas Foster. "The Gospel According to LaRouche" by Dennis King, reprinted with permission of author. Illustration reprinted with permission from Marshall Arisman.

"Let Them Eat est": Reprinted from *Mother Jones,* December 1978, pp. 41–54. © 1978 by Suzanne Gordon. "Where Erhard Launders the Money" by Arnold Levinson, reprinted with permission of author. Cover reprinted with permission from *Mother Jones.*

"The Boomerang Crime": Reprinted from *Mother Jones,* November 1979, pp. 40–48. © 1979 by David Weir. Illustration reprinted with permission from *Mother Jones.*

"The Bechtel File": Reprinted from *Mother Jones,* September/October 1978, pp. 28–38. © 1978 by Mark Dowie. Illustration reprinted with permission from Lou Beach.

"The Party's Over": Reprinted from *New Times,* July 10, 1978, pp. 23–47. © 1978 by Kate Coleman. Cover reprinted with permission from *New Times.*

"Operation Wigwam": Reprinted from *New West,* December 1, 1980, pp. 25–38. © 1980 by Dan Noyes, Maureen O'Neill, and David Weir. Opening page reprinted with permission from *New West.* Copyright 1980 by *New West.*

Library of Congress Cataloging in Publication Data

Weir, David.
  Raising hell.

  Consists of 8 magazine articles reprinted, each
accompanied by an investigative story.
  Includes index.
  Contents: Nuclear nightmare / by Michael Singer and
David Weir—Citizen Scaife / by Karen Rothmyer—
Teamster madness / by Douglas Foster—[etc.]
  1. Reporters and reporting.   2.   Center for Inves-
tigative Reporting (U.S.) I. Noyes, Dan. II. Title.
PN4726.W44 1983   070.4'3   83–11922
ISBN 0–201–10858–5
ISBN 0–201–10859–3 (pbk.)

Cover design by Mike Fender
Text design by Patricia Lowy
Set in 11-point Times Roman by Kingsport Press, Kingsport, TN

ABCDEFGHIJ-DO-86543
First printing, September 1983

Contents

*To our parents
and to the next generation of muckrakers—
especially Laila, Sarah Daisy,
and Peter*

Acknowledgments

This book is in many ways the product of the entire staff of the Center for Investigative Reporting. In particular, we owe a special debt of gratitude to Mark Schapiro, who helped us develop the concept of a book based on the Center's major investigative stories. Other Center staff members contributed in many ways to the research and writing, and we thank them all for their criticisms, suggestions, and support: Doug Foster, Tracy Freedman, Diana Hembree, David Kaplan, Laura Lent, Karen O'Neill, Maureen O'Neill, Liza Cohen Pike, and Matt Rothman. We especially thank Howard Kohn, who skillfully reviewed all sections where we wrote about ourselves (Weir and Noyes) in the third person to check for accuracy and consistency, and to remove as much as possible the awkward self-consciousness that inevitably creeps into that kind of writing. We also express our gratitude to the energetic interns at the Center who enthusiastically helped with the research and fact checking: Ann Scott Knight, Susan Ferriss, Ida Landauer, Jeanette Valentine, and Jim Dupont. Center associates Alec Dubro, Jonathan King, Eve Pell, Angus Mackenzie, and Seth Rosenfeld also made suggestions. In addition, independent publisher Andrew Fluegelman devoted his considerable skills to helping us develop this project in its early stages.

Beyond the Center staff and associates, many friends and relatives helped us pull this book together; Janie Kelly and Alison Weir in particular read early versions of chapters and suggested changes. A third of the book was drafted at Sanibel, Florida, where we are grateful to Ty Symroski, Leonard E. Symroski, Bob Dormer, Lisa Baldwin Dormer, Tom Weir, and Anne Weir for logistical help, including housing, transportation, supplies, and encouragement. Also, we are deeply indebted to the late Grace M. Symroski for the help she gave during this and many other projects.

To the many funders and supporters of the Center, far too numerous to list here, we are deeply grateful for the aid provided over the long, trying years of building the Center. Many associates, interns, former staff members, and supporters also deserve our gratitude for the parts they have played in the stories included here and for helping us build a strong institution that supports the difficult work of investigative reporting.

Among these are some we cannot fail to mention. They include: Lowell Bergman, Tamara Baltar, Deborah Begel, Henry Weinstein, Trenace Thompson, Raul Ramirez, Stan Sesser, Melinda Rorick, Sherry Reson, Evelyn Shapiro, Sandy Close, Warren Green, Herb Gunther, Richard Parker, Elizabeth Eudey, Becky O'Malley, Ben Bagdikian, Peter Schrag, David Hunter, Phil Stern, Mae Churchill, Bob Greene, Jack Tobin, Howard Bray, Alvin Duskin, Don Devereux, Steve Goldin, W. H. Ferry, Carol Ferry, Mike Kepp, Judy Kaye, Maryanne Mott, Herman Warsh, Bob Maynard, Irene Moosen, Howard Rosenberg, Ken Kelley, Michael Oliver, Diana Kohn, Bob Alvarez, Tom Layton, Elliott Buchdruker, Saul Bloom, Betty Medsger, Marc Beyeler, Michael Castleman, Judy Coburn, Ken Connor, Laura Daltry, Fred Goff, Terry Flash, Joel Gurin, John Harris, Elaine Herscher, Zoia Horn, Craig Pyes, Sandra Katzman, Jan Legnitto, Susan Lyne, Joan McCarthy, Judy Austermiller, Chris Paine, Sandra Sutherland, Drummond Pike, Philip Scheffler, Jerry Dougherty, Charles Koppleman, Amy Rennert, Anita Rook, Naomi Schiff, Ralph Shikes, Mark Shwartz, John Steiner, Lee Thorne, Bill Wallace, Harvey Wasserman, Cora Weiss, Anne Zill, Steve Rees, Fred Branfman, Alan Ramo, Kay Regar, Marty Teitel, Viola Weinberg, Jeff Carter, Ron Dellums, Scott Kaufer, Sally Lilienthal, Toby McLeod, James Canty, Brian Wainwright, Peter Skewes-Cox, Adrian Price, Pillsbury, Madison & Sutro, David Helvarg, Nick Allen, David Kinley, Jacob Scherr, Maureen Hinkle, Barry Castleman, Skip Stiles, Kathy Ellison, David Dickson, Jon Stewart, Anne Hurley, Lori Lieberman, Cynthia Kasabian, Scott Zonder, Ros Davidson, Robin Updike, Norman Solomon, Tom Morgan, Paul Cohen, Laura Bernstein, the Fund for Investigative Journalism, David Marash, Andy Abraham, Patrick Ellis, Sophie Mirviss, Abigail Norman, David Pingitore, Bob Rodriguez, Caroline Young, Michael Abeshouse, Paul Glickman, James Hurlitz, Maggie Roth, Letty Belin, Brad Bunin, Russ Richeda, Leonard Sellers, Michael Levett, Chris Cook, Diana

Sperrazza, Adam Hochschild, Frank Browning, Jon Larsen, Linda Lotz, Jon Carroll, John Markoff, John Culliney, Margery Tabankin, Smith Bagley, Leeda Marting, The Youth Project, Victor Honig, Wade Greene, Davis Haines, Monica Melamid, Melinda Marble, Stewart Mott, James Kettler, Richard Boone, Jay Harris, Lorraine Honig, Frances Moore Lappe, Josh Mailman, David Ramage, Margaret Standish, Rebecca Sive-Tomashefsky, The Playboy Foundation, Katharine Tremaine, Kitty Tucker, Joel Bernstein, Marianne Edmunds, David Fenton, Christine Doudna, Sarah Lazin, Jeff Gerth, John Gofman, Joan Lovett, Allan Maraynes, Andrew McGuire, B. K. Moran, Jessica Mitford, Victor Navasky, John Nelson, David Newman, Kathy Robbins, Susan Silk, Amanda Spake, William Kistner, Kathy McDonald, Anne Hurley, Loren Stein, David Bank, and Peter McMillan.

At Addison-Wesley, we owe special thanks to Doe Coover for believing in the project from the beginning, when there were plenty of reasons to have doubts, and for her support and encouragement throughout the editorial process. Also, thanks to Robin Manna for her enthusiasm and editing skills. She improved the manuscript with every move of her pencil, particularly in the introductory chapter. We would also like to thank our copyeditor, Kathie Ness, and the designer, Patricia Lowy, for their vital roles in making this book as good as it is.

Finally, we thank the nonstaff authors whose work helped make this book possible: Suzanne Gordon, Mark Dowie, Karen Rothmyer, Barbara Newman, Paul Avery, Kate Coleman, Terry Jacobs, Dennis King, Michael Singer, and Arnold Levinson.

Foreword
by Mike Wallace

You are about to embark on a series of first-rate short stories—detective stories, in a sense. Some of them have the crisp kinetic energy of a good film chase; others, the gritty wisdom of lessons learned hard at first hand. If it all adds up to a "textbook," it's the most engrossing one I've read in quite a spell.

I'm not sure that I'm the most appropriate choice to introduce *Raising Hell: How the Center for Investigative Reporting Gets the Story,* for I'm to some degree a figure out front now, a funnel through which the work of a variety of reporters is currently brought into darkened living rooms across the land. It is all of us—the producers, their associates, the researchers (and myself along with them)—who engage in the endlessly fascinating pursuit of not "just the facts, ma'am," but along with the facts, the sketches of those assorted individuals who people our filmed inquiries on *60 Minutes.* And it is those characters, and not simply their adventures, who make our work as satisfying as it is. Their motivations, their fears, their evasions, their greed, their posing, their lying, and the pleasure we take in our pursuit of them—all of that combines to make our chore as addictive as it is.

That's what motivates most good reporters, I think. Pursuit. I'd be too lonely to do it by myself; as a matter of fact, I'm not sure I could, for I am, at heart, a collaborator. I like to rub up against the pals, the colleagues, the camera crews, who travel the motel circuit like a gypsy troupe. And we in turn rely on those stay-at-home film editors who've seen it all on their Steenbecks and their tape machines to tell us when to stop and how to make it clearer, what works, and what doesn't. In sum, I guess I'm saying that I admire lonely print reporters, but I wouldn't want to be one.

Now, about the enterprise called investigative reporting, that redundancy that Woodstein put into the popular lexicon. Lots of us who make our living that way deplore the phrase for the simple reason that most reporting, of course, is investigation of a sort. Few of us are content to serve just as handout rewriters. Most reporters I know are professional skeptics in any case, and so investigation comes with the territory. How much investigation you are drawn to, or are willing to get bogged down in, separates the Woodsteins from the rest.

Can you train to be one? I imagine that a legal background, an accountant's background, a scientific background can help. But I have a hunch that a communications background won't help you much. Liberal arts, lots of reading and writing, languages, government, economics, history—all this is bound to make you a better reporter in the long run, "investigative" or otherwise. I'm not sure that journalism schools do much that you can't learn in your first six months on almost any job. A Graduate Journalism School, I guess, can be useful if you work at it and if your teachers are resourceful and bring in itinerant professionals as guests to stir things up. But I think you learn best on the job.

I don't know that there's a lot more I can say by compelling way of introduction. What you're about to read is fascinating and instructive, about as eloquent an understanding of what it is we do—in print and television—as I have come across. My sole fear is that it will trigger too many more of you to try to wind up doing what we do, and already there aren't enough jobs to go around.

Welcome nonetheless!

Introduction

This is a book about power—about those who wield it and those who watch it. It describes the work of a small organization devoted to a particular journalistic approach to watchdogging power popularly known as investigative reporting.

This book is our chance to reexamine from the reporter's perspective a selection of the journalism produced during the first five years of the Center for Investigative Reporting's existence. We hope to pass on some of the lessons we've learned, as well as provide an inside look into how power and information are used in our society.

Investigative reporting is uneconomical, prestigious, controversial, satisfying, lonely, labor-intensive, time-consuming, sometimes hazardous work. For most investigative journalists, it is a calling as well as an occupation. Though often more than a job, to be successful it has to remain less than a mission. A reporter's zeal must be directed to uncovering and documenting facts, not to getting revenge or attracting attention. But since there is a certain passion in bringing the powerful to account, investigative journalism has always had an activist tinge. Underlying the work is the belief that things are rarely as they seem, and seldom as they should be. The radicalism often associated with the reporting stems from the perpetual search for root causes of events—and from a low tolerance for injustice.

There is always the hope that new information can spur changes, create reforms, and curb abuses of power. But first, investigating the powerful requires getting the facts straight. Those reporters who don't do so face a limited future in this line of work. Those who would shape the facts to reflect their own biases lose their credibility and their ability to publish. Those who indulge in outright fabrication may be publicly humiliated—a recent example is Janet Cooke at the *Washington Post,* whose Pulitzer Prize was rescinded when it was discovered that she had created a fictitious character to tell about drug abuse.

Investigative journalists, therefore, are keenly aware of the dangers of inaccuracies and take elaborate precautions to avoid them. At the Center for Investigative Reporting, and at most of the publications that we write for, stories are subjected to a rigorous fact-checking process before publication—wherein a researcher independently verifies each fact in a story. The eight magazine stories reprinted in this volume have withstood both the challenge of time and the scrutiny of those who would gladly have undermined the stories' impact. The people and organizations described all were worthy subjects for journalistic attention at the time of publication, and most could use a follow-up check today.

Eight "stories-behind-the-story" accompany articles reprinted here. Collectively these constitute a semicontinuous narrative, populated by a revolving pool of more than a dozen journalists, working alone or together over a five-year period. All told, they represent a selective history of the work of the Center for Investigative Reporting as told by the reporters involved. In addition, the stories contain a cross-section of the methods and techniques used to produce investigative journalism.

If we have been guided by any common philosophy in pursuing these stories, it was that captured by Pulitzer Prize–winning columnist Mary McGrory in her advice to reporters: "Ask, go back; be nice to people, but not to power."

Traditions of Investigative Reporting

Investigative reporting is a grand tradition in American journalism. The modern-day version grew out of the "muckraking" reporting produced at the beginning of this century. Many prominent names in American journalism have been attracted to this reportorial school, which combines strong social criticism with in-depth reporting. At some point in their careers, Walter Lippmann, Lincoln Steffens, Theodore Dreiser, John Reed, Jack London, Upton Sinclair, I. F. Stone, Ida Tarbell, Rachel Carson, Carey McWilliams, and Jessica Mitford have all engaged in "muckraking."

The rise and fall of investigative reporting over the years has depended on multiple social, political, and economic forces. The work has thrived during periods of social unrest and reform movements. Its development has depended on mass audiences educated enough to desire comprehensive, detailed reporting; on a healthy economy that could support a luxury of information; and on a social and political atmosphere that was tolerant of critical views.

These forces combined to create a journalistic explosion on the American scene in the early twentieth century. Lincoln Steffens unofficially ushered in muckraking in 1902 with the first installment of *The Shame of the Cities.* His book exposed corruption in big-city government across the country and helped establish the muckraking journal *McClure's.* One month later, the first installment of Ida Tarbell's long-planned *History of the Standard Oil Company* effectively revised commonly accepted notions about this country's largest company. Mass circulation magazines like *McClure's, Collier's,* and *Cosmopolitan* captured the public's attention. They ran exposés about the fraudulent practices of the patent medicine industry, the special interests that corrupted and ruled the Senate at the turn of the century, and the wave of labor racketeering that struck cities from Chicago to San Francisco during the early 1900s.

World War I, the changing economics of journalism, and public perception that the muckrakers' charges had not caused true reforms contributed to a decline in muckraking during the 1920s and 1930s. By the end of World War II, the United States had embraced a Cold War mentality in which alternative views and political criticism were considered unacceptable, even illegal. Soon McCarthyism pointed out the weakness of uncritical journalism: Senator McCarthy's unfounded charges of Communist subversion were reported in many instances without any attempt to scrutinize their validity.

McCarthy's eventual disgrace and the country's entrance into its most unpopular war helped begin a new age of muckraking that culminated with Watergate and the resignation of President Nixon in 1974. During the 1950s and 1960s, some of the memorable examples of the craft were Edward R. Murrow's brilliant television exposés of McCarthy and of migrant farm labor, and Paul Jacobs's reporting on the effects of atmospheric atomic testing on the civilians of Nevada and Utah. In addition, Rachel Carson published her book *Silent Spring* on the new manmade destruction of the environment, and I. F. Stone explored the roots of the Korean War. During these years, other journalists concentrated on organized crime. Investigations into the Teamsters Union and its investments in Las Vegas, the rise of the Mafia, and the growth of an illegal drug trade gave new legitimacy to the investigative reporter. With these successes, investigative reporting gained a new foothold and made editors and readers more certain of its value.

Investigative reporting today stands somewhat apart from "objective reporting," a concept that has developed during this century and seems to mean different things to different people. In the 1920s, proponents of objective reporting attempted to establish journalism on a professional basis with accepted standards. By removing the value system implicit in the work, they hoped to broaden newspaper audiences and essentially homogenize the news for wire service copy. The idea was to assure a story's acceptance throughout a city or the entire country. Therefore, the owners of news organizations trying to expand their markets pushed "objective reporting" hard. Journalism schools started teaching these professional standards, and newsworkers displayed their new formal training by avoiding personal involvement or judgment in their stories.

Gradually, however, working journalists have come to see the flaws in a reporting method that allows only the "official version" of a story to emerge. Others noticed these drawbacks, too. The private Commission on Freedom of the Press, a benchmark review of journalism, concluded in 1947 that objective reporting as taught in universities could obscure facts as well as uncover them. One problem is that individuals in positions of authority, both in government and in the private sector, have increasingly come to rely on a corps of what could be called "counter-journalists." These public relations experts are paid by individuals, companies, and government agencies to screen and present information to the public and the press. Today, journalists commonly are prevented from talking directly to politicians and executives; instead they must go through "official channels."

Meanwhile the public has come to mistrust government

statements, press releases, and even official reports. Skeptical public reaction to the Report of the Warren Commission on the Assassination of President Kennedy is one example of this trend. Furthermore, the Watergate scandal demonstrated to Americans that the highest officials in the land sometimes lie and deceive the public. Today, many investigative reporters believe that "objective" reporting can be a smokescreen for the powerful that results in the distribution of official views without critical analysis. Interpretive, in-depth reporting that probes the reasons behind official statements is an effective antidote for this kind of journalistic lethargy.

Accordingly, in the 1970s the "new journalism" of Norman Mailer and Tom Wolfe gained popularity among reporters. The acceptance of this style demonstrated that readers are interested in an author's viewpoint and good writing, as well as a balanced presentation of the facts. Reporters began to introduce themselves into their material, alert the reader to their points of view, and admit that they had motivations for writing their stories. The "new journalism" made journalists more visible and allowed them greater freedom to include their analyses in their stories. Occasionally this style led to excesses, of course, but by and large it represented an improvement in the craft.

Good investigative reporting provides a kind of middle ground between "objective" and "advocacy" journalism (where a cause is uppermost in the reporter's mind). The facts still hold the upper hand in investigative journalism, but when a reporter selects and emphasizes those facts in writing, personal value judgments clearly enter the process. And although an author may not wish to pretend that his or her work is "objective," this doesn't mean it isn't fair. Fairness is quite another concept, and one that strikes to the heart of the methodology of investigative reporting. As demonstrated in the narratives that follow, journalists are forever considering facts and opinions that diverge from their own. One rule of thumb for all journalists is that the subject of an investigative article must have a chance to respond to any charges before they are published or broadcast.

Rejecting the ironclad notion of "objectivity" does not mean that "truth" has been similarly discarded or that objectivity has no role in journalism. Rather, the investigator has no higher responsibility than to delve beneath the surface of events to root out as much "truth" as possible—never claiming it is the final word. It is challenging work, and this book is designed to highlight the way investigative reporters go about that quest today.

CHAMPAGNE DICK
JOHN GREGORY DUNNE

NEW WEST

NUCLEAR NIGHTMARE

Your Worst Fears Are True

BY MICHAEL SINGER AND DAVID WEIR

THIS *is a true story. Although much of it has the ring of fiction, of doomsday novels and disaster movies, it is real. If you lived in Los Angeles in 1975, you lived through the nation's first full-scale peacetime nuclear alert.*

And that's not even the frightening part . . .

Dear Mr. Hartley:
There is a nuclear device with a potential of 20 kilotons concealed on one of your valuable properties electronically controlled in Los Angeles County. . . . [Turn to Page 15]

1

Nuclear Nightmare

by Michael Singer and David Weir
with Barbara Newman

Dear Mr. Hartley:
  There is a nuclear device with a potential of 20 kilotons concealed on one of your valuable properties electronically controlled in Los Angeles County . . .

It is Tuesday, November 4, 1975. Jean Brady is opening the morning's mail. Her boss, Fred Hartley, chairman of the board of Union Oil, is out of town. It is the routine beginning to what promises to be a routine day. About halfway through the stack, she comes to an air-mail envelope without a return address. Curious. She opens it and takes out a single piece of paper. The letter is very carefully typed on a Tangier-Tippen typewriter.

  . . . You will not call the authorities or use any electronic surveillance equipment. You could trigger the bomb accidentally and it will be very dirty . . .

Jean Brady calls her supervisor, who, in turn, calls Union Oil's chief of security, Paul Schooling. Schooling is already a little jumpy. Union Oil's California property has, in recent months, been damaged by a mysterious bombing, a bombing still unsolved. Schooling reads the threatening letter, but he knows he has no choice. Calls go out to the Los Angeles Police Department and the FBI.

> . . . If you fail to carry out all of these orders we will send a copy of this letter to the news media with instructions to evacuate California, we will then trigger the device, there will be billions of dollars of damage and Los Angeles will be sterile for a long time. —FISION

Surprisingly, in view of the fact that "Fision" has placed a time limit of six days on the note, the Los Angeles Police Department and the FBI begin squabbling about jurisdiction. Although the FBI has precedence in the case under the Atomic Energy Act, LAPD Chief Ed Davis tells the FBI to "keep the hell out." Then L.A. Sheriff Pete Pitchess, who has been recently assigned to coordinate the county's emergency response plans, finds out about the crisis and jumps in. It takes all of November 4 and most of November 5 for the FBI to flex its federal muscle and take charge of the case.

It is now 3 P.M. on the afternoon of November 5, 30 hours after the letter to Hartley was opened. The FBI, now running the show, plays it by the book—its officers call in officials of the Energy Research and Development Agency (ERDA) to determine whether or not the threat is credible.

ERDA's analysts note that the letter is not a hurried job—it is clear and rational. They note that the sum of money requested, $1 million, is not impossibly large. They note that the instructions for delivering the money (small bills—nothing over $100—in two suitcases) are realistic. The money would fit. It is also possible, as the letter claims, to build a 20-kiloton bomb and conceal it. It could be transported in a van without being detected. "Fision" says that the bomb can be detonated by remote control, and this, too, is credible—some bombs can be detonated by a simple telephone call from another city. In addition, the fact that the threatener refers to the bomb as "dirty" adds credibility: Crude bombs *are* dirtier (they disperse more radioactivity per kiloton) than military bombs.

Within 50 minutes, ERDA responds to the FBI: Yes, it's a credible threat. There may be a bomb.

Officials at ERDA's round-the-clock Emergency Operations Center also call a few other people: the White House Operations Center, the National Military Command Center and the Joint Congressional Committee on Atomic Energy. Now officials at the highest levels of government know that ERDA thinks that there is a possibility that Los Angeles will blow up sometime within the next 108 hours.

It is now 6:30 P.M. on November 5. The decision has been made at the FBI to search for the bomb. There are six major Union Oil properties in Southern California: a skyscraper in downtown Los Angeles; two tank farms, in Torrance and San Pedro; one tank farm refinery in Wilmington; and two dockside port facilities in the L.A. harbor. There is not enough equipment and manpower in Los Angeles to complete the search quickly and thoroughly. The FBI asks ERDA for the services of the Nuclear Emergency Search Team (NEST), a little-known government organization designed to cope with just this sort of situation.

At 6:45, ERDA officials call the NEST headquarters in Las Vegas. Ironically, when the order to "scramble" comes, NEST members are already gathered in a conference planning a mock nuclear emergency exercise. Senior officer Jack Doyle remembers, "Suddenly, everybody's adrenalin was pretty high."

By 7:30, Doyle and two others are airborne, on their way to Los Angeles. All night long, special planes are dispatched to pick up NEST members and bring them to L.A. Bomb experts are flown in from nuclear weapons laboratories in New Mexico and Northern California. By dawn, 30 operatives have been assembled for the search—and 45 more are on the way.

It is now 8:20 A.M. on November 6. As the official ERDA chronology has it, "ground search commenced." NEST secretly deploys its personnel to the six Union Oil sites. Only top management and security agents at Union Oil are alerted. For all the other workers, it's just another day on the job.

NEST sets up its own emergency command post at Los Alamitos Air Station in Garden Grove, installing four special unlisted telephones for communication with field operatives.

All day long, helicopters equipped with sensitive detection pods buzz over Union Oil tank farms and port facilities. Men in business suits stride briskly down the corridors of Union Oil's corporate headquarters carrying black briefcases. Inside those briefcases are miniaturized, supersensitive Geiger counters tuned to wireless earplugs. When a radioactive source is discovered, the NEST operative will hear its "signature" buzzing in his ear.

At 2:30 P.M. a NEST searcher picks up a radioactive "signature" from one of the executive office suites. The source is soon discovered: a souvenir chunk of uranium. At 4 P.M. a searcher at another plant discovers a "hot" railroad car parked on a spur just outside the perimeter of company property. Armed with detectors, NEST operatives gingerly open the railroad car to peer inside. Nothing. The signal was apparently produced by radioactive residue on the floor of the car.

Meanwhile, ERDA is directing other phases of the operation. Naval and LAPD ordnance disposal units are ordered to stand by, although neither of the units has ever had to dismantle a nuclear bomb before. The FBI is developing a plan for trapping the extortionist, but it is clear that the L.A. bureau is unprepared for this big an emergency—one agent is repeatedly called away to deal with bank robberies in his district.

It is now 8:30 P.M. on November 6. All reports from the field are still negative. In Washington, it is near midnight. Sleepy ERDA officials are surprised when one of the agency's top administrators stops by the Emergency Operations Center for advice. What should he tell the press? Everyone agrees that a low profile must be maintained. Even though the threatened 20-kiloton bomb is about the size of the one that destroyed Hiroshima, killing or injuring 150,000 people and leaving a four-and-a-half-square-mile area around ground zero completely burned out; even though L.A.'s famous inversion layer might trap the radioactivity in the basin and create an atomic cloud no one could survive, ERDA officials quickly agree that the danger of panic is worse than the possible consequences of not releasing the information. An official scribbles in the official chronology, "No public release."

As a consequence, during this week in November, the citizens of Los Angeles read in the *Times* that John Robinson is the new USC football coach, that Francisco Franco is fading fast, that Patty Hearst's trial for bank robbery will soon begin; but they do not read that the government is taking very seriously a nuclear extortion plot directed against their city.

NEST continues its covert search. The constant buzzing of helicopters near Long Beach prompts residents to complain to City Hall officials, who demand to know what's going on. Federal officials brief them and urge them to keep the secret. They agree.

It is now 3 P.M. on November 7. All Union Oil sites have been searched. There is nothing more that NEST can do. If the extortionist has been smart enough to shield the bomb with lead or water, then NEST, with all its sophisticated equipment, will probably not find it. If nothing happens in the next three days, the incident will be officially judged a hoax, and it will be up to the FBI to catch the perpetrator. ERDA orders its field teams to wrap up the operation.

The Unlikely Extortionist

Seven months later, a federal grand jury indicted Frank James, a 63-year-old car-leasing salesman with no previous criminal record, for "use of [an] instrument of commerce to threaten to destroy property." During a brief, virtually unreported trial in October, 1976, the details of how the FBI caught the man charged with precipitating the first all-out nuclear alert in this nation's history were revealed.

About 30 agents participated in the operation on November 10, 1975—the day the extortionist had demanded that the money drop be made. Following instructions given in the threat letter, a classified ad was placed in the *L.A. Times:* "Fision, we do not want FO [fallout] on L.A." A telephone number, allegedly Union Oil's but in fact one of the FBI's many unlisted numbers, was included.

That evening, FBI agents maintained surveillance at telephone booths where the extortionist had told them to wait for his call. Frank James was seen entering a phone booth nearby at about the time the extortionist called with instructions for the money drop. An FBI agent, posing as a Union Oil executive, did take the extortionist's call, and it was recorded by agents in a room at Pacific Telephone. But James's voiceprint was never introduced into evidence, and no one has conclusively proved that the voice on the other end of the line giving instructions for the money drop was Frank James's.

The following day several agents swooped down on a houseboat in San Pedro, where James lived with his wife. Their search failed to turn up the esoteric foreign-brand typewriter on which the extortion note had been typed, nor did the agents find any other physical evidence that James was the extortionist.

Nevertheless, James, whose son is a policeman, was convicted of "threatening to destroy property"—not quite the same thing as extortion—and became the only person ever found guilty in a nuclear threat incident. "As far as the government was concerned, the less said about it the better," the assistant U.S. attorney who prosecuted the case remembers. Accordingly, he didn't even issue a press release about the conviction. James's appeals lawyer, a former Orange County deputy district attorney, says his client is "totally inconsistent with the profile developed by the feds [of a nuclear extortionist]. He has no particular interest in environmental or political issues." When his appeals proved unsuccessful, James was sent to prison, but he was released within six months after suffering two heart attacks. To this day, he maintains that he was the victim of an "FBI frame-up."

Whether James is guilty or innocent, the implications of the case are alarming. If he is guilty, then the question is: What drove him to it? Why would a man with no previous criminal record, no grievances against the government or Union Oil and no interest in politics suddenly decide to hold up an entire city for ransom? And how was a man with no special knowledge of nuclear bombs able to write such a convincing note, a note that galvanized the entire government into action?

Look at it the other way. If James is not guilty, if the FBI was participating in a frame-up or merely mistaken, then there's a nuclear extortionist still out there, a terrorist who probably has some sort of nuclear expertise, perhaps waiting for another chance.

But all right. Let's assume that the FBI got the right man. Let's assume that the government was right when it decided not to tell the citizens of Los Angeles about the threatening letter and the possible consequences. The question is: Why did the government take it all so seriously? Isn't a nuclear bomb hard to make? Isn't the technology of nuclear explosions beyond the reach of all but the most sophisticated governments?

The answer is no.

Nuclear weapons are easy to make. At least 10,000 physicists, and virtually any well-educated person with the will to learn certain details, are capable of designing—and making—such a weapon.

This is another true story . . .

The Dangerous Professor

Not long before the NEST team packed up its gear and flew to Los Angeles, a 35-year-old professor of physics (now at Louisiana State University) named Peter Zimmerman finally got around to reading a book called *The Curve of Binding Energy*. Written in 1973 by John McPhee, the book described Ted Taylor's private nightmare about nuclear terrorism. As early as a decade ago, Taylor, one of the top U.S. nuclear bomb designers, had become concerned with how easy it was for someone to build a crude nuclear bomb. After reading McPhee's book, Zimmerman began to worry about the same thing. From 1976 through 1977 he carried on a reasonable and persistent dialogue with Department of Energy officials about the problem.

During this time he met Forrest Frank, an aide to the House Subcommittee on International Security and Scientific Affairs. The two discovered that they shared the same concern about nuclear terrorism and began thinking about ways to make the government pay attention to them. They decided to write a paper which Zimmerman would deliver before the prestigious American Physical Society in the spring of 1979.

What Zimmerman set out to prove was that a particular form of plutonium—plutonium oxide, a carcinogenic powder that is extracted from waste in nuclear power plants—could be made to explode in a crude nuclear bomb. Though the government had ignored Taylor's assertion to this effect years before, they could hardly ignore Zimmerman: He worked out the calculations that turned Taylor's assertions into a mathematical certainty. The kind of crude bomb Zimmerman figured out how to make represented a great leap backward—from the clean, high-tech laboratories in Los Alamos, New Mexico, to a dark basement or machine shop in any American town. It is kid's play compared to the designs of Harvard college student Dimitri Rotow and Princeton student John Aristotle Phillips—the plans for sophisticated military bombs that got so much attention in the media last year. It is far simpler than the H-bomb plan printed in *The Progressive* magazine after the U.S. government withdrew its suit to prevent publication. (The cost and skills involved in producing an H-bomb are beyond the means of a single individual.)

In the course of researching his paper, Zimmerman made a number of requests to the Department of Energy for data to which he was entitled under the Freedom of Information Act. By doing so, he came to the attention of officials in the DOE's Department of Classification. DOE officials called Zimmerman and asked him what he was doing. He told them about the paper. His interrogators asked him to submit it to the DOE so that the department could decide whether or not the information should be classified, as defined in the Atomic Energy Act of 1954. (DOE has the authority to declare any weapons-related information classified until it rules otherwise. Such information is referred to as "born classified.") Zimmerman planned to deliver the speech from note cards, but DOE officials insisted that the speech be written down—word for word—and submitted for review. Zimmerman continued to work out his calculations and the wording of the speech. In one conversation with DOE officials he asked if he would be breaking the law if he passed the speech on to his secretary for typing. The answer was "maybe." Zimmerman typed the speech himself.

He arrived in Washington a week prior to his scheduled appearance at the meeting of the American Physical Society and immediately received an invitation to appear at the DOE offices at 20 Massachusetts Avenue. There followed a tense but cordial discussion about the contents of the paper. DOE officials asked Zimmerman to remove certain information from the speech. When he asked why, he was told that the answer to his question was classified. He stood his ground and insisted on an answer. The DOE officials then appealed to Zimmerman's conscience, raising the question of whether *he* wanted the information in the public domain. After lengthy discussion, Zimmerman agreed that he did not, and deleted portions of his speech.

One of the things that the DOE got Zimmerman and Frank to delete voluntarily was all reference to a design scheme for a crude bomb in which the plutonium oxide could be made to fission (detonate) by a method so simple it would shock not only some in the weapons establishment but also lawmakers and citizens who understand anything about nuclear bomb technology.

So, although the public wasn't aware of it, one of the government's worst nightmares had come true: Here was a bright physics professor who, with no access to classified information and with no help from the military establishment, had come up with the plan and the mathematical calculations necessary to make a simple, low-yield (in the one-kiloton range) nuclear bomb. Nuclear critics had argued that such a thing could happen, and now it was incontrovertibly true.

A Very Simple Bomb

For years it was accepted that the military had a monopoly on nuclear bomb-making. Indeed, it is impossible for a single individual to build a military-style bomb, in part because of the need to convert plutonium or uranium to an enriched "weapons-grade" metal, a process that involves a series of expensive engineering, chemical and metallurgical techniques. (Weapons-grade metal is a more enriched form of plutonium than plutonium oxide.) Another difficulty involves the construction of the trigger, or implosion system, which consists of a series of high-explosive charges that are placed strategically all around the metal sphere surrounding the nuclear material. They must detonate within microseconds of each other and with equal force and pressure in all directions in order to compress the nuclear material to the point where a nuclear explosion occurs. The complex system is essentially an engineering miracle.

The complexity of these two steps gave many weapons experts confidence that a crude bomb could not be built. However, a four-month investigation conducted by *New West* reveals that:

- The necessary calculations to build such a bomb are within the reach of second-year physics students. With proper reference materials, the calculations can be done in 30 minutes.
- The materials necessary for constructing the bomb are available in a well-stocked hardware store, at a cost of less than $2,000. Tools required to thread, cut and shape the metal can be rented.
- One fissionable material, plutonium oxide, requires no processing. The amount needed would fit in a household bucket.
- It is possible to detonate plutonium oxide with high explosives from a *single source*, thus eliminating the need for complex implosion systems.
- One person, working alone, could build a bomb in two easily assembled sections, each light enough to be carried by a person of average strength. The bomb could be taken to a target site where the fissile materials are stored and could then be armed in minutes.
- The total volume of a one-kiloton bomb could be less than fourteen cubic feet; the bomb could fit in the trunk of a car (as opposed to the convoy needed to transport 1,000 tons of TNT).
- Construction of the bomb would require no highly technical

procedures. The few dangerous steps involved in handling high explosives and fissile material can be circumvented with information available to the public.

- Even more frightening, there is a strong possibility that an infinitely simpler nuclear device could be constructed. This device would require no mathematical calculations at all, no special tools, and would be even dirtier than the crude nuclear bomb mentioned above. While *New West* was unable to obtain definite confirmation of the feasibility of this astonishingly simple nuclear device, at least three of the experts we interviewed confirmed that such a device is entirely within the realm of possibility.

The information that *New West* has gathered about the size and nature of these crude nuclear devices is far more specific than we are willing to reveal. For obvious reasons, we do not feel it is appropriate to print the exact plans for these "kitchen-table" bombs. In this matter, you will have to take our word for it—or, more precisely, you'll have to take the experts' word for it. These things can be built by anyone. They are simpler than anything described in *The Curve of Binding Energy*. As one government official commented, "It's so damn crude, it seems impossible. But it gives me nightmares because I'm afraid it would work."

The Single-Point Syndrome

Interviews with many weapons experts familiar with the Zimmerman situation have led us to conclude that a principal implication of the Zimmerman/Frank paper is that if a terrorist gained access to plutonium oxide, he or she could detonate that material in a relatively simple way. Sources stated that the original paper contained information indicating that plutonium oxide could be detonated from a single high-explosive source, thus eliminating the need to build a complex implosion system. This radically simple method of detonation is known as single- or one-point initiation.

The implications of this formulation are devastating. Plutonium oxide can be stored right now in as many as eighteen sites around the country: There are three such sites in California, one in New York and three in Pennsylvania. If obtained by a terrorist, this material could be poured into a prefabricated nuclear bomb in minutes and detonated from a single point. The high explosives needed for single-point initiation can be purchased by almost anyone, almost anywhere in the United States. A crude bomb may not disintegrate a city, but it could take off the top 100 floors of the World Trade Center or pulverize every government building in the immediate area of L.A.'s Civic Center. Its radioactive fallout would leave a deadly substance in the lungs of many suburban dwellers in the vicinity.

The government will not publicly comment on the credibility of any bomb design. However, several knowledgeable sources, including General ("Ink") Gates, manager of the DOE Nevada underground testing program (testing above ground stopped in 1962), and Donald Kerr, head of Los Alamos Laboratory, where prototypal nuclear weapons are designed, conceded in interviews that it might be possible to get a fission explosion from a single-point initiation using plutonium oxide. (Documents released under the Freedom of Information Act indicate that in some cases, single-point tests have *indeed* yielded nuclear explosions.) In fact, General Gates oversees a program called single-point safety testing.

In addition, while government officials may not publicly acknowledge the reality of crude bombs, they've got names for them: In nuclear establishment lingo the bomb is a CFE (clandestine fission explosive), IND (improvised nuclear device) or "gadget." It is a weapon that a political terrorist, criminal or any other alienated person can use. In the government lexicon, such people are "nonstate" or "subnational" adversaries.

Government officials who do know all the details relating to the construction of such bombs have misled the public about how easy it is to design and build them. Experts who have tried to confront the government about this problem have been ignored, harassed or muzzled. The government explains that such actions are necessary to protect national security. But *New West* has discovered other reasons for the secrecy:

- The government's ability to discredit any nuclear threat is severely hampered by the fact that so much bomb-grade nuclear material is unaccounted for that it can never again be certain this material is not in the hands of a terrorist or a deranged individual.
- If and when a crude nuclear bomb is built, the government may not be able to detect its location.
- Even if the bomb is found, experts may not be able to disarm it.
- Bomb-grade uranium and plutonium remain inadequately protected because the Nuclear Regulatory Commission has not provided sufficient safeguards at nuclear facilities.
- If a crude nuclear bomb is detonated in a major urban area, government analysts predict the following consequences: mass deaths and radioactive contamination, and the possible suspension of certain constitutional guarantees.
- The country's vulnerability to nuclear terrorism, however great it is now, will dramatically increase under the "plutonium economy"—the next stage of nuclear power, planned for the 1980s, in which plutonium is the primary source of energy.

Plutonium Valley
There's a radioactive wasteland 80 miles from Las Vegas

It's off limits. You don't go there. One doesn't go there if one has any sense. It's just fenced off. And no access."

The speaker is General Mahlon ("Ink") Gates, a DOE official who oversees the government's single-point safety testing program in Nevada, and he's talking about what is now called "Plutonium Valley," a desolate stretch of desert 80 miles north of Las Vegas. Plutonium Valley is where the government used to test atmospheric nuclear weapons (above ground) to determine whether they were "one-point safe," that is, whether they would explode if they were dropped off a truck. No one in the government will comment officially on the results of the tests, but according to documents released under the Freedom of Information Act, at least one bomb has "gone critical" (yielded a nuclear explosion), dispersing plutonium over the ground.

So now the citizens of Las Vegas seem to be stuck with a poisonous wasteland a little more than an hour's drive away. Given plutonium's extreme toxicity (lung cancer can result from inhaling .000001 grams), the question arises as to whether the radioactive substance, helped by the desert winds, might "migrate" to Las Vegas or other communities.

"That's a possibility," says Troy Wade of DOE's Nevada operations, "but we have taken the soil and fixed it with an epoxy spray or asphalt so it can't move around. Really, it's a zero possibility."

Plutonium has a radioactive half-life of at least 24,400 years. Assuming that the plutonium is glued to the ground as the DOE says—and *New West* has no interest in making an on-site inspection—then Plutonium Valley will merely be an uninhabitable no man's land for the next thousand generations. But if epoxy and/ or asphalt decays quicker than plutonium—that is, sometime within 244 centuries—then Caesars Palace may just have to relocate to Tierra del Fuego.

The Men Who Knew Too Much

It seems almost inconceivable: the high school bomb, the people's bomb, the small and dirty bomb. A bomb, furthermore, that the government may be virtually powerless to detect and disarm. But government officials did not learn about such a bomb from Peter Zimmerman's paper. They've known about it for quite some time. For over a decade, a secret and extraordinary struggle has been raging in government circles over the issue of how easy it is to build crude nuclear bombs.

When Ted Taylor began worrying about the problem, his superiors at what was then the Atomic Energy Commission discounted his fears. In 1968, he went to see then Undersecretary of State Nicholas Katzenbach. "I had a one-hour meeting with him," Taylor remembers, "and it really sounded like he was going to do something. But nothing ever came of it. The Vietnam war must have closed in on him." It was shortly after that that Taylor started to collaborate with John McPhee on *The Curve of Binding Energy*.

Taylor maintains that he has been unable, despite repeated efforts, to sit down with government officials in a classified context and discuss why he thinks it is easy to build a bomb. Taylor went so far as to offer to recant his position publicly if government scientists could prove he was wrong. He made that proposal eighteen months ago to NRC Chairman Joseph Hendrie and Commissioner Peter Bradford and has never received a reply. Donald Kerr, head of the Los Alamos nuclear weapons laboratory, defends the NRC, claiming that any discussion with Taylor would force the government to reveal information it wants kept secret.

Though the government never publicly conceded anything to Taylor, in 1975 the NRC did assign a middle-level official named James Conran to study the state of nuclear "safeguards." Conran took the job seriously, and what unfolded over the next three years was a war of gigantic proportions between Conran and the upper management of both the NRC and the DOE. The battles were waged in memos, studies, congressional and grievance hearings, in the headlines, on television and in the consciences of people who knew that Conran was onto something. The catalogue of concerns which Conran was later forced to turn into accusations grew from a fundamental conviction on his part that the whole safeguards system was inadequate. As Conran put it in an open letter to the NRC and President Carter in the spring of 1977, safeguards were "afflicted pervasively by serious and chronic weaknesses which pose serious potential hazard to the public health and safety, and which even appear to threaten (potentially, at least) the national security."

By gaining access to then-secret DOE files, Conran discovered that 381.6 pounds of bomb-grade material were missing from a nuclear facility in Apollo, Pennsylvania. The CIA believes that the majority of the material was smuggled to Israel for the purpose of constructing an atomic bomb. (The smuggling incident became a major scandal in 1977.)

In addition, Conran challenged the safeguards status quo by postulating an "on-site" scenario: A terrorist group builds a nuclear bomb and brings it to a nuclear facility. They then penetrate the site (which the General Accounting Office says is possible) and steal bomb-grade material. Within minutes they can arm the bomb. In a crisis like this, the NRC would have to rely on the local police. As one safeguards analyst explained, "It could very easily develop into a confrontation within the site boundary while these thugs are on their way out. It would boil down like this—'Stand back, you bastards, I've got an A-bomb!' 'Like hell you do; let's get 'em!'—and you'd easily have a catastrophe." Using a crude bomb against a nuclear facility would magnify the bomb's destructive power exponentially.

Conran argued that his NRC superiors failed to grasp the importance of the on-site scenario because they didn't understand how easy it was to make a bomb. Therefore, in 1976, he proposed that the Jasons, an independent group of university-based scientists who work on national security problems, do a comprehensive study of crude nuclear bombs. Hal Lewis, a Jason and a physicist at the University of California, Santa Barbara, proposed that the Jason study explore the use of single-point initiation and plutonium oxide in a crude bomb. But ERDA officials refused to allow the study. Former NRC safeguards official Maurie Eisenstein told *New West*, "The reason the study never got done was that it was a very sensitive issue."

Conran's preliminary findings, published in a draft report in April, 1976, attacked almost every aspect of the NRC's safeguards program. The ensuing controversy led to the creation of a special NRC task force and to several rounds of congressional hearings. Conran himself, however, was never allowed to finish his study. At one point, according to information filed in the NRC Public Documents Room, a safe in his office containing classified material was confiscated without a proper "accounting." (Under NRC regulations, whenever secret documents change hands, a written record has to be made.) Conran was transferred unceremoniously out of the Division of Safeguards, even though the NRC task force supported many of his preliminary conclusions. When Conran filed a grievance concerning his transfer, his union representative said he was pressured by the NRC acting general counsel into withdrawing it. Within the past year, according to one congressional source, Conran has signed an agreement prepared by the NRC which restricts him from communicating with congressional oversight committees—a move which in effect muzzles him.

But why would the government not want to learn about information so vital to national security? One scientist involved in the struggle explained it this way: "The government is scared shitless to find out. . . . They don't want to put it on paper and have their faces rubbed in it. . . . They're afraid to find out officially. They're afraid to have a record."

The Boston Bomb

Why this fear? Because, among other reasons, there have been, including the Los Angeles incident, 55 nuclear threats against American cities since 1970. Four of them, including the one in Los Angeles, triggered high-level responses. One of these was in Orlando, Florida, where a fourteen-year-old boy eventually admitted to making the threat. (See box, page 28.)

Another occurred in Boston, Massachusetts, on April 26, 1974.

> We are taking this opportunity to inform you that a certain quantity of plutonium has fallen into our hands for reasons we don't feel we have to go into. . . .

When Boston Police Commissioner Robert di Grazia received this threat message on April 26, 1974, NEST had not yet been created. The threateners claimed to have an atomic bomb 25 times as large as the one that devastated Hiroshima. They demanded $200,000 and four airline tickets to Rome; if their demands were not met, they said, the bomb would be exploded on the night of May 4.

The letter, which was addressed to "law enforcement officials, elected officers and whoever else this may concern," was turned over to the FBI, which alerted other branches of government, including the White House. Roger Mattson was the technical assistant to one of the five AEC commissioners at the time, and because his boss was out of town, Mattson got deeply involved in an incident he otherwise might never have heard about.

"I told acting chairman William Anders, 'You can't ignore these things and say they're trivial acts of malcontents. If on Saturday that bomb goes off, how are you going to live with yourself?' "

Anders agreed, and called together the AEC's safeguards experts and "grilled and cross-examined them," according to Mattson. Their answers to his probing questions were disturbing.

ANDERS: "Is anything missing today that wasn't missing yesterday?"

STAFF: "We can't be sure."

ANDERS: "If something *is* missing, how could we find the device?"

STAFF: "We'd have to fly low over the city."

ANDERS: "Wouldn't that scare people?"

STAFF: "Yes, and furthermore, if we sent helicopters with radioactive sensors down a street, every doctor's or dentist's office with an x-ray machine would trip [the sensors] off."

While AEC officials were "staying up nights," according to Mattson, worrying about this threat, they couldn't tell whether the FBI was taking it seriously or not. So Mattson and two AEC colleagues went to FBI headquarters to brief Director Clarence Kelley.

Meanwhile, the search and detection component of the AEC (which would soon become NEST) was put on special alert. When the FBI requested help, a contingent of about 50 men flew to Griffiss Air Force Base in Rome, New York, to await orders to "overfly" Boston. Then, as NEST senior officer Jack Doyle recalls, "We just sat there and froze. All of our personal luggage was lost by the airline." The search was eventually called off when the FBI decided that the threat was a straight extortion attempt. A dummy package of money, left at the dump site, was never claimed.

"We discovered that we had a lot of faults in our system during that incident," says Mattson. "Most of all we realized that every government is vulnerable in this nuclear age. You know what scares me? It's that single, irrational guy, working alone—he worries me."

The Boston incident marked a turning point in the government's awareness of its weaknesses in countering nuclear threats. Then-President Gerald Ford, who was rumored to be personally outraged by the government's lack of preparedness, ordered that a new emergency response apparatus be set up.

The Plutonium Perplex

Regrettably, the government's response to the reality of nuclear terrorism and the imminent possibility of someone making a simple, dirty bomb has been less than ideal. While publicly denying that any real threat exists, government officials have chosen to put their faith in flashy, sophisticated technology— the same sort of technology that proved ineffectual during the Vietnam war. They have chosen limited, mechanical solutions to complex philosophical and moral problems. Above all, they have avoided doing anything—such as limiting the supply of plutonium—that would harm the nuclear power industry.

While people like Taylor, Conran and Zimmerman have been muzzled or ignored, government officials have quietly set up an elaborate operation in the DOE called the Emergency Action and Coordination Team (EACT), which exists to counter just such a threat. Among its components is a threat assessment team to analyze all available information; the highly mobile NEST search teams headquartered in Las Vegas and in the Washington, D.C., area; and a weapons analysis group of bomb designers from the Los Alamos and Lawrence Livermore nuclear research laboratories. The bomb experts are responsible for determining how a clandestine bomb is designed, what its likely yield would be and whether it could be dismantled. However, despite the fact that EACT has been assigned such responsibilities, extensive interviews with administrators, field personnel and knowledgeable critics reveal that EACT, established in 1976, is vulnerable to smart terrorists.

Teenage Terrorist
Who was that kid—and what's he doing now?

Nine years ago the Orlando police received a letter that threatened destruction of their city by means of an H-bomb. The chief of police at the time recalls, "It was one of the things I will always remember . . . sitting up all night, holding a piece of paper, wondering if the community is about to blow up."

When the FBI eventually identified the perpetrator, he turned out to be a precocious tenth-grade student who told one reporter, after his arrest, "When it comes to nuclear physics, I don't know why, I just can't get enough of it."

Several years later, while in the Air Force, the young man enrolled in nuclear weapons school and completed three-quarters of the course before his commanding officer realized the significance of the "incident" in his past and ordered him to see a psychiatrist. Shortly thereafter, he left the service.

The young man was bitterly disappointed: He was fascinated by the beauty and power released by nuclear bombs. He left the Air Force and went to work at a truck stop in Georgia, where, he muses, "Lots of nuclear bomb material comes through almost every day."

Rand Corporation analyst and expert in nuclear terrorism Brian Jenkins points out that as more and more countries go nuclear, the amount of available fissile materials increases, and safeguards in some countries may be even less adequate than those in the United States. Large quantities of nuclear materials have been stolen in India. A nuclear plant was seized by guerrillas in Argentina. As Jenkins puts it, "One's confidence in a flat statement that they [terrorists] do not have material is loaded. It becomes more and more difficult to make that statement."

EACT is organized around the progressive stages of a nuclear threat. In the first stage, EACT assesses the credibility of the threat. Is the message grandiose and hurriedly composed, or is it rational and consistent?

Of course, the threat is even more serious if a bomb design is submitted. Government officials admit that designs have been submitted in at least two threat incidents, and those plans were assessed by weapons experts. (In the Orlando case, the fourteen-year-old boy submitted plans for an H-bomb, after he sent the letter.) Given the relative simplicity of designing a nuclear bomb, it is easy to understand that even the crudest of drawings must be viewed with a very serious eye. Also, there is more and more information on the public record describing how to design a nuclear device. One expert told us that in one of ERDA's own publications, a 1977 issue of *Nuclear Safety* magazine, a scientist, in his attempt to *disprove* that it is easy to build a homemade bomb, revealed enough information about the plutonium "to shave weeks of work for a terrorist trying to build a sophisticated plutonium bomb."

EACT also uses a speculative technique called "psycholinguistics" to try to learn something about the threatener from the way the threat letter is worded. Government psychiatrists are trying to develop a profile of the nuclear terrorist, but this process is handicapped by the lack of solid information about who has made the 55 nuclear threats recorded in the past decade.

If EACT determines that a threat is credible, its next defense is to send out the NEST team. NEST is equipped with extremely sensitive detection equipment that can be carried in briefcases, trucks or helicopters. The devices can pick up signals from any radioactive source. But, as Jack Doyle, senior operations officer for NEST, says, "You can certainly plan scenarios where this approach doesn't get it." The reason is that anyone can shield nuclear material or a bomb with a sheet of lead, as an extortionist claimed to have done in a 1976 nuclear threat in Spokane, Washington. And as Ted Taylor said, "It's also easy to shield with water—down in a swimming pool. . . . To say we have instruments to fly around with a high assurance of finding a bomb—that's false."

In addition, the natural background radiation in cities can complicate NEST's search. "If I had to look in a building that was made out of granite from the White Mountain area of New Hampshire—that's the really 'hot' stuff [granite from that area contains more radioactive material than other building materials]—[it would] be a bit tricky," says Doyle. A search for a hidden bomb in the cities of New England, therefore, might be particularly difficult. "And a lot of the western United States," continues Doyle, "is high in natural uranium and thorium."

If a NEST or FBI search does happen to locate a nuclear device, EACT is faced with a whole new set of problems. The team must get close enough to the bomb to analyze what's in it and how it might work. Taylor says a bomb might be impossible to inspect because of "any kind of booby-trapping that would signal a physical approach to the weapon. Or it could be a bomb that requires a code detonator, and if you start manipulating the thing, it's geared to be detonated."

There are two possible outcomes to an attempt to disarm a nuclear bomb, Kerr says: "You either become confident that you can disarm it, or you begin to figure out how to mitigate the consequences." Kerr explained that Los Alamos experts are looking into techniques that would "focus the force of the explosion." Since fissioned particles adhere strongly to vermiculite (an inflammable material used as insulation or as mulch in seed beds), tractor trailers filled with this material might be used to surround a blast site. Unable to disarm or move the bomb, the government would have to detonate it under controlled conditions. Such an event would demand extraordinary measures on a scale unknown in the history of this country.

There is another scenario that leaves the population and the government completely powerless. "We may not get an indication of the thing until we see the first flash," Doyle worries. "The guy may just punch it off and say, 'See what I've done here? Now I want to make you a deal.' "

As a matter of policy, the U.S. government refuses to make concessions to terrorists. That policy is rooted in the belief that once the government gives in to one terrorist's demands, others will seize the opportunity to force similar concessions.

Robert Kupperman, until recently the chief scientist of the U.S. Arms Control and Disarmament Agency, has studied the possibility of a terrorist threat to a major city. "Should the destruction of a major city be considered a real possibility, the government would have little choice but to consider major concessions," Kupperman believes—"concessions that could potentially undermine its ability to govern."

The "two-bomb scenario," for instance, has Kupperman and other analysts especially worried. First, terrorists explode a bomb in a desert area, establishing their credibility. Then they threaten a city. The public would panic, and the government would be forced to bargain.

DOE's Kerr suggests an even simpler scenario. "It would seem to me the simplest thing is not to set off a bomb but to send a letter that contains the [fissionable] material, and watch the system stew."

The problem for the government, according to Kupperman, is how to make enough concessions to mollify the terrorists (or at least buy time until they and their bomb could be located) without undermining the government's "political or financial stability." Terrorists making outrageous demands could not be seriously bargained with. But, Kupperman continues, a clever group might simply ask for a series of "incremental policy shifts . . . over a period of time within the context of administration policy. In such a case it might be possible to negotiate without overtly undermining national sovereignty. The government might [be] forced to accede—partially or in full."

The implications of Kupperman's statements are staggering. If a serious nuclear threat were to be made, the government would have *no choice* but to break policy and bargain. Then, we would no longer have government as it is presently conducted, but government by terrorism.

Because of what he sees as a dangerous lack of preparedness, Kupperman fears that the government may overreact to the first credible threat—resorting to "repression on a broad scale." The specter of press censorship (recently tested by magazines and newspapers that published the secrets of the H-bomb) is real, since, as Kupperman observes, "Should the threat become public or should there even be rumors of the threat in the press, widespread panic could result." Of course, terrorists may choose to make their threat known, deliberately using a panicked public to further pressure the government.

Another terrorism analyst, David Krieger, fears that clever

instigators may use this method to "catalyze" repression, or even to trigger international war. This latter possibility could be triggered if they exploded a bomb without warning and then misidentified the source as the USSR, provoking a panicked retaliatory response. "One wonders," says Krieger, "whether or not national leaders would be capable of responding intelligently under possibly panic conditions." Given the awesome nuclear arsenal possessed by both superpowers, nuclear war would be hard to stop once it got started.

Who's Got the MUF?

Because it never occurs to most people in government that nuclear power could be abandoned, they believe the only way to prevent a catastrophic nuclear terrorist scenario is to keep plutonium and uranium out of the "wrong" hands. But the government has a problem in this area, too, and it's called MUF—nuclear "material unaccounted for." NRC officials claim that most of the MUF has gotten stuck in the pipes as the material is reprocessed. They also claim it is impossible to check all the pipes since there are thousands of miles of pipes in one reprocessing facility. But since the NRC admits that thousands of pounds of nuclear material are unaccounted for, it cannot rule out the possibility that some plutonium or enriched uranium is in unauthorized hands.

The MUF problem is one of the basic issues raised by Taylor and Conran years ago. In addition, there have been a number of what the government euphemistically calls "events," which illustrate the fundamental difficulties of safeguarding nuclear materials. In one case, a truck containing an unassembled nuclear weapon was seized by hijackers in the Southwest. But the fact that authorities recovered the truck with its cargo intact led them to speculate that the hijackers weren't even after plutonium: They may very well have been after a truckload of furs. In other cases, casks containing plutonium have been lost in transit and have later turned up in the wrong places: One shipment of highly enriched uranium disappeared in transit between New York's Kennedy International Airport and Frankfurt, Germany. Five days later it turned up in London. These and other, similar incidents corroborate Taylor's contention that it would be much harder to steal gold in this country than plutonium.

Since 1974, one government-financed report after another has concluded that the safeguards threat is so serious that security for the nuclear industry, now in the hands of private guards, should be transferred to U.S. military personnel or to a federal guard service. The NRC has not acted on these recommendations in the past. A 1976 NRC report pointed out that "this reluctance [to protect plutonium and enriched uranium against determined violent assaults] stems from industry beliefs that (1) this level of threat should be a federal responsibility, and (2) the necessary levels of defense would be damaging to company images." Taylor explains that "there is a tendency on the part of the government not to want to disrupt the nuclear industry, which is a commercial enterprise. There is also a weapons connection, a possible one, and the nuclear industry doesn't like that."

After the Blast

In the aftermath of the accident at Three Mile Island, the government and the media have focused public attention on the problem of making nuclear power plants safe. But there is a deeper, more troubling question underlying the nuclear debate that is not publicly addressed: What kind of world will the nuclear society create?

"The focus on safety issues is incorrect," says NRC Commissioner Victor Gilinsky, "because the true vulnerability of the system is in nuclear safeguards. Safeguards are the thorn in the side of nuclear power."

The reason is simple. To do a conscientious, responsible job of safeguarding bomb-grade nuclear material, government officials feel they might have to assume powers that will fundamentally alter the nature of our society. They will need to wiretap, bug, and open the mail—perhaps on an everyday basis—of those whom they suspect might be nuclear terrorists.

The 1975 Barton Report, commissioned by the NRC, envisioned the evolution of a nuclear police state. It predicted the emergence of a special police force empowered to conduct domestic surveillance without a court order, to detain nuclear critics and dissident scientists without filing formal charges and, under certain circumstances, to torture suspected nuclear terrorists.

In 1974, twenty years after the passage of the Atomic Energy Act, government officials planning for the future convinced Congress to add an amendment to the original legislation allowing the government to probe the "character, associations and loyalty" of plutonium workers. But security checks and covert surveillance would not be likely to detect a sophisticated and determined infiltrator who took care to present himself as a loyal worker. Furthermore, at least one psychologist who has studied the problem says that even the most systematic safeguards may not detect the events in a loyal worker's personal life that might turn him into a plutonium thief. He might become angry or depressed, suddenly find himself in debt, be converted to a new religion, be influenced by a political argument, or simply be *tempted* by the prospect of possessing such power. The black-market value of plutonium could approach that of any known substance.

According to a government-funded study conducted in 1976, "Communities subjected to [nuclear] terrorism will accept increased safeguards and the concomitant decrease in civil liberties. The paramount concern of society is to protect itself from known consequences. . . ." The study observes that "the tendency toward overreaction . . . outweighs that of underreaction, creating a real risk that civil liberties will be sacrificed for a minimal derived value in terms of societal protection."

If these scenarios sound far-fetched, it may be sobering to learn that many in the government don't think they are. Officials in Washington are preparing contingency plans for dealing with a new version of the "unthinkable"—a peacetime nuclear emergency. The plans call for a division of responsibilities (some of which are gruesome and dangerous) among many branches of government, all coordinated through the Federal Emergency Management Agency (FEMA), an emergency agency created by the government only seven months ago. FEMA has the responsibility for dealing with all sorts of possible crises. To combat nuclear crises, the agency is developing a Federal Response Plan for Peacetime Nuclear Emergencies (FRPPNE, pronounced "fripnee").

To date, only an interim working plan has been produced under FRPPNE, but it gives us some insight into just what government officials are preparing for. As explained in a few short lines in the preliminary FRPPNE report, it is the responsibility of the Department of Justice to "minimize, both in scope and duration, the restraints, if any, that the exigencies of a dire peacetime nuclear emergency might necessitate with respect to the free exercise of constitutional and other basic rights and liberties." And, further, to "preserve and/or reconstitute, as quickly as possible, representative constitutional government." What the report is alluding to is the necessity for martial law following a nuclear threat.

"The sort of thing that comes up," explains Donald Kerr, "is, What if you had to evacuate an area? You would in effect have to impose the equivalent of martial law. You would remove people from their homes, for their own protection. What if someones tells you they won't go? Probably the humane ethic [would] say, 'I don't care what you think your rights are; for your own good we're going to take you away.' "

At least one high EACT official is confident that civil liberties will not be allowed to stand in the way of strong action if and when the crisis comes. "We're convinced that if there ever was a real incident," he says, "either by high-level decree or command, all these little gnats will be swept out of the way."

"Post-theft recovery measures would create a situation approaching civil war," Russell Ayres has predicted in a Harvard legal publication, "with the government arrayed against the perpetrators of the nuclear threat and with innocent citizens caught in the middle."

In case a bomb does go off, FRPPNE has assigned the rest of the federal government specific responsibility for various functions. The Department of Agriculture is to dispose of contaminated livestock and issue food stamps. The Treasury Department is to consider whether to place a moratorium on banks, and whether to print more money. The Securities and Exchange Commission will decide whether to suspend the stock exchange. Health and Human Services (HHS; formerly HEW) will establish mental health centers and condemn or embargo food. The FBI, U.S. Postal Service and HHS share the responsibility for identifying the dead and attempting to reunite families. Commerce will decide whether to implement antihoarding measures. Labor will determine whether a wage/price freeze is necessary. The General Services Administration must try to protect fine arts and museums. The Environmental Protection Agency is to draw up plans for decontaminating water, food and buildings, and to decide how to dispose of the dead, who may be highly radioactive.

"The kinds of questions we have to face," says Harry Calley, of the EPA's Office of Radiation Programs, "are, What do we do after a blast with the radioactive buildings? Do we try to clean them up? What if that's ten times as expensive as knocking them down and rebuilding? Also, what about contaminated wheat fields? Should we harvest that wheat and store it? Plow it under? Mow, bale and bury it? Or eat it?"

The Plutonium Economy

As many as 20 or 30 years may pass before we can detect the individual human cells exposed to radiation that have gone "berserk" and caused cancer. In much the same way, we are only now, on the eve of the 1980s, having to confront the social and political fallout of the Manhattan and "Atoms for Peace" projects of the 1940s and 1950s. That legacy, if the nuclear industry has its way, will be the "plutonium economy." All the enriched uranium and plutonium produced to date is insignificant when it is compared to what is planned for the future.

As the end of the first generation of nuclear power plants (those which, in simplified terms, use uranium as fuel and produce plutonium as waste) approaches, we face a second stage, which the industry dubs "plutonium recycle." The concept is simple and logical: "mine" the plutonium from the waste products of the first-generation plants and "recycle" it as an even more efficient fuel into refurbished old plants or into a new type of nuclear plant—the "breeder reactor."

Plutonium literally "breeds" more plutonium—a regenerating process that might ultimately offer a partial solution to overdependence on other sources of energy, such as oil. But, on the negative side, this means that a vastly increased amount of material would be moving around the country. The NRC has estimated that as much as 200,000 pounds of special nuclear materials could be produced by 1990, and much of the future plutonium would be in the form of plutonium oxide, giving terrorists or organized criminals the opportunity to intercept bomb material in transit.

The plans for plutonium recycle and the breeder were blocked by President Gerald Ford, who was concerned about the government's inability to safeguard bomb-grade material. President Carter also opposed development of the breeder, but Congress passed authorization of funds—over his objections.

Although the White House and Congress have taken contradictory stances on when and how to launch the plutonium economy, those within the nuclear establishment are already taking it for granted. Kerr and others believe that "co-locating" various plutonium processing facilities in giant "nuclear parks" (similar to the ones the government already operates at Oak Ridge, Tennessee, and Hanford, Washington) would eliminate many transportation worries. But this concept would create problems in the long-distance transmission of the electricity to the cities where it is needed most. It would also make the nation's electricity supply highly vulnerable to war or sabotage.

Hal Lewis of the influential Jasons believes that the plutonium economy is inevitable. "The world is going to go to a plutonium economy, whether or not we want it to. Simply because the world has a better recognition that it's at war with the oil-producing countries than we seem to have. So there will be a plutonium economy. And we better plan accordingly."

The Beginning of the End

The picture is indeed bleak. We have a bomb that anyone can make; we have a government placing its faith in high-tech devices that are probably inadequate; we have an increasing amount of bomb-grade nuclear material unaccounted for; we have a large number of experts convinced that sometime, somewhere, probably pretty soon, a terrorist bomb will go off and level a large portion of a major American city.

It seems obvious that only a basic reordering of national priorities can prevent one of these grotesque scenarios from becoming a reality. As difficult as it may be, as much economic hardship as it may cause, the fierce momentum of the plutonium economy must be altered and reversed. Already there are a few hopeful signs—the moratorium on the licensing of new nuclear power plants; the possibility that some existing plants may be closed—but halfway, reformist measures are not enough. We have become convinced that the government is trying to regulate the unregulatable, limit the unlimitable. The simple truth is: Nuclear technology is out of control. Any sane governmental policy must be founded on that central fact.

Behind the Story

The chairs in the living room were a little too comfortable for David Weir. He had been conducting interviews all day and was still jet-lagged from the cross-country trip to Washington, D.C., the night before. Now he began to doze off during this late-night interview. But his partner, Michael Singer, had the stamina to overcome his own exhaustion and ask a few last questions of the secretive "whistle blower" sitting across the room.

Their government source, Barry Steel,* mentioned that the government had secret strategies "for preventing unauthorized use of weapons-grade material by terrorists or other 'subgovernment units.'"

"Has anybody like that ever gotten their hands on nuclear material?" Singer asked.

"I remember an incident up in Massachusetts a couple of years ago when there was a bomb threat against the city of Boston which the government took very seriously," Steel answered. "The White House Situation Room was on around-the-clock alert."

By now Weir was sitting up, suddenly wide awake.

"What happened?" he asked.

"Well, it turned out to be a hoax, but not before a lot of people got very nervous. Something happened that made us think that a Middle Eastern terrorist organization may have been behind the Boston threat. But the FBI could never pin it down."

Weir and Singer pressed Steel for more details. He declined, citing restrictions under the Atomic Energy Act against discussing security matters. So they decided to make a few visits to the Public Document Rooms at the Nuclear Regulatory Commission (NRC) and the Department of Energy (DOE). They were looking for reports or letters that might corroborate this and other allegations they had picked up in two days of interviewing members of the government's nuclear bureaucracy.

Their trip to the capital had begun inauspiciously. Three times in twenty minutes they had driven past the garish Mormon temple

* Not his real name. "Steel" was a confidential source.

which sits above the Capital Beltway like the Emerald City of Oz. They were lost and they knew it. It was a moonless June night, and the two West Coast reporters became frantic trying to find their exit into the rural Maryland countryside, all the while losing more time.

With a road map and a little luck they finally turned up the driveway to an unimposing tract home with a house trailer outside and plenty of Stroh's beer in the refrigerator. Ron Clary, a structural engineer working for the NRC, had evidence that the Rancho Seco power plant in California was not constructed well enough to withstand an earthquake along a fault that ran underneath the facility.

Clary's house was just the first stop on a circuitous investigative path that was to take many unexpected twists and turns before yielding "Nuclear Nightmare" six months later—the first of many trips around the Beltway and into the homes of officials who were afraid to meet with reporters in their offices during work hours. It was also their first glimpse into the shadowy world the Atomic Age has created in the capital—one that is pervaded by secrecy, fear, rumors, intimidation, and behind-the-scenes maneuvering. It is a world that, in the words of one of its most revealing catchphrases, was "born classified" and remains largely so to this day.

The officials Weir and Singer were seeking hold "Q" clearances, the highest civilian classification granted by the U.S. government. In addition, many hold military appointments—visible signs of the semisecret role Pentagon officials play in almost every aspect of nuclear regulation. The people the two reporters interviewed invariably spoke in tightly controlled low voices, choosing their words carefully and responding to questions with the nervous precision of witnesses being interrogated in court. One mistake and they could lose their jobs. Worse, if they were found to have violated the provisions of their "Q" clearance or of a particularly draconian section of the Atomic Energy Act, they could go to prison.

"Nuclear Nightmare" began in early 1979, when Jim Harding, an activist at the San Francisco–based Friends of the Earth, received internal NRC files from Ron Clary. Harding turned the material over to Singer, whom he had met during political organizing work for California's Nuclear Safeguards Initiative campaign in 1976.

Singer, a freelance reporter whose main experience was in newspaper writing, showed the documents to a friend at the *Los Angeles Times,* Henry Weinstein. The files were interesting but inconclusive, so Weinstein recommended that Singer go to the Center for Investigative Reporting. There he met with David Weir, who immediately became interested in the allegation of a widespread pattern of hazards in nuclear plants across the country.

The pair approached one national magazine, but the editor there was not interested in financing what could become a long and fruitless investigation. Still, public and media interest in safety at nuclear power plants was high, and the Center was able to raise two grants of $1,500 each to fund the risky research phase of the story. With this money, the two reporters checked out the leads from the NRC files during several exhausting days in Washington, where they cut costs by staying with friends and working almost around the clock.

Clary became a key link in the chain of individuals who eventually helped Singer and Weir put the story together. He called a number of other friends inside the NRC and introduced them to the reporters. Late on the second night of that Washington trip, Singer and Weir drove across the Maryland countryside to the home of one of those friends, Barry Steel, who provided the Boston lead.

The remaining days in Washington turned up many interesting items but nothing solid enough to guarantee a story. Their money spent, they returned to California. Soon thereafter, Weir received a telephone call from the editor of *New West* magazine, Jon Carroll. In the wake of the accident at Three Mile Island, he had become keenly interested in stories about nuclear power. Judy Coburn, a freelance writer in Los Angeles and a mutual friend of Carroll and Singer, had told him about the nuclear leads Weir and Singer were investigating.

Carroll asked the reporters to visit his office in Beverly Hills, where they could discuss the story possibilities at length. The two reporters met for several hours with Carroll and managing editor Meredith White. By the end of lunch, Carroll and White were excited by the story, and Weir and Singer had a financial commitment to fund the next stage of their investigation.

Over the next six weeks, the pair sifted through their voluminous files, searching congressional reports and NRC and DOE papers for details about nuclear safety and safeguards issues. Carroll agreed to finance a return trip to Washington so that they could expand their list of sources and further check out the leads they'd developed on the first visit.

By the time they returned to California in late July, Singer and Weir had narrowed their focus to three separate stories: Clary's allegations about the construction problems at the Rancho Seco nuclear power plant, Steel's story of the Boston nuclear bomb threat, and a third lead about a plutonium release at a midwestern nuclear facility. They agreed to split up the work that was needed for each story. Judy Coburn, the writer who had told Carroll about the reporters, agreed to write the Clary story ("How Safe Is Rancho Seco?" *New West,* November 1979); Weir and Singer decided to concentrate on Boston; and the third story was filed for possible future investigation.

Few cities are as humidly uncomfortable as the nation's capital in midsummer, so Singer and Weir checked into an air-conditioned hotel near Dupont Circle and rented an air-conditioned car for their trips into the surrounding countryside. These two refuges from the heat became their mini command posts during the next stage of the investigation.

Except for some occasional backup help for Coburn, Weir and Singer now concentrated exclusively on the Boston case. They interviewed two top officials in safeguards at the NRC, one a former FBI agent, the other an ex–Secret Service man. Both were stiff and suspicious. They were unwilling to admit that any nuclear threats against American cities had ever occurred, even though Weir and Singer knew by now that government investigators had logged a long series of such threats.

The two safeguards officials were more than guarded in their answers. When asked a question about a nuclear threat such as the one in Boston, they looked at each other in Laurel and Hardy fashion and exclaimed: "Did we ever know about that? No, we never heard of that. Sorry, can't help you on that one."

After an hour of questions, Weir and Singer left the NRC, abandoning the "front-door" approach for the duration of the investigation. Clearly the NRC had too much at stake to admit what the reporters already knew to be true: (1) that a huge amount of bomb-grade material was missing and unaccounted for and (2) that dozens of nuclear threats had been received by mayors, governors, the White House, other high government officials, and corporate officials during the 1970s.

Next the reporters decided to try the FBI. They telephoned the Bureau and made an appointment with the chief of counterintelligence in Washington. They signed in at the massive new J. Edgar Hoover Building on Pennsylvania Avenue, were issued identification badges, and were greeted by a junior agent—an intern at the Bureau. The young man was cordial but formal. He led them through a maze of hallways and elevators toward the counterintelligence offices. Noticing that the new FBI headquarters was across the street from the old building, Weir innocently asked the junior agent whether an underground passage connected the two buildings. "I am not authorized to answer that question" was his curt reply.

Weir and Singer were ushered into a large office where seven men waited. The door was closed as introductions were made around the room—the head of counterintelligence, a specialist in nuclear questions, the Middle East expert, and so on. Singer and Weir realized that they had walked, not into an interview *of* the FBI, but into an interrogation *by* the FBI.

The reporters had had to offer a fair amount of information to obtain the interview in the first place. So the Bureau knew that they had heard of a "nuclear threat in Boston, possibly involving a Middle Eastern terrorist group." Now the agents wanted to know more, including where they had obtained this information and what else they knew.

Singer and Weir "stonewalled" the agents on these questions. For their part, the agents denied knowing anything about the Boston incident. Like the NRC officials, the FBI men were not interested in releasing information about what was obviously a sensitive subject. But they did ask repeatedly for the source of the reporters' tip.

There was an element of intimidation in the situation because at that time *The Progressive* magazine was under a government-sought, court-ordered injunction not to publish an article on how to make an H-bomb. Weir and Singer felt that the story they were chasing (which included information about the ease of making a small "clandestine" bomb) might be similarly subjected to prior censorship by the government.

None of the seven agents hinted at that possibility, however. Leaving the room, Weir even managed to extract a smile from one older man, a former cop from Boston, who seemed slightly less formal than his younger colleagues. "I guess you don't have much to do these days since there are hardly any terrorists around anymore, eh?" Weir asked. The ex-cop smiled and said, "Maybe that's because we do our job so well."

"Maybe I'll call back sometime," Weir suggested.

"Sure."

It was a connection that would prove useful.

Back at the hotel, Singer and Weir set up a "boiler room" command post in their adjoining rooms. Files were sorted into stacks on the desks and beds, and both telephones were in use almost constantly. They were trying to find a source in any law enforcement agency who could tell them more about what had happened in Boston five years earlier. Finally, after three days and a $250 phone bill, there was a breakthrough. A consultant to another news organization, who was himself a security expert, gave Weir the name and number of an FBI agent in the Bureau's Boston office. By mentioning the intermediary's name, Weir was able to persuade the agent to do something he wasn't technically allowed to do. He "pulled" the file on the case and read it over the phone.

It was an interesting story but not good news for Weir and Singer. The agent read a copy of the threat letter. The FBI had investigated the threat but had found neither a bomb nor the perpetrator. A phony money "drop" had been made, but nobody came to pick up the satchel, which the FBI kept under surveillance long after the extortionist's deadline had passed. Further investigation had cast suspicion on a college fraternity house, but charges were never pressed. No Middle Eastern group was mentioned in the file.

For Weir and Singer it was a disappointing moment. They had spent a good-sized expense budget courtesy of *New West,* and suddenly they had very little to show for it. They decided to go back to their original source on the Boston case, Barry Steel.

By checking through volumes of NRC and DOE studies they had come across the report of an incident at an airport in the Northeast: a shipment of nuclear material had been lost for several weeks right around the time of the Boston threat. Putting the two cases together, Weir and Singer realized that government investigators might have been worried that the Boston extortionist had a weapon to back up his threat. For that reason the investigators had treated the threat more seriously than they need have. But Weir and Singer were never able to find a Middle Eastern connection. They explained all of this to Steel, who was impressed with the thoroughness of the reporters' investigation and now agreed to supply further information.

As Singer later explained, "We now knew the right questions to ask. The more you know, the more you find out. Barry Steel knew about other incidents besides Boston, but he didn't say anything about them at first because there was no reason for him to."

Steel said that a producer at ABC News named Barbara Newman had researched nuclear terrorist threats extensively and knew about several other serious incidents besides the one in Boston. Singer and Weir called Newman, who agreed to meet with them at her home on the outskirts of Washington. An energetic and skilled producer for ABC's *20/20* program, Newman led Weir and Singer up to her third-floor loft, which was cluttered with boxes and books and film cartridges left over from her investigation. She readily agreed to supply her files and help the writers do the story "right," since much of her material had not been aired.

Newman's style was astonishing. As Singer put it, "Barbara would call up anybody anywhere and ask them anything." While they were looking through her files on nuclear terrorism, Newman placed a few calls. "How's my favorite general?" she started one conversation. "When are you going to tell me what happened on your base out there last summer? You know, that accident everybody's trying to hush up?"

Weir and Singer returned to their hotel room and spent an entire day organizing the new information and integrating it with their own. By now they had perceived the outlines of a story that had several aspects. Weir became interested in the civil liberties implications. "It's almost as if the government is creating these weapons to protect a society that won't be worth protecting anymore," he told Singer, after studying what would happen to the Bill of Rights if a nuclear terrorist ever did explode a bomb. While Weir followed the political and social effects of nuclear weapons, Singer became fascinated with learning the technical aspects of fission explosives.

In the NRC Public Documents Room the reporters had unearthed a list of forty-four nuclear threats in U.S. cities. With Steel's help they zeroed in on one of those cases—the Los Angeles incident at Union Oil—for further work. Steel said that the government had taken the Union Oil threat as seriously as the Boston one, and that on technical grounds it was even more believable. *New West* editor Carroll was happy to authorize further investigation by the pair, even though the Boston story was not very good. Everyone agreed that the Los Angeles incident would be more relevant to the magazine's readership, which was concentrated in southern California.

Weir and Singer quickly discovered a unique aspect of the LA case: it was the only one of the forty-four nuclear threats in which somebody had been convicted as the perpetrator. Newman said she thought the case against the man, Frank James, was weak and that the actual perpetrator might still be at large.

As they broadened their investigation into the LA case, they outlined the emerging contours of the story:

- There had been a whole series of nuclear threats.
- The government felt vulnerable to these threats.
- The government had created an elaborate response mechanism that endangered civil liberties.
- The problem was about to grow worse with the advent of the plutonium economy.

It was the last element that gave the story its urgency, according to Weir. "We realized that as reporters we would be acting preventively. We were about to try to intervene in the historical process and get this information to the public while there is still something that could be done about it. We both realized that within ten or fifteen years, or whenever these big nuclear terrorist events

occur, freedom of the press is going to have to be curtailed, because
the consequences would be too disastrous."

During the fall, Weir and Singer continued to interview their
sources by telephone from their offices in California. They also
made short trips to Las Vegas, site of the NEST headquarters,
and to Los Alamos, New Mexico, site of the nuclear weapons
laboratory.

Singer read and reread various documents. But he kept returning
to a letter from Peter Zimmerman, a Louisiana State University
physicist who had written to the NRC about something called
"single-point initiation." A congressional source in Washington had
told the reporters that another paper Zimmerman had been
scheduled to give before the American Physical Society was
suppressed by the DOE.

When Singer called, Zimmerman told him the information in
the paper was classified. Frustrated, but feeling he was on to
something, Singer thought of another approach. He telephoned a
source who was privy to the Zimmerman affair and confronted
him on the subject of the professor's suppressed paper.

"I think he could not give the lecture because he was going to
talk about single-point initiation," Singer stated, remembering the
NRC letter but without any evidence to back up his question—
and not really understanding the term. The tactic worked. The
source was silent, then said, "Mr. Singer, you said that, I didn't."
The source agreed to fill in the details because he assumed that
an inside source at the NRC had given Singer the information.
As a result, Singer was able to piece together the story of how it
was much simpler to explode nuclear material than the government
wanted the public to believe.

He first went to a physicist friend who taught at the University
of California in Berkeley and convinced him to give a private lecture
on the workings of the nuclear bomb. Singer taped his friend's
explanation, which he and Weir studied until they had mastered
the elements of assembling and exploding a nuclear bomb, at least
well enough to write about it in their article.

Again *The Progressive* case affected their investigation. The
reporters, as well as their editors at *New West,* felt that the
information they had uncovered—how to build a simple, crude bomb

that could be detonated from a single point—was far more dangerous than *The Progressive*'s complicated H-bomb directions. The materials needed for the latter were prohibitively expensive for all but national governments. The simple terrorist bomb, however, could be made for a few thousand dollars from materials available in any "well-stocked hardware store," according to one source.

Therefore, Weir and Singer feared that the government would stop the magazine's distribution if it found out about their story ahead of publication. This made it difficult to obtain official confirmation of some of their information without alerting officials.

On a trip to Las Vegas, Weir and Singer interviewed Jack Doyle, a senior official with NEST. He had participated in the Los Angeles incident at Union Oil and, more important, had a strong commitment to the public's right to know. When they asked him a question, he answered, without the tension and suspicion the reporters had encountered so often in Washington. Doyle agreed to be quoted by name—another important aid to a story that was relying so heavily on off-the-record sources.

Doyle supplied an insider's view of the Los Angeles threat. He also verified many other allegations that the reporters had gathered from Steel, Newman, and their other sources, including NEST's inability to detect a bomb shielded by lead or water. Doyle took the reporters on a short tour of the hangar where NEST kept its helicopters and equipment, and he patiently explained to them how the elaborate NEST structure worked. He was a rare find—a government official who actually believes in the public's right to know. His help was crucial to the success of the investigation.

Weir returned to San Francisco while Singer stayed on to interview DOE official General "Ink" Gates. Far less candid than Doyle, Gates nonetheless supplied an important piece of corroboration for the story when he was surprised by Singer's question, "Where is Plutonium Valley?"

"It's off limits," Gates sputtered before the aide stationed in the room could stop him. "You don't go there. One doesn't go there if one has any sense. It's just fenced off. And no access." Gates then confirmed that single-point testing had been conducted at Plutonium Valley.

For the final information needed on single-point initiation, Singer

traveled to Los Alamos, in the hills of New Mexico. The site of
planning for the Trinity test—the government's first successful effort
to explode a nuclear bomb during World War II—Los Alamos
remains one of the key centers of the government's secret nuclear
weapons establishment. There Singer conducted a tense interview
with Donald Kerr, head of the Los Alamos operation. Singer was
ushered to a chair facing Kerr. A group of what Singer called
"flacks" sat behind him, in a position where Kerr could see them
but the writer couldn't. Throughout the interview, according to
Singer, the flacks gave signals to the cautious Kerr before he
answered the questions. After about forty-five minutes of this cat-
and-mouse exchange, Kerr finally admitted that single-point
initiation existed.

Singer returned to California and the two writers started drafting
their story. Once they looked at each other's sections, however,
they realized that the two styles did not mesh well, so they asked
Weir's longtime friend and colleague Howard Kohn for editing
help. Kohn blended the two styles, and the writers then redrafted
the piece before heading to Los Angeles for the final stage of their
project.

New West set Weir and Singer up in the magazine's conference
rooms, eight floors above Los Angeles, and booked rooms for them
at the Beverly Wilshire Hotel, one block away. One of the magazine's
lawyers flew out from New York to assess whether the magazine
faced a government injunction or any other kind of legal jeopardy
from the story. With their files spilling out of boxes stacked around
a long conference table, the writers began the fact-checking process
with *New West* staffer Laura Bernstein.

Good fact-checkers are more responsible than most magazine
writers like to admit for guaranteeing the quality of the reporting
in long investigative pieces such as "Nuclear Nightmare." Bernstein
was, in Singer's description, "a pugnacious, wonderful, tough
woman who was not going to be bowled over by our story, or
David, or me, or anything else." Bernstein started the painstaking
process of isolating and verifying every factual statement, name,
date, event, title, agency, quote, and assessment in the story. In
order to check their facts, and to comply with the editing changes
being suggested by Jon Carroll and Meredith White, Weir and Singer

placed a new round of telephone calls to many of their key sources. One of Weir's calls was to the ex-policeman he had met at the FBI months before. Weir wanted confirmation of the jurisdictional squabble between the FBI and LA police chief Ed Davis. He asked seven or eight innocuous questions, then sprang the important one, and finished up with a few more unimportant questions so that his source would not realize the reason for the call. The FBI confirmation that Weir obtained convinced Bernstein and the editors to include the jurisdictional fight in the story.

A disagreement between the editors and writers broke out over the conclusion to the article. Carroll's version ended on a note of hopelessness, to which Weir and Singer strongly objected. "The whole point of writing the story," Singer explains, "was to inform people so that something could be done." The two sides quickly compromised, however, on the version that appears here.

New West's talented art director, Roger Black, in an unusual move for one in his position, invited the authors to participate in his design plans for the story. He showed them several graphics under consideration and listened to their views before making his decisions. Often the editorial and art departments in magazines are at odds, and sometimes these two elements of a story seem to contradict each other. Black, however, is savvy enough to avoid this pitfall. One result is that his designs have consistently won awards for *New West* and the other magazines where he has worked.

It was Friday, and the magazine had to "go to bed" for its Monday publication date. The fact-checking was completed, the design was finished, the headlines had been written and pasted up. There were still a few last-minute editing changes, partly to fit the gargantuan story into the magazine's limited copy hole. So while Singer was flying back to San Francisco, Weir drove back on Interstate 5 with a car full of files and an eye for the next telephone booth. Every couple of hours he dialed the *New West* office to consult with managing editor White over her changes. By evening, Weir and White had settled on the final few adjustments to the piece.

"Nuclear Nightmare" was released the following Monday simultaneously in *New West* and *New York* magazines, both of which were then owned by Australian publisher Rupert Murdoch. Besides a front-page story in the *San Francisco Chronicle* based on the article and a wire service story confirming the threat at Union Oil, little public reaction was generated.

The issue of nuclear terrorism has continued to interest and concern the public, however. About a year after "Nuclear Nightmare," the *New York Times Magazine* published an article by Larry Collins called "Combatting Nuclear Terrorism" that began, as had "Nightmare," with the actual words of a nuclear extortion threat—this one against New York City in July 1975. A novel about nuclear terrorism by Larry Collins and Dominique Lapierre, *The Fifth Horseman,* became a best-seller when it was published in Europe and was considered by Paramount Studios for a possible film offer. *Time* magazine reported that "the most hair-raising detail [in the book] is the revelation that there have actually been more than 50 attempts at nuclear blackmail in the U.S."

There are some signs that the U.S. and other governments now take the threat of nuclear terrorism more seriously than they did before "Nuclear Nightmare" appeared. Senator Alan Cranston (D–Calif.) warned at a news conference in February 1981 of the dangers of revolutionary groups' acquiring a nuclear weapon. In October 1982, Congress passed legislation to strengthen the laws governing security of nuclear materials. The bill implemented a 1981 Senate ratification of the Convention on the Physical Protection of Nuclear Materials that obligates signatory countries to adopt domestic safeguards for nuclear materials. A task force of senators and House members interested in nuclear nonproliferation was organized in 1982 and met that August to discuss nuclear terrorism.

Other officials still remain unconvinced of the dangers. The director of the State Department's Office for Combatting Terrorism reportedly told the task force that nuclear materials would be too difficult to obtain and hazardous to handle and therefore were an unlikely terrorist weapon. This official then admitted that the Nuclear Emergency Search Team, which had spent over $100 million since 1974, was not included in policy decisions on nuclear proliferation.

Meanwhile the threats continued. In an August 1982 interview with Center researcher Jeanette Valentine, Robert Burnett, Director of Safeguards at the NRC, revealed that two five-gallon containers of low-enriched uranium were stolen from a uranium processing plant in North Carolina in 1979. Around the time of the incident, according to Burnett, the plant manager received an extortion note. The FBI "assumed investigative jurisdiction" and arrested a suspect who was later convicted. This was the first confirmed non-hoax threat of nuclear terrorism in U.S. history.

Hank Boudin, a spokesman for the Department of Energy, believes that the safeguarding of nuclear materials has been strengthened in recent years. "The DOE always puts heavy emphasis on safeguarding because we know the danger involved. We know evil forces are trying to get ahold of the material."

Since the publication of "Nuclear Nightmare," Michael Singer has produced freelance magazine articles, newspaper stories, and television exposés in San Francisco. His work exposing police corruption won an Emmy and a Radio Television News Directors Association regional award in 1983.

When Weir had lunch with *New West* editors Jon Carroll and Meredith White six months after "Nuclear Nightmare" appeared, they said they were surprised that more action had not resulted from the article. Carroll said that the situation reminded him of another investigative story *New West* had done that failed to achieve immediate impact. That other story was the exposé of Jim Jones and the People's Temple just before they left San Francisco for Guyana.

2

Citizen Scaife

by Karen Rothmyer

Five years ago, George Mair was bored with his job as editorial director of KNX, the CBS radio affiliate in Los Angeles. As Mair recalls it now, he and John E. Cox, Jr., an aide to Republican congressman Barry Goldwater, Jr., hit on the idea of starting a nonprofit organization aimed primarily at improving relations between business and the media. The one thing they didn't have was money, so when they heard that Richard Larry, an administrative agent of the Scaife Family Charitable Trusts, was coming to town, they called up to see if they could talk to him.

"The only reason he agreed to have dinner with us is that he thought Jack was another man named Cox he was supposed to be meeting," Mair, now an editorial columnist for the Los Angeles Times Syndicate, says with a laugh. "But he was very polite and listened to our ideas. He came again a few months later and we had lunch. He gave us a check. When we opened it, it was far, far beyond our wildest dreams—one hundred thousand dollars."

Thus was born the Foundation for American Communications, one of a large number of organizations that owe their existence to the generosity of one of the richest men in America,

Richard Mellon Scaife. Scaife, a great-grandson of the founder of the Mellon empire, has made the formation of public opinion both his business and his avocation.

Over the past twelve years, Scaife, whose personal fortune is conservatively estimated at $150 million, has bought or started a variety of publications, mainly in the Pittsburgh area. But he has increasingly turned his attention from journalism to other, more ambitious efforts to shape public opinion, in the form of $100 million or so in grants from Scaife charities to conservative, particularly New Right, causes. These efforts have been dramatically successful. Indeed, Scaife could claim to have done more than any other individual in the past five or six years to influence the way in which Americans think about their country and the world.

Since 1973, Scaife charitable entities have given $1 million or more to each of nearly a score of organizations that are closely linked to the New Right movement. These range from the Institute for Foreign Policy Analysis, a Massachusetts think-tank that examines political and military issues, to California's Pacific Legal Foundation, the oldest and largest of a dozen conservative legal groups, all Scaife beneficiaries, which function as mirror images of the Nader-inspired public-interest law groups.

The press has generally overlooked Scaife, even when reporting on organizations that are financially dependent on him. For example, Scaife is the single largest donor to the Mountain States Legal Foundation—$200,000 toward a $1-million budget in 1980—as acknowledged by Mountain States officials. Yet, earlier this year, when James Watt, then president of Mountain States, was up for Senate confirmation as Interior Secretary in the Reagan cabinet, the press reported—on the basis of available information—that Mountain States was primarily funded by timber, utility, and mining interests.

Similarly, officials of The Heritage Foundation, a conservative think-tank that supplied eleven members of the Reagan transition team, acknowledge that Scaife is a far larger contributor than Joseph Coors, whose name has been the only one mentioned in most press reports on the group. Scaife, who joined with Coors to launch Heritage seven years ago, gave

close to $900,000—three times Coors's gift—to help meet the
current $5.3-million Heritage budget.

"They're playing all sides of the street: media, politics—
the soft approach and the hard," says George Mair, referring
to Scaife and his advisers. Mair left the Foundation for American Communications just over a year ago, forced out, he
claims, over the issue of what he regarded as the group's increasingly conservative bias. FACS president Jack Cox says,
"The decision was made by the board of trustees to sever
Mr. Mair's relationship with the foundation and that decision
was not based on any political or ideological disputes."

Scaife himself has never publicly discussed his motivations
or goals. Indeed, he has repeatedly declined requests for interviews, as he did in the case of this article. Officials of most
organizations that receive money from Scaife charities say they
rarely if ever see Scaife himself, but deal instead with aides
like Richard Larry, who has also been unavailable for comment. Most of the more sensitive Scaife donations are made
through a family trust that is not legally required to make
any public accounting of its donations, and most institutions
that receive money from Scaife, like their more liberal coun-
terparts, do not volunteer information about their contrib-
utors. The story of Scaife and his activities has to be pieced
together from public records, such published reports as exist,
and conversations with people who for the most part decline
identification—some because of business or professional reasons, others because they fear retaliation. (Shortly after this
article was completed, the *Pittsburgh Post-Gazette* published
a four-part series on Scaife. Written by staff writer David Warner, the series detailed Scaife's publishing and some of his
New Right connections, relying in part on documentation also
privately made available to this reporter.)

Scaife's secretiveness is but one aspect of a complicated
personality. A handsome man in the blond, beefy style one associates with southwestern ranchers or oil millionaires, the
forty-eight-year-old Scaife dresses like a Wall Street executive.
His astonishingly blue eyes are his most striking feature. A
friend from an early age of J. Edgar Hoover and a long-time
admirer of Barry Goldwater, Scaife is said by those who know

Meeting Mr. Scaife

Richard Scaife rarely speaks to the press. After several unsuccessful efforts to obtain an interview, this reporter decided to make one last attempt in Boston, where Scaife was scheduled to attend the annual meeting of the First Boston Corporation.

Scaife, a company director, did not show up while the meeting was in progress. Reached eventually by telephone as he dined with the other directors at the exclusive Union Club, he hung up the moment he heard the caller's name. A few minutes later he appeared at the top of the Club steps. At the bottom of the stairs, the following exchange occurred:

"Mr. Scaife, could you explain why you give so much money to the New Right?"

"You fucking Communist cunt, get out of here."

Well. The rest of the five-minute interview was conducted at a rapid trot down Park Street, during which Scaife tried to hail a taxi. Scaife volunteered two statements of opinion regarding his questioner's personal appearance—he said she was ugly and that her teeth were "terrible"—and also the comment that she was engaged in "hatchet journalism." His questioner thanked Scaife for his time.

"Don't look behind you," Scaife offered by way of a goodbye.

Not quite sure what this remark meant, the reporter suggested that if someone were approaching it was probably her mother, whom she had arranged to meet nearby. "She's ugly, too," Scaife said, and strode off.

---

him to be fascinated by military and intelligence matters. At the same time, he is so shy and so insecure about his intellectual capacities, according to one business acquaintance, that "he never speaks business without two, three, four people around him."

David Abshire, who as chairman of the Georgetown University Center for Strategic and International Studies, a major Scaife beneficiary, has known Scaife for nearly twenty years, describes him as "likable, enthusiastic, and a very fine, public-spirited individual." A Democratic officeholder in Pittsburgh, on the other hand, views Scaife as a "lone wolf" whose clout "is through his money and nothing else." Pittsburgh acquaintances add that Scaife is rarely seen on the social circuit, and suggest that Scaife's relations with most of the other Mellons tend to be less than cordial. Certainly that holds true within his own family: Scaife has only one sibling, Cordelia Scaife May, and he has not spoken to her for the past seven years.

One small insight into Scaife's personality is provided by Pat Minarcin, a former editor of the now-defunct *Pittsburgher* magazine, which Scaife financed. "We were talking one time after a meeting and I said to him, 'Is money power?' " Minarcin recalls. "He paused three or four seconds and looked at me really hard. He's just not used to people speaking to him on that level. He said, 'I didn't use to think so, but the older I get the more I do.' "

Certainly money is very much the stuff of which Mellon family history is made. Judge Thomas Mellon, the son of an Irish immigrant farmer who settled in the Pennsylvania countryside, rose to prominence in Pittsburgh during the latter half of the nineteenth century through shrewd real estate investments and a lending business that became the Mellon Bank. In time, the family holdings came to include, in addition to the bank, substantial blocks of stock in Gulf Oil and Alcoa, among other companies. By 1957, when *Fortune* magazine tried to rank the largest fortunes in America, four Mellons, including Scaife's mother, Sarah Mellon Scaife, were listed among the top eight.

In 1965, when his widowed mother died, Richard Scaife— in his early thirties, married, and the father of the first of two children—had no real career. After flunking out of Yale (he later finished at the University of Pittsburgh), Scaife had followed in the footsteps of his father, a retiring man from a local industrial family, and been given a variety of titles but little real power in several Mellon enterprises.

Just looking after his personal affairs could have become a full-time job. At the time of the last public accounting, in 1978, Scaife was the second-largest stockholder (after his second cousin Paul Mellon) in the Mellon Bank, one of the top twenty banks in the country. Until 1978, he was a bank trustee, having been elected to that post at the age of twenty-six. Among Scaife's other personal sources of wealth is the income from two trusts set up for him by his mother—probably amounting to around $8 million a year. He has homes in Pebble Beach, California, and in Pittsburgh, and a large estate in Ligonier, Pennsylvania, and he flies from coast to coast in a private DC-9—a plane so big that in commercial service it carries up to 100 passengers.

After his mother's death, Scaife began to take an increasingly active role in the family's philanthropic activities. Scaife family entities currently engaged in giving money to charity include the Sarah Scaife Foundation, set up by Scaife's mother; the Allegheny and Carthage Foundations, set up by Scaife; and the Trust for Sarah Mellon Scaife's Grandchildren (who number only Scaife's two, because Cordelia Scaife May has none). Taken together, these four groups have assets of more than $250 million, and current annual income of at least $12 million. (Eventually, Scaife's children will get the income from their trust, as Scaife now gets the income from his trusts.)

Gulf Oil company stock makes up a large part of the Scaife fortune. If one were to count in not just Richard Scaife's personal holdings in Gulf, but also those of the various Scaife charitable entities, the total would probably rank as the second largest holding (after Paul Mellon) in the company. By the same rough yardstick, Scaife and Scaife family entities account for about 6 percent of the stock (all nonvoting) of First Boston Corporation, a major investment banking firm. Scaife was elected to the First Boston board last year. The Mellons and Scaifes as a whole hold about 13 percent of the First Boston stock, an investment second in size only to that of Financière Credit Suisse.

The Heritage Foundation

A November 17, 1980, *New York Times* story on conservative think-tanks reported that "When the Heritage Foundation announced the other day that it was forwarding to Mr. Reagan a suggested 'blueprint for a conservative American government,' requests for details poured into the foundation's Capitol Hill office, and a dozen reporters from the nation's major papers and broadcasting networks showed up for the briefing." The article went on to quote Hugh Newton, a Heritage official, as saying, "We've never had this kind of attention before. . . . A lot of people who used to toss our stuff into the trash can are going to have to start reading it."

There is certainly plenty to read. Heritage, with a staff of sixty and a budget this year of $5.3 million, is probably the most media-oriented of the New Right research and policy study groups, producing a steady stream of reports and publications aimed at both policymakers and the news media. Richard Scaife has given almost $4 million to Heritage—including seed money—since it began operating seven years ago. This year, Scaife grants total about $900,000, including money specifically allocated to an editorial briefing series, distribution of the *National Security Record,* and a Distinguished Journalism Fellow program.

The day-long, twice-yearly editorial briefings for journalists cost about $15,000, of which Scaife gives two-thirds. About fifty to sixty journalists attend the sessions. Recent topics have included Enterprise Zones (a Reagan-backed urban revitalization plan), the Heritage "alternative budget" prepared for Reagan, relations with China and Taiwan, and the SALT II treaty.

The *National Security Record,* aimed primarily at Congress, is a monthly report on defense and national security issues. As an illustration of the *Record*'s influence, the foundation's September/October 1980 newsletter noted that "Liberal Carl Rowan devoted two columns in a single week to an attempt to refute the assertion in the July *National Security Record* that the Soviets were manipulating events in the Caribbean through the Cubans and other surrogates. Shortly thereafter, John Chamberlain, [Joseph] Kingsbury-Smith and [Smith] Hempstone wrote columns bolstering the *National Security Record*'s argument—all citing the Heritage research." Chamberlain, a King Features syndicated columnist, was chosen by Heritage last year as its Distinguished Journalism Fellow.

Other Heritage activities include serving as a consultant to WQLN, the public television station in Erie, Pennsylvania, which espouses free-market economics.

Heritage also publishes a quarterly, *Policy Review,* and produces a twice-monthly column, *Heritage Foundation Forum,* which it says is used by more than 450 newspapers.

According to John Von Kannon, assistant to the president of Heritage, Scaife and his aides rarely participate in Heritage functions. "They look for organizations they agree with," he says, and then leave them alone.

The Small-Bore Publisher

It was newspapers, however, not the world of finance, that
eventually captured Richard Scaife's interest. In 1969, he made
a successful offer of almost $5 million for the Greensburg,
Pennsylvania, *Tribune-Review* (daily circulation: 41,500),
which was part of an estate being handled by the Mellon Bank.
Greensburg, a town of 20,000 people about thirty miles east
of Pittsburgh, is the county seat of Westmoreland County,
which is a curious mix of, on the one hand, working-class,
mob-infiltrated towns, and, on the other, rolling hills where
Mellons ride to hounds.

Scaife apparently has not scrimped on costs at the paper,
including salaries. He has lured at least two people from the
Pittsburgh dailies, and his Harrisburg bureau chief, J. R.
Freeman, says that it is his understanding that he can "go
anywhere in the world and stay as long as I want." The
paper, housed in an attractive, modern building on a Greensburg side street, routinely features staff reports on Pittsburgh
politics as well as local affairs, depending on the wires for
most national coverage.

Despite his vast resources, Scaife has not moved into the
big leagues of publishing. During the Nixon years, he was
urged by at least one high official in the White House to bid
for *The Washington Star,* but he never did. Pittsburgh acquaintances say that several years ago Scaife talked about buying
The Philadelphia Inquirer; however, Sam McKeel, president
of Philadelphia Newspapers, Inc., the Knight-Ridder group
that owns the *Inquirer,* says Scaife never made any overtures.
Last year, Scaife entered into negotiations to buy *Harper's*
magazine, but nothing came of those talks.

Instead, Scaife has settled for a modest collection of holdings
which include, in addition to the *Tribune-Review,* the *Lebanon*
(Pennsylvania) *Daily News* and *Sunday Pennsylvanian;* two
Pennsylvania weeklies, *The* (Blairsville) *Dispatch* and the *Eliz-
abethtown Chronicle;* until recently, a city magazine, *Pittsburgher,* which folded early this year; and a new monthly
business Sunday supplement called *Pennsylvania Economy,*

which began publishing last October. Elsewhere, he owns half of two weeklies in California and half of *The Sacramento Union,* his largest (circulation: 106,000) and only nationally known acquisition. Scaife bought the half interest in late 1977 from John McGoff, a Michigan publisher who is under investigation by federal authorities in connection with alleged secret payments by the South African government to permit him to buy news properties.

Various explanations are offered for Scaife's failure to acquire a major national publication. Some acquaintances speak of his dislike of publicity; others of his unwillingness, despite his wealth, to spend the sums required. Pat Minarcin, the former *Pittsburgher* editor, suggests another aspect of Scaife's personality that may be relevant. "Here is a man who is as rich or richer than any other man in the country, who has a hunger to be accepted as a journalist and a responsible member of society," says Minarcin. "Yet he has this fatal flaw—he keeps shooting himself in the foot."

In the case of the *Tribune-Review,* the "shot" was Scaife's firing of a young reporter, Jude Dippold, in October 1973, two days after Dippold had remarked to the newsroom upon reading of Spiro Agnew's resignation as vice-president, "One down and one to go." Within hours of Dippold's firing, ten of the paper's twenty-four-person editorial staff resigned. They charged in a statement that Scaife (a $1-million contributor to Nixon's re-election campaign and a $47,500 contributor—according to Justice Department records—to the illegal Watergate campaign fund known as the Townhouse Operation) had "continually, in the opinion of the professional staff, interjected his political and personal bias into the handling of news stories."

Six years later, another chapter was added to the "Citizen Scaife" saga. This time it involved the firing of a young editorial cartoonist, Paul Duginski, at *The Sacramento Union.* According to Duginski, on December 3, 1979, he was called in by editor Don Hoenshell, who has since died, and shown a letter from Scaife complaining about several unflattering cartoons Duginski had drawn of California's conservative lieutenant governor, Mike Curb. According to Duginski, the letter instructed Hoenshell to restrict Duginski to doing cartoons on local issues. Duginski accepted the restriction but told his story to *feed/back,* the San Francisco State journalism review. Shortly after *feed/back* published an article on the matter last spring, Duginski was told that he was being laid off for economic reasons.

As in the case of Jude Dippold, Duginski's colleagues rallied to his defense. In addition to presenting him with a T-shirt that announced "I've been Scaifed," twenty-seven of them signed a petition offering to donate part of their salaries so that Duginski could continue to be employed. Management declined the offer. Duginski still has not found another full-time cartooning job.

Scaife's one foray into international publishing represents perhaps the most curious of his publishing enterprises. In 1973, he became the owner of Kern House Enterprises, a U.S.-registered company. Kern House ran Forum World Features, a London-based news agency that supplied feature material to a large number of papers around the world, including at one time about thirty in the U.S. Scaife abruptly closed down Forum in 1975, shortly before *Time Out,* a British weekly, published a purported 1968 CIA memorandum, addressed to then-director Richard Helms, which described Forum as a CIA-sponsored operation providing "a significant means to counter Communist propaganda." The Forum-CIA tie, which lasted into the seventies, has been confirmed by various British and American publications over the years, and it was confirmed independently by a source in connection with this article.

Helms is a member of the same country club near Pittsburgh as Scaife. "Unfortunately," Helms says, "I really don't know him." On the matter of Forum and a possible CIA link, he adds, "I don't know anything about it. And, if it were true, I wouldn't confirm it."

Scaife's involvement with Forum began at a time when he seems to have begun to recognize that newspapering might not represent the most effective way to make his mark on the world. Perhaps it was frustration at his lack of clout as a publisher that led Scaife to cast around for other areas in which to play a public role. This search coincided with the birth of a powerful new movement, one that was to culminate in the election of Ronald Reagan—the New Right.

Overlooked Maecenas to the New Right

Many leaders of the New Right are, like Scaife, men in their thirties and forties who, for one reason or another, see themselves as outside the old conservative establishment. They share not just a traditional free-market, anti-Communist view of the world, but also a sophisticated ability to analyze the forces that shape American society. This analysis has led to the creation of myriad New Right lobbying groups and think-tanks whose techniques are drawn directly from citizens groups and New Left organizations of the 1960s. ("Ten years ago the liberals kind of had a copyright on organizations outside of government," says Leon Reed, an aide on defense matters to Senator William Proxmire. "At some point the Right realized that all of the things like shareholder resolutions and testifying before Congress can be used by anyone.") This analysis also accounts for the tremendous emphasis the New Right puts on the news media, particularly television. No longer, as in Spiro Agnew's day, are the media seen simply as the enemy; rather, they are regarded as an institution which, like any other, is capable of being influenced as well as intimidated.

Scaife, with his money, his interest in politics and the media, and his long-held conservative views, quickly became a key New Right backer. Indeed, the rise of the New Right coincided with a substantial increase in Scaife's power to assist it. In 1973, he became chairman of the Sarah Scaife Foundation; within a year, a total break occurred between him and his sister. Since their mother's death, Cordelia Scaife May had tried to restrain her brother from shifting family charitable donations away from Sarah Scaife's priorities—population control and art—and toward conservative causes. After the break, she apparently gave up.

Scaife beneficiaries take pains to draw a distinction between Scaife as an individual and the Scaife charitable entities, each of which is presided over by several trustees, of which Scaife is but one. The virtually complete shift from Sarah Scaife's priorities to Richard Scaife's is, however, clear evidence of his overriding influence. The New York–based Population Council, for example, has been given no further Scaife funds since 1973, after receiving nearly $16 million during the previous thirteen years.

The Sarah Scaife Foundation, the Carthage Foundation, and the Allegheny Foundation, whose donations are a matter of public record, do give to many civic projects as well as to Richard Scaife's political charities. The Allegheny Foundation in particular has been a generous benefactor of such local causes as a major restoration now in progress in Pittsburgh. But the clearest indicator of which charities lie closest to Richard Scaife's heart is the giving pattern of the Sarah Scaife Grandchildren's Trust. Trusts, unlike foundations, do not have to give any public accounting of how they spend their income. According to information privately made available, the grandchildren's trust has virtually ceased giving to organizations other than conservative and New Right groups.

Total donations from Scaife's entities to conservative causes currently run about $10 million a year. (This amount, of course, does not reflect any personal contributions Scaife may make, about which no information is publicly available.) Among better-known conservative funders, the John M. Olin Foundation gave a total to *all* causes of $5.2 million in 1979, while the Adolph Coors Foundation gave away $2.5 million. Among funders perceived as left of center, Stewart Mott, heir to a General Motors fortune, gives away, through a trust, an average of between $700,000 and $1.3 million a year, according to an aide, while the Haymarket Peoples Fund gave $191,400 in 1979.

Sometimes, of course, a small amount of money at the right time is of more value than millions later on. Since 1973, Scaife entities have provided seed money to as many as two dozen New Right organizations.

The power of Scaife money is well appreciated by those who come up against it. An official of a large foundation concerned with arms control says that whenever he and other foundation executives interested in military issues discuss possible projects, they "always inevitably think about all that Scaife money and what it's doing." The official adds that the conservative groups "have a heck of a lot more influence [in defense matters] than the left-wing groups.

"A group like the National Strategy Information Center, which invites young academics to Colorado every year, can reach a lot of people very effectively," he says. "There is no analogous program on the left. The left-wing groups are constantly scraping for money. And they're badly splintered. The only thing that is anything like a match for the right-wing groups is the Institute for Policy Studies." The IPS budget for 1980 was $1.6 million.

Drawing Up the Agenda

Military and intelligence think-tanks and academic programs like the National Strategy Information Center have been particularly favored by Scaife; a catalogue of Scaife recipients over the past few years would contain virtually every significant conservative defense-oriented program in existence in the U.S.

Groups devoted to free-market economics—like the Law and Economics Center at Emory University, which has provided all-expenses-paid economics courses for 137 federal judges—have been the second-largest beneficiary since 1973.

Because they have been able to attract big names—people like former Navy Secretary Paul Nitze, now chairman of policy studies of the Committee on the Present Danger, and economist Milton Friedman, a frequent lecturer at the judges' seminars— many Scaife-funded defense and economics organizations command media attention. This attention has increased with the movement of a number of people from New Right groups into the Reagan administration—among them Interior Secretary Watt, from the Mountain States Legal Foundation, and presidential counselor Edwin Meese, one of the founders of the Institute for Contemporary Studies. Both groups describe Scaife as their largest donor, and the institute says Scaife provided its seed money of $75,000 in 1973.

Where the Money Goes

Some of the larger or better-known conservative and New Right groups to which Richard Scaife has given substantial funding since 1973 are listed below. Amounts, which include grants from the Carthage and Sarah Scaife Foundations and the Trust for the Grandchildren of Sarah Mellon Scaife, are approximate.

DEFENSE

The Center for Strategic and International Studies, Georgetown University (Washington, D.C.)	$5.3 million
The Committee for a Free World (New York)*†	$50,000
Committee on the Present Danger (Washington, D.C.)†	$360,000
Hoover Institution on War, Revolution and Peace, Stanford University (Stanford, Calif.)	$3.5 million
Institute for Foreign Policy Analysis (Cambridge)*†	$1.9 million
National Security Program, New York University†; and National Strategy Information Center (New York)†	$6 million

ECONOMICS

Foundation for Research in Economics and Education (Westwood, Calif.)	$1.4 million
International Center for Economic Policy Studies (New York)†	$150,000
International Institute for Economic Research (Westwood, Calif.)*†	$300,000
Law and Economics Center, originally at Miami University, now at Emory University (Atlanta)*†	$3 million
World Research, Inc. (San Diego)	$1 million

MEDIA

Accuracy in Media (Washington, D.C.)	$150,000
Alternative Educational Foundation (*The American Spectator* magazine, Bloomington, Ind.)	$900,000
The Media Institute (Washington, D.C.)*†	$475,000
WQLN-TV (Erie, Pa.)	$500,000

THINK-TANKS

The Heritage Foundation (Washington, D.C.)*†	$3.8 million
The Institute for Contemporary Studies (San Francisco)*†	$1.7 million

POLITICAL RESEARCH/EDUCATION GROUPS

American Legislative Exchange Council (Washington, D.C.)†	$560,000
The Free Congress Research and Education Foundation, Inc. (Washington, D.C.)†	$700,000

LEGAL GROUPS

Americans for Effective Law Enforcement (Evanston)	$1 million
National Legal Center for the Public Interest, plus six affiliates (Capital Legal Foundation, Washington, D.C.; Mountain States Legal Foundation, Denver; Mid-Atlantic Legal Foundation, Philadelphia; Great Plains Legal Foundation, Kansas City, Mo.; Mid-America Legal Foundation, Chicago; Southeastern Legal Foundation, Atlanta)*†	$1.8 million
Pacific Legal Foundation (Sacramento)†	$1.9 million

† denotes that the group recently received a contribution equal to 10 percent or more of the current or most recent available budget, as based on public or private records and/or confirmation by organization

* denotes that the group is known to have received seed money from Scaife

---

Not just names but numbers count. With so many conservative groups active in defense and economic matters, vast quantities of facts are constantly being generated and large numbers of seminars and briefings are constantly under way. "You can't underestimate the effect of a simple paper avalanche," says Leon Reed, the Proxmire aide. "One of the most important things groups like this can do is to give information to the people in Congress who support you. Groups can also provide people to speak at press conferences, testify before committees, things like that."

One example of the kind of "paper avalanche" to which Reed refers is the number of facts and figures generated by conservative groups at the time of the start of the 1979 congressional debate on the SALT II treaty. A quick check reveals at least eight studies of the issue, all critical, by groups that receive substantial Scaife backing. In addition, the Scaife-assisted Georgetown Center for Strategic and International Studies held a two-day briefing for twenty key European journalists on the issue, and The Heritage Foundation held an all-day session for members of the U.S. press. According to Herb Berkowitz, Heritage director of public relations, that press briefing "really kicked off the debate." The arms limitation treaty was not ratified.

Other examples of the potential impact of names and numbers abound.

- In its September 17, 1979, issue, *Time* devoted two pages to a report on a Brussels conference on NATO sponsored by the Georgetown Center and chaired by Henry Kissinger, a counselor in residence at the center. The article gloomily asserted: "The North Atlantic Treaty Organization received a thorough physical and psychological checkup last week and was found to be less than robust at age 30. The general diagnosis: flabby nuclear muscle and a creeping inferiority complex."
- In August 1980, a United Features Syndicate column by Virginia Payette reported that "terrorism has become a fact of American life." The article went on to explain, "It doesn't have to be that way, according to Dr. Samuel T. Francis, an expert on international terrorism of The Heritage Foundation. . . . Not if we give the FBI and the CIA a chance to stop it. . . . The way things are now, he warns, the FBI and the police are not only hamstrung by red tape, they are themselves being hauled into court for violating the civil liberties" of known terrorists.

- On December 15, 1980, *The New York Times* carried a full-column report, datelined San Francisco, which began: "A group of conservative black businessmen and educators, meeting here over the weekend with representatives of President-elect Ronald Reagan, advocated a reduction in the minimum wage, the elimination of rent control laws and a thorough reorganization of many social programs." In the seventh paragraph, the article reported that the sponsor of the conference was the Institute for Contemporary Studies (to which Scaife is the largest donor).

- Among a plethora of news articles last year on weakened U.S. military capabilities—which appeared at the same time as Scaife-backed organizations were turning out at least a dozen studies on the subject—probably the most breathless was an October 27 *Newsweek* cover story entitled "Is America Strong Enough?" The article, which quoted few people by name, depended heavily on such sources as "defense experts" and "a respected American military analyst." It reported in apocalyptic Pentagonese that "experts say Soviet advances in missile guidance now threaten the security of Minuteman ICBM's that constitute the land-based leg of America's nuclear triad—opening a 'window of vulnerability' that threatens to subject the United States to nuclear blackmail, if not a Soviet first strike, by as early as 1982." The only expert named in a two-page spread entitled "Sizing up the Soviets' Might," was Jeffrey Record from the Institute for Foreign Policy Analysis. In the old days, Record explained, "Our nuclear superiority gave the Russians pause because they knew we could blow them out of the water. Now our trump card has been canceled." Scaife provided the largest single portion of the institute's seed money ($325,000) in 1976, and continues to be the institute's single largest donor, providing about one-third of its current $1-million budget.

Such examples suggest how layer upon layer of seminars, studies, conferences, and interviews can do much to push along, if not create, the issues which then become the national agenda of debate.

A Bead on the Media

While the defense and economics groups funded by Scaife court the news media and, by the very nature of what they do, attract coverage, Scaife has also shown himself to be interested in groups that specifically produce or scrutinize news or try to affect the newsgathering process itself. Contributions in this area do not approach those going to the other two areas; but they are substantial, and growing.

Some insight into the thinking of Scaife's advisers regarding the media is provided by George Mair, formerly of the Foundation for American Communications. "They always wanted me to tell them about how things work at CBS," Mair recalls. "They seemed fascinated by the media and loved to hear all the gossip. But, at the same time, they had a conspiratorial view of how the media work."

To date, FACS has received more than $700,000 from Scaife, including about 20 percent of its current $650,000 budget. According to FACS president Jack Cox, Scaife remains the organization's single largest donor. Besides sponsoring conferences which have been attended by close to 500 journalists, FACS runs seminars for nonprofit organizations and businesses on how to deal with the media. Cox estimates that 3,000 to 4,000 executives have attended these sessions. FACS also sends a newsletter free to about 6,000 people, including the op-ed editors of all metropolitan dailies and all news directors of commercial radio and television stations.

Recent events sponsored by FACS include an April seminar for business executives cosponsored by the UCLA Graduate School of Management (itself the recipient of a $1 million grant from the Sarah Scaife Foundation three years ago), and a December conference for journalists on nuclear energy cosponsored by the Gannett Newspaper Foundation.

Jack Scott, president of the foundation, describes FACS as "a balanced organization" with no perceptible bias. "Cox is a conservative; there's no blinking at that," Scott says. "But he is very reluctant to project his political opinions. I don't think that as an organization they have a philosophy."

Llewelyn King, publisher of *The Energy Daily,* based in

Washington, D.C., was a panelist at the December nuclear conference. He says that he believes that the reporters at that conference, whom he describes as having come, by and large, from small papers, "would have liked to have heard more from people opposed to nuclear power." At the same time, he says, "I don't think anybody got brainwashed."

Michael Rounds, a business reporter for the *Rocky Mountain News* who attended a FACS seminar on economics last year, says, "I felt it was very well done. Where else would I get a chance to meet Paul Samuelson?" He adds, "I saw it as business-supported—that's why I went. The economists weren't what I would call liberals. The organizers were trying to educate a bunch of journalists like me, trying to give them and me a sense of how business works and to deal with perceived anti-business bias."

Education of journalists is also a part of the work of another Scaife-backed media group, the Washington-based Media Institute. The institute's president, Leonard J. Theberge, also was a founder of the National Legal Center for the Public Interest, the umbrella group for six conservative legal groups funded by Scaife. Institute board members have included Herbert Schmertz, vice president, public affairs, of Mobil, and J. Robert Fluor, chairman of Fluor Corporation. Scaife's assistance began with a $100,000 donation in 1975, the first year of the institute's existence, and is around $150,000 this year, or about 15 percent of the budget.

Frank Skrobiszewski, second in command to Theberge, describes the main objective of the Media Institute as being "to improve the quality of economic reporting, particularly on network television." To this end, the institute has published, for example, a study of television news that concludes that the networks have increased the public's fear of nuclear power. It also runs lunch seminars for journalists and puts out a newsletter.

The institute's newest project is the Economic Communications Center, which began operating last October. Its purpose, according to Skrobiszewski, is to provide journalists with quick analyses of current economic issues and easy access to experts in the field. "For example, when news comes out on something like the wage-price index, we can have an analysis prepared in one-and-a-half to two hours and have an economist ready to discuss it," Skrobiszewski explains. "Journalists often complain that they have no one to go to outside of government. This closes that gap." Skrobiszewski cites as an example of the center's quick acceptance the fact that its analysis of Iranian assets prompted interviews with the expert who prepared it by, among others, ABC, the AP, and UPI.

Scaife's funding not only makes possible a critical scrutiny of television programs; it also helps to create programs. Between 1976 and 1977, Scaife entities supplied $225,000 (the second-largest grant after Mobil) to WGBH, the Boston public broadcasting station, for a series that examined topics including the CIA, defense, and foreign policy. Scaife later supplied $110,000 in pre-production grants for a series on intelligence issues, based on a script by former CIA deputy director Ray Cline, now a top official at the Georgetown Center for Strategic and International Studies. According to Peter McGhee, WGBH program manager for national productions, the series currently is in limbo because only half of the needed $2 million has been raised. He says he is unsure how much of that, if any, was pledged by Scaife.

Closer to Pittsburgh, Scaife supplied $500,000 to public television station WQLN in Erie, Pennsylvania, to help underwrite *Free to Choose,* a ten-part series featuring Milton Friedman.

On the print side, Scaife has helped to underwrite a number of magazines. In the past decade, for example, Scaife has given more than $1 million to the publishers of *The American Spectator,* a monthly whose views range across the conservative spectrum.

The most prestigious of the periodicals with which Scaife has been associated is *Daedalus,* the journal of the American Academy of Arts and Sciences. Three years ago, Richard Pipes, a Harvard historian who is now a member of the National Security Council staff, approached *Daedalus* with a proposal for a special issue on U.S. defense policy, with himself as guest editor. Pipes also provided a proposed backer, in the form of a Scaife charity that was willing to put up $25,000 immediately and $25,000 to $50,000 later.

Pipes was keenly interested in defense policy, having been chairman of the so-called B-team, a group of ten outside experts convened by George Bush while Bush was CIA chief to make an assessment of Soviet military strength. The B-team conclusions, delivered in late 1976, included an estimate of Soviet defense spending that was twice as high as previous government estimates and an assertion that the Russians were bent on nuclear superiority. The conclusions, which were widely accepted as official, played a major role in shaping the current defense debate.

The *Daedalus* project proposed by Pipes was agreed to, but funding was sought from the Carnegie Endowment for International Peace to provide balance to the Scaife donation, and the issue of Pipes's editorship was left unresolved. As the essays began to come in, according to one source close to the project, it became evident that many were "under the influence of Pipes and the B-team mentality. It became clear that this was to be the B-Team's riposte to earlier liberal critics." Eventually, it was agreed that the project would have a board of advisers but no guest editor.

At some point following that decision, Scaife withdrew from the agreement to supply additional funds and insisted that the Scaife name not be associated with the project. Stephen R. Graubard, *Daedalus*'s editor, says his recollection is that Scaife aides were unhappy about several things, especially a time delay in the publication of what turned out to be two special issues, Fall and Winter 1980. "They never said Pipes had to be guest editor or we'll take our marbles and go home," Graubard says. Others recall things differently. A second source close to the project says, "The Scaife people said their understanding was that Pipes was to be the sole guest editor and strongly implied bad faith. They were, in effect, trying to dictate what was to be in the magazine. They wanted to give the cold-war hard line."

In the end, it is difficult to say what lessons, if any, can be drawn from the story of Richard Mellon Scaife and his activities. While such a recounting suggests that journalists should treat the rich and their creations—the foundations, the trusts, the charitable organizations—with as much curiosity and skepticism as they treat government and political groups, the fact is that the size of Scaife's fortune and the narrowness of his interests make him unusual, if not unique.

Beyond this, the fact that Scaife—virtually unnoticed—has been able to establish group after group whose collective effect has been to help shape the way Americans think about themselves and their nation's problems raises a concern addressed by Walter Lippmann nearly sixty years ago. "On all but a very few matters for short stretches in our lives, the utmost independence that we can exercise is to multiply the authorities to whom we give a friendly hearing," Lippmann wrote in *Public Opinion*. "As congenital amateurs our quest for truth consists in stirring up the experts, and forcing them to answer any heresy that has the accent of conviction. In such a debate we can often judge who has won the dialectical victory, but we are virtually defenseless against a false premise that none of the debaters has challenged, or a neglected aspect that none of them has brought into the argument."

By multiplying the authorities to whom the media are prepared to give a friendly hearing, Scaife has helped to create an illusion of diversity where none exists. The result could be an increasing number of one-sided debates in which the challengers are far outnumbered, if indeed they are heard from at all.

Behind the Story

In 1975, Karen Rothmyer, then a reporter for the *Wall Street Journal,* arrived at a J. P. Stevens textile factory in North Carolina to check out the working conditions. She was met at the gate by several company officials, who accompanied her throughout the plant, eavesdropping on her every conversation. When she asked the workers, who were mostly women, what they thought of conditions inside the facility, they glanced nervously at the officials before answering, "Everything is fine." Exasperated, Rothmyer finally told the officials she had to visit the ladies' room. Once there, she stayed a long time, interviewing each worker who came in the door. Rothmyer got her story while the guards waited helplessly outside.

This kind of determined resourcefulness makes Karen Rothmyer one of a select breed of reporters—a "lone wolf" hunting down stories that are too tough or complicated for others to tackle. She is persistent, systematic, and unrelenting in her attention to detail.

"Citizen Scaife" actually started out as a small follow-up piece to an earlier *Columbia Journalism Review* (*CJR*) story that Rothmyer had written about John McGoff, an American publisher who allegedly received South African funds to help him buy American newspapers. In that piece Rothmyer presented evidence that one of McGoff's goals was to influence U.S. policy in favor of the South African government. When she started the Scaife piece, she had no idea that it would grow into a major award-winning investigative article, one so important and unusual that the editor of the *Washington Post* would call with praise. At first she was simply curious about Scaife, then intrigued, and finally, in the way of all good investigative reporters, obsessed. Along the way, she got a batch of secret documents, an interview with a former head of the CIA, and finally a stormy confrontation with Scaife himself.

Scaife co-owned a newspaper with John McGoff—that is how Rothmyer became interested in him. Routinely, when writing her McGoff article, she had checked the library for background on Scaife. But she found very little, considering his wealth and influence as an heir to the Mellon family fortune. *Who's Who* revealed almost nothing. The only newspaper clip she could locate mentioned that Scaife had been a large contributor to Richard Nixon's campaign. Phone calls to people who should have known about Scaife produced little additional data beyond the fact that he owned some small newspapers in the Pittsburgh area.

A leftover lead from the McGoff investigation concerned a London-based operation called Forum World Features, which the British press had exposed as being secretly funded by the CIA. Richard Mellon Scaife bought and then closed down this mysterious news organization just about the time the CIA revelations surfaced. Rothmyer wanted to find out more.

"Somebody had told me that Scaife or his family operated two or three foundations," Rothmyer recalls. "But I'd never written anything about foundations before. It was a totally new area. That's true with every story: you suddenly have to become an expert in things you didn't know anything about until yesterday."

During the McGoff story Rothmyer had learned about Wesley McCune, a researcher based in Washington, D.C., who maintains files on right-wing groups. In a call to McCune, Rothmyer learned the names of three Scaife-connected foundations—Carthage Foundation, Allegheny Foundation and Sarah Scaife Foundation. McCune also mentioned a resource library called the Foundation Center, which has offices in New York and other cities. A trip there produced a list of organizations that Scaife's foundations supported with grants.

Meanwhile, Rothmyer discovered an article written by freelance reporter John Friedman in *The Nation* about a public television series that had been partly funded by another CIA-linked group, the Smith-Richardson Foundation. Friedman's article mentioned Scaife briefly, so Rothmyer called him. Friedman listened to Rothmyer's list of Scaife-connected foundations and remarked that one seemed to be missing—the Scaife Family Charitable Trust. He explained that the trust, also known as the Trust for Sarah Mellon Scaife's Grandchildren, had been the other major funder of the suspect British television series, and that it too might be linked to the CIA.

At this point, Rothmyer remembers, "I thought perhaps I had a story about some guy who was a semi–CIA cooperator, a publisher who helped out the CIA on the side. I still had no idea of his immense involvement with the New Right."

Rothmyer mailed a request to the IRS for the tax returns of the three Scaife-connected foundations and the trust. (Under the law these records of tax-exempt organizations may be released to the public.) The IRS sent returns for the foundations, but stated that it had no record of a Scaife Family Charitable Trust.

"So I figured then that there really wasn't any such thing as the trust," Rothmyer explains. "I thought it was just sort of an overall name for the various family philanthropic activities."

As the next stage of her research Rothmyer thumbed through volumes of *Editor and Publisher,* the annual publication that lists all U.S. newspapers, their owners, and their employees. After identifying Scaife's Pittsburgh-area newspapers, Rothmyer tediously copied the name of every editor or reporter who had worked for them and left. She also asked a colleague at Columbia University's Graduate School of Journalism, where she was teaching, for the names of any journalists in Pittsburgh, "because I did not know a soul there; I'd never even been to Pittsburgh."

Soon Rothmyer had a long list of names, and she tried reaching some of them by telephone. One name led to another and another, until she found herself talking to a former Scaife employee now working in Miami. "In every investigative story," she explains, "you've got to have one big break. And in this case, the big break came quite early on. I got this phenomenal piece of luck. I was talking to this guy in Miami, asking him what it had been like to work for Scaife, and so on, when halfway through the conversation he suddenly said to me: 'You know, it's funny. Somebody else was asking me about Scaife just a couple of weeks ago.' " The Miami reporter told her the second man's name and phone number, unaware that he had just given Rothmyer the most important contact of her entire investigation.

The Miami journalist sensed that the man from up north had a "gripe" against Scaife, but that was all he knew about him. So Rothmyer phoned him to ask if she could visit. He agreed.

Before making the trip to a nearby northern city where the man worked, Rothmyer "checked him out as well as I could." She figured out "what his ax to grind" probably was and prepared to scrutinize carefully whatever information he might offer. The mystery of the situation attracted her.

"I prepared as well as I could and played it extremely cool. This was a guy who was no fool. To this day I don't know the whole story of what his involvement with Scaife had been, or why he had taken the trouble to fly to Miami and perhaps elsewhere to talk with people who knew about Scaife. But he took my measure for a couple of hours, and then he showed me a whole bunch of clips and other material relating to *his* problem with Scaife. He felt Scaife had caused him extreme problems—legal and otherwise— and that Scaife had really made his life miserable. Most of the stuff he gave me, then, was on his own issue with Scaife. And then, almost as a throwaway, he handed me some papers and said, 'Here is something you might want to take a look at too.' "

This "something," after much checking and verifying, turned out to be the internal minutes of the Scaife Family Charitable Trust. There was also a report prepared specially for the directors of the trust, listing all the donations made since the trust had been set up, some twenty years before.

By now Rothmyer had discovered that trusts are different from foundations. Trusts don't have to provide a public accounting of their donations, and that is why the IRS had no record of the Scaife trust. Some states have minor reporting requirements, but these are seldom complied with. "So in fact," Rothmyer notes, "it's practically impossible to find out what a trust is up to."

Except, of course, when somebody hands over internal records. "As I looked through this list of donations, there were literally hundreds of names, and it blew my mind, just leafing through it. It took me a few minutes to absorb what I had and meanwhile stay cool. . . . Then I asked, 'Can I borrow this, make a copy, and give it back to you?' And he said, 'Okay.' "

Later Rothmyer learned that her source, whom she agreed to keep confidential, had also provided the same documents to at least two other reporters. One of those reporters would later release a story just before her *CJR* piece appeared.

Rothmyer studied the lists of groups supported by the trust for days before patterns started to emerge. "I had no idea what many of the organizations were—they all sounded the same at first. Some

were totally innocuous-sounding; others sounded like something
I'd vaguely heard of before. Most of them did not appear in
any newspaper clips either. There were a few I recognized—like
the Heritage Foundation. But since this was before Reagan was
elected, the Heritage Foundation was not exactly a hot news item
yet."

Rothmyer's first step was to write individual letters to dozens
of the organizations, asking for information. "A lot of them
responded, a lot didn't. But I began to understand, as I got back
these replies, what it was I was dealing with here."

Rothmyer realized that the groups fell into three broad categories:
military/defense-oriented organizations, conservative economic
organizations, and media-oriented groups. By matching the trust's
internal list with the publicly available list of groups receiving
donations from the three Scaife foundations, she saw where there
was overlap.

The organizations that Rothmyer examined most carefully were
those that received monies but no public foundation backing, like
the Heritage Foundation. "It seemed to me that Scaife or his advisers
had made a decision that they didn't want it to be known publicly
that they were funding these things."

At this point Rothmyer began to realize that she was investigating
a network of organizations that formed the backbone of the New
Right. And all were secretly funded by the Scaife Family Trust.
As a whole, this nationwide hookup amounted to a master plan
to influence public opinion and public policy on an unprecedented
scale. (Nearly a year later, when Rothmyer's exposé was published
in July 1981, Ronald Reagan had been elected president, and the
political mood of the entire nation had swung dramatically to the
right. Few Americans, however, had any inkling of the behind-
the-scenes role played by one very wealthy and powerful
individual—Richard Mellon Scaife—in these public events.)

Meanwhile, Rothmyer was also trying to trace Scaife's publishing
empire. "I continued locating people who had worked for him,
finding out what sort of guy he was as a newspaper publisher.
You look for people who are no longer there, of course, because
their jobs are not endangered by talking. I did talk to some people
still working for him. But one had to be careful. Eventually I got

enough to feel that as a newspaper publisher he was not the big
time."

She also put effort into figuring out whether he had any local
political clout. She started by asking an acquaintance in the
Democratic party in New York for the name of a Democratic "big
wheel" around Pittsburgh, "because, presumably, they'll know
something about Scaife since he's a big Republican donor.

"I realized fairly soon that as a local political figure in Pittsburgh
he wasn't much," Rothmyer explains, "though he would have liked
to be; that was the story I got from everybody."

By now Rothmyer was actively trying to analyze her material,
a process that illustrates the intellectual side of investigative
reporting. Many hours are spent building patterns and matching
facts, looking for inconsistencies or errors, reviewing documents
and interviews, in order to achieve an *analysis* that binds all the
data together. Without this analysis, another reporter possessing
the same facts failed to create the impact Rothmyer made with
her work. It is the *interpretation* of the facts that gives this work
its significance.

"Because of my conclusion that Scaife was not much as a
publisher," explains Rothmyer, "and that he did not have a lot
of political clout locally, I made the decision to concentrate on
his national funding strategy. It seemed to me, the more I analyzed
the material I'd been given, that he seemed to be giving money to
every organization that had sprung up on the Right."

Next came another demanding exercise. "For several weeks, I
called up every organization I wanted to use in my piece and
squeezed any information I could out of them." She had obtained
some of their budgets from IRS filings or annual reports, although
she found most of these financial data surprisingly sketchy. Then
she matched these figures with the list of Scaife's donations to each
group. "I called them up and said, 'Okay, look, I know your budget
is such-and-such and that Richard Scaife has given you x amount
of money. This means he gave you fifty percent of your budget
last year, is that right?' "

In most of these cases, Scaife had donated the money on the
stipulation that he not be identified as a funder. But as reporters
often find, having a little information can help dislodge more, or

at least confirm what they already know. "In most cases, they would simply say, 'Yes, that's right, he's the largest funder.' But they weren't going to volunteer anything new," Rothmyer recalls.

"That confirmation was important to me, though, because without it, for all I knew, there might have been some funny business going on with the record of donations from the trust. I had to get verification."

In a cautious style befitting the careful investigative reporter, Rothmyer also went back to the man who had supplied her the list of trust donations and asked him for names of people who could verify its authenticity. Among the names was one Rothmyer recognized, and she was able to persuade that person to see her. (This man's identity also must remain confidential.) When Rothmyer showed him the trust list, he confirmed that it was authentic and then made a special effort to prove to her that he was not the source who had originally leaked the document. He pulled out of his desk his copy of the list—an original, of which there were supposedly only six in existence—handing Rothmyer in the process the final verification she was looking for.

Rothmyer considered her interview with this man—"confidential source No. 2" as she calls him—to be the most important of her investigation. "He was somebody in a position to know how the Scaife financial empire was set up. Although I had studied what stocks were in which trust, which stocks were in the foundation, who held what percent of the voting power, where the family money came from—all sorts of things—I really had a lot of questions just about the mechanics of it all.

"I had gone as far as I could in trying to understand it myself. I talked to a couple of trust lawyers in New York, but I had no explanation of what was in the Scaife Family Charitable Trust, or when it was set up, or by whom."

Rothmyer says that she had "prepared as thoroughly as I could for this interview. I mean really prepared. And it paid off because basically this man didn't want to tell me anything more than a little bit beyond what I knew. He would verify conclusions I had reached based on my analysis of the documents. He would also elaborate on it slightly sometimes.

"But he was a man who did not want to say anything that might

help somebody reading the story figure out who had given the
information. He shows up in absolutely no way in the story. Nor
would he have helped me, I think, if I hadn't already known eighty
percent of what I needed to know. For example, he was so relieved
to know that I had talked to trust lawyers in New York, because
he felt that meant that the information in the story could have
come from somebody other than him. I promised him that there
would be no way that anybody could put two and two together
and figure out who he was."

Rothmyer feels that her background as a business reporter for
two years at the *Wall Street Journal* impressed both of her
confidential sources. "Just having worked for the *Journal*—I could
have been a bozo in a lot of ways—creates in people's minds perhaps
the misconception that one is really on top of everything serious
that happens in the world. I don't know what a Eurobond is much
more than the next person, but people like these two sources don't
want to talk to an idiot journalist who needs to be led by the
hand from square one."

One other factor in Rothmyer's success with source No. 2 was
her decision "not to ask him about anything except what I absolutely
had to. There were other people who could give me their assessment
of Scaife the man, and so on. So we strictly talked about technical
points in this interview—partly because I didn't know how much
time he would give me." This strategy allowed Rothmyer to
concentrate on preparing her financial questions—a job she did
so well that the interview lasted only thirty minutes.

Rothmyer's rules for journalists approaching key interviews are
"Be prepared at all times" and "Don't pick up the phone until
you're ready." An experience near the end of her Scaife investigation,
when she broke her own rules, illustrates her point.

Although the story had changed drastically from her earliest lead
that Scaife might be somehow connected to the CIA, Rothmyer
still felt compelled to wrap up the Forum World Features–Scaife–
CIA connection. To accomplish this, she needed to interview
Richard Helms, who had been head of the CIA at the time the
reports surfaced in Britain. The British newspaper accounts were
based on a memo purported to be from the London CIA station
chief to Helms. "So I had prepared questions for Helms weeks in

advance of my trip to Washington, and I had been trying to get an appointment with him," Rothmyer remembers. "But I didn't think he was ever going to see me. So here I am in Washington and I'm running around from appointment to appointment, and I think, Tomorrow's my last day here; let me try to reach him one last time.

"Now I was in a department store in downtown Washington at the time I remembered this. Right outside the ladies' room were some phone booths, the kind that you stand at with the glass at the side, not even a booth. But I thought, Hell, I'll just call his office.

"I called, reached his secretary, and said, 'Hi, I'm the person who has spoken to you several times, I'm trying to reach Mr. Helms.' And so she says, 'Well, just a minute, he's right here, let me put him on.' Oh, shit. Helms gets on the phone and says, 'What do you want to ask me?'

"I didn't have my notebook, I didn't have a pencil, I didn't have my questions. Here I was standing at a pay phone outside the ladies' room in a downtown department store talking to the former head of the CIA, and what the hell did I want to ask him?

"Rummaging through my purse I found my eyeliner—that's the first thing I found—and I started flipping open my book, and luckily I had the wits to remember the one basic thing I wanted to ask him. And he claimed he really hardly knew Scaife at all and said he did not know anything about the London operation. So I got all of that written out in smudgy eyeliner.

"After I got off the phone, I said, 'Rothmyer, let that be a lesson. *Never* do that. Anytime you call you've got to have your questions there."

By now Rothmyer knew what she wanted to write, so she started trying to make an appointment with Scaife himself. "I didn't think he would talk to me, because when I had been doing the McGoff piece I had tried repeatedly to talk to him and the closest I got was when his secretary conveyed the message that he didn't want to speak to me.

"This time, however, I couldn't even get that. Nobody ever called me back to say he didn't want to see me. But I kept calling. When I was in Pittsburgh I could have tried to 'doorstep' him. But I

decided to save that as my final tactic. And it was after the story
was actually written and handed in at *CJR* that I decided to try
my last card, which was to catch him in Boston."

Scaife was due in that city to attend the annual meeting of First
Boston Corporation, of which he was a director. But Rothmyer,
aware of the secrecy that Scaife sought while conducting his
business, was worried that he might not make an appearance at
an event as public as an annual stockholders meeting. So she placed
a call to Scaife's Pittsburgh office, once more trying to arrange an
interview. "I may be in Pittsburgh Tuesday. Can I interview him
then?" she asked Scaife's secretary.

"Sorry, he'll be out of town."

With this evidence that Scaife might well be in Boston, Rothmyer
convinced her editors at *CJR* to pay her travel expenses. (She had
long since exhausted an initial $1,500 research grant sponsored by
the Center, which had covered the earlier phase of her investigation.)
"I got to the meeting site early and dressed correctly, a copy of
Business Week in my hand. Not very many people were standing
around, and the chairman of First Boston came over, introduced
himself, and said, "Hello, I don't believe we've met."

"I responded, 'Hello, I'm Karen Rothmyer.'

"He stood there awkwardly, literally shifting from foot to foot,
and then finally left."

Scaife never showed for the stockholders meeting, and during
the board meeting that followed, Rothmyer waited in a chair behind
a potted palm near the elevator, hoping Scaife would finally make
his appearance. "But all the directors left, and still no Scaife. I
was discouraged."

Many reporters would have given up at this point. But Rothmyer
went back to the telephone, this time to dial the First Boston office.

The secretary answering the call heard an officious woman's voice.
"Hello, I've missed meeting Richard Scaife at the meeting. Is he
there?" Apparently assuming this was one of Scaife's assistants (who
else would make such a call?), the secretary gave Rothmyer the
extension of a private room in the Union Club where Scaife and
other directors were meeting over lunch.

From a phone booth at a luncheonette next to the club, Rothmyer
dialed the private room. "I'd like to speak to Mr. Scaife."

He came on the line.

"Hello, this is Karen Rothmyer."

He hung up.

Rothmyer ran out of the phone booth to where her mother was waiting ("I had arranged to meet my mother for lunch and go shopping with her afterward") and yelled "Yippee!" because at last she knew she would be able to "doorstep" the man she had been seeking for so long. "I knew he was in there and I knew he couldn't get out without passing me. Before placing the call I had checked the back of the Union Club building and saw that there was no exit. Now, I knew I'd be seeing him, but would it be a long wait or a short one? Well, I needed to go the bathroom and I thought, Should I? and I decided, Better not."

Instead Rothmyer rushed around to the entrance to the club, and suddenly there he was—Richard Mellon Scaife. "Rather than finishing his lunch, Scaife had left immediately after the phone call. He appeared outside, at the top of the stairs, a minute and a half after I made the phone call. If I had gone to the bathroom I would have missed him. When he came out and saw me at the bottom of the stairs and I saw him at the top of the stairs, we both sort of froze for five seconds. I think neither of us could quite believe the situation." What happened next is described in the box on page 58.

"It was ninety percent hard work and ten percent luck, I guess. If you can remember just to go that last sort of mile—even when you don't want to and your mother is waiting and you need to go to the bathroom, but you say, All right, just one more thing . . . But you do need to have that tiny bit of luck, too."

Every story has a "lag time" between when it is written and when it is actually published. While Rothmyer waited for her Scaife piece to come out, she had one scare that all her work might have been for naught. A reporter who had been given the documents about the trust and its list of grantees released his story just before hers was due to appear. "I was kind of sick when I found out it was coming out, because I thought, There goes my piece. But although this reporter did a lot of work and put together every little tidbit about Scaife he could find, he didn't really understand who Scaife was in political terms because he hadn't done the research to find out who a lot of the groups were on the list." Because his story lacked this perspective, it did not achieve an immediate national impact.

Rothmyer's article, by contrast, attracted widespread attention. Within several days of publication, *Washington Post* editor Ben Bradlee called the reporter to congratulate her on the piece. Soon after, the *Post* reprinted nearly the entire article on the front page of its widely read "Outlook" section. Editors from various magazines and book publishers around the country started calling. And readers from all over phoned, asking about Scaife or the New Right in general. The piece was a first of its kind. It charted the course for reporting about the New Right, a group currently so significant in contemporary American politics that many reporters have followed Rothmyer's lead.

Since the story appeared in *CJR,* Richard Mellon Scaife has continued to play a major role in the funding of the New Right. His media involvement expanded in early 1982, when Scaife became the sole owner of the *Sacramento Union* by purchasing John McGoff's one-half share. More recently, Scaife bought radio station KQV in Pittsburgh, a news format station.

Scaife remains convinced that the American media have a leftist slant that needs to be counteracted by his news organizations or by others that he assists financially. In a rare interview published in *Today,* the *Philadelphia Inquirer*'s magazine, Scaife was quoted as saying, "I think the most important thing I'm doing is . . . to educate people so they don't have a liberal bias." Perhaps with that end in mind, Scaife's seed money in the past two years has included $200,000 to a new conservative literary magazine, *The New Criterion,* and $100,000 to *This World,* a conservative religious journal. Scaife has also helped fund conservative campus magazines at Yale and Dartmouth.

The *Inquirer* interview may signal a decision by Scaife to be more public with his concerns and to become more of a national figure than he has been in the past. Currently he is a member of the board of directors of the privately funded Committee on the Present Danger, and he served as a member of the President's Commission on Broadcasting to Cuba. The commission recommended establishing a station modeled on Radio Free Europe to be called Radio Marti and aimed at Cuba.

As these two appointments suggest, Scaife's main concern continues to be the perceived menace of the Soviet Union. This concern is reflected in Scaife's trust and foundation activities. Since 1981 the family trust has given $300,000 to the Washington-based Institute for Religion and Democracy. That amount represents about half of the institute's total financial support during its first two years. The institute figured prominently in a January 1983 CBS *60 Minutes* program which attempted to show that substantial money from established Protestant church organizations is being used to fund Marxist groups in Central America. A January 1983 *Reader's Digest* article on the same topic also cited the institute as an agency that opposes this funding.

Karen Rothmyer continues to teach at Columbia University's Graduate School of Journalism in New York and occasionally pursues freelance magazine stories. For her work on "Citizen Scaife" she received an Investigative Reporters and Editors Award for Magazine Writing in 1982—an especially noteworthy honor in that it was given by her peers.

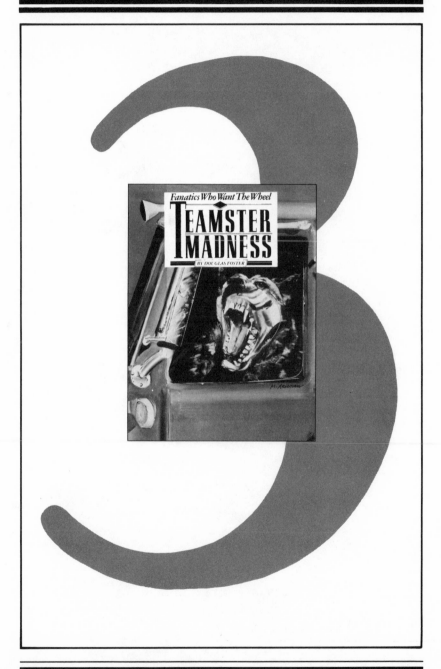

Fanatics Who Want The Wheel

TEAMSTER MADNESS

BY DOUGLAS FOSTER

C H A P T E R

3

Teamster Madness

by Douglas Foster

Shortly before he died of cancer in May 1981, Frank Fitzsimmons, then president of the Teamsters, sent an urgent message to his underlings about a nefarious conspiracy to rip his organization asunder. The "intelligence report" Fitzsimmons sent along to his international executive board warned of a "full-blown freakout from the entire 'Get the Teamsters' network." The report said this "freakout" had been sparked by the election of Teamster ally Ronald Reagan. It described the anti-Teamster network as a Big Business/Red Menace combine that included Wall Street financiers, "press prostitutes," and international Socialists—all prepared to join hands and spend "countless millions of dollars on the war against [the Teamsters] to stop their role for economic development and improved standards of living."

As shocked as they were by the Fitzsimmons mailing, sent along with a personal cover letter, most of the officials who received it ignored the most salient fact: the report had been produced not by the union's research department but by a bizarre right-wing cult—the U.S. Labor Party—led by Lyndon LaRouche. For LaRouche, a fixture of the political fringe, approval from Fitzsimmons, president of America's largest union, capped a ten-year effort to wield influence in the labor movement.

LaRouche's attempt to attain power in the American labor movement has been marked by acts appropriate to those of political "hired guns":

- His followers have been responsible for intimidation, phony letters, fake newspaper articles and other cleverly constructed "dirty trick" campaigns against Teamster reformers and progressives in other unions, including Leonard Woodcock, former president of the United Auto Workers.
- Hate-filled, often inaccurate "intelligence" information on the supposed "enemies" of organized labor has been transmitted to union leaders with no indication that the information reflects the bias of the increasingly reactionary U.S. Labor Party or its spinoffs. This activity echoes both the style and substance of the intelligence that LaRouche and company have provided to corporations and government intelligence agencies.
- Through the *American Labor Beacon,* a widely circulated glossy magazine, LaRouche associates are now trying to effectively propagandize not only union leadership but rank-and-file workers. Locals in at least four different unions have already responded favorably to the *Beacon,* and several union local presidents or past officials have taken up the magazine's line. The *Beacon* flatly denies affiliation with LaRouche or the U.S. Labor Party, even though its editor and publisher are both Labor Party regulars.

The Politics of LaRouche

You may have learned of Lyndon LaRouche from tripping over his followers as they campaigned for nuclear power in airports behind strident banners ("Feed Jane Fonda to the Whales!" and "More People Died in Ted Kennedy's Car Than Have Been Hurt By Nuclear Power"). Perhaps you've heard of his people buttonholing businessmen to sell $400-a-year subscriptions to their *Executive Intelligence Review.* Or you may

have read of them offering their "intelligence" about progressive activists to police departments.

LaRouche has run for the presidency twice, in 1976 and
1980, on platforms best described as a progressive's nightmare:
he calls for immediate construction of 120 nuclear power
plants, blames the B'Nai B'rith Anti-Defamation League for
funding the Nazis and calls publicly for an "American Whig"
coalition of business and labor to turn the country around
while secretly seeking a military solution to the nation's problems.

LaRouche's own political odyssey has been an odd one.
He began on the Left, in 1948, as a member of the Trotskyist
Socialist Workers Party (SWP) and drew fleeting notice in
the late 1960s only when he abandoned the SWP, was expelled
from the Students for a Democratic Society for disruptive behavior and founded, with the help of 30 followers, the National
Caucus of Labor Committees. Little of substance was heard
from the NCLC for four years or so, as the organization grew
slowly to an estimated 2,500 members and—like so many "vanguard" parties of the time—busied itself with rhetorical attacks
on capitalism and predictions of revolution.

Then, in 1973, LaRouche swung radically rightward. His
followers conducted "Operation Mop-up," a series of brutal,
chain-swinging attacks on left-wing groups, such as former
SWP friends and the Communist Party USA, and NCLC members began schooling in guerrilla training. Classes in guerrilla
warfare reportedly included education in "political" techniques
like garroting, knifing and booby-trapping. During this period,
LaRouche also came to terms with capitalism, constructing
a multi-million-dollar series of computer businesses (including
the now-bankrupt Computron Technologies of New York)—
a mainstay of LaRouche's political survival.

From 1973 on, LaRouche and his followers targeted trade-
union chieftains for special attention and, through a plethora
of front groups, began to emphasize the importance of reform-
ing labor. A former *New York Times* editor remembers receiving scores of telephone calls at the time from businesspeople
who wanted to find out more about LaRouche. "These industri-
alists got a long pitch about how LaRouche wanted to reform

labor along constructive lines," the editor recalls. The quiet methods employed by LaRouche to infiltrate labor have avoided headlines, but the "constructive lines" of reform have become clear in the intervening years.

The Gospel According to LaRouche

In dozens of books and articles since 1977—on military, political, historical and aesthetic topics—Lyndon LaRouche and his followers have signaled the key elements of a neo-Nazi outlook, including:

- a pathological hatred and fear of Jews as alleged usurers and terrorists and as carriers of moral corruption and diseased philosophies;

- a belief that wealthy Jews such as the Rothschilds (and, by implication, the world Jewish community) comprise the core of a subhuman species, apart from the human race;

- a conspiracy theory of history that blames the world's political and economic problems on machinations by these subhumans (who are allegedly plotting genocide on a world scale); and

- a militant program for (1) the "immediate elimination" of Jews from American public life and their subsequent indictment for alleged treason against the Republic, (2) the establishment of a fascist-style "industrial-capitalist" dictatorship under LaRouchian leadership, and (3) the "total mobilization of the entire nation" to prepare for "total war" (a line from Joseph Goebbels), with the aim of establishing "firm-handed" LaRouchian regimes throughout the world.

The LaRouchians, like many neo-Nazis in West Germany today, use code words and elliptical arguments to conceal some of the nastiest implications of their propaganda. But they also have produced a vast quantity of overtly anti-Semitic literature, attacking the "Jewish lobby," the "Jewish bankers," "Jewish hypocrisy," the Anti-Defamation League of B'nai B'rith, Nazi hunter Simon Wiesenthal, Israel and Zionism. LaRouche himself traces the "problem among Jews" back to ancient times, to the "tradition of the Jews who demanded the crucifixion of Jesus Christ . . ."

LaRouche and his followers also rant against the "British," an obvious code word. The "British" in LaRouchian propaganda usually have Jewish surnames, and LaRouchian writers carefully point out that the "City of London" is the headquarters of the Rothschilds and other Jewish "oligarchs."

In one key article, LaRouche lists a string of wealthy British families (all but one Jewish) and then defines "Britain" as "these same families' interests." LaRouche and his followers spare no adjectives in excoriating the biological-racial characteristics of the "British." Writes LaRouche: "The ruling British elite . . . are clever animals, who are masters of the wicked nature of their own species, and recognize ferally the distinctions of the hated human species." Elsewhere, LaRouche hails himself as the "potential destroyer" of the "evil species."

Overtly favorable references to Nazi Germany crop up in the military writings of LaRouche. For instance: "During 1939–1941, there was a sound and intense German nationalist enthusiasm in Germany for defeating Britain." And this one, published in 1978: "England was then, as now, the enemy of continental Europe, including the German nation."

The LaRouchians mix their pro-Nazi statements with statements that give a superficial impression of anti-Nazism, their attacks on the Rockefellers as "Nazis," for instance. But such usage is mere trickery. When the LaRouchians call for the "immediate elimination of the Nazi Jewish lobby" from American public life, they are using the word *Nazi* to disguise their own advocacy of a Hitler-style policy.

The first target of this policy, apparently, is to be the "British." A LaRouchian editorial says that if the British do not end their nefarious activities (such as encouraging Israel against the Neoplatonic-humanist Arabs), they should be subjected to the "treatment" meted out "to Japan in 1945." As to the Soviet Union, LaRouche suggests that the United States can achieve "total victory" via ABC "paving" (*ABC* means atomic, bacteriological and chemical warfare, combined) "to the purpose of exterminating every possible means of opposition."

—Dennis King

A Disinformation Campaign

In February of 1980, a sophisticated forgery of *The Pittsburgh Press* front page appeared in union halls across Michigan during the heat of hard-fought local union elections. The headlined story linked a small band of union reformers known as Teamsters for a Democratic Union (TDU) with the Ayatollah Khomeini and militants holding American hostages in Iran. It was attached to a leaflet that advised, "[No one] should even *talk* to people who give aid, comfort and publicity to enemies of the United States."

In 1981, the Teamsters for a Democratic Union was again the target of dirty tricks. Hundreds of union locals received copies of a forged letter purportedly written to TDU leader Peter Camarata, a dockworker from Detroit, by Reed Larson, the president of the vehemently antiunion National Right to Work Committee.

The letter read: "Dear Pete . . . I believe the discussion concerning the merger of PROD [Professional Driver's Association] and TDU to make a stronger anti-Teamster movement, as agreed, will be greatly beneficial to the National Right to Work Committee." It added that a $25,000 check was enclosed, further assurance "that you are going to have the NRWC's total effort of support in your upcoming effort to disrupt the Teamsters' Convention and discredit Fitzsimmons and the hierarchy of the Teamsters Union."

The contents of the letter targeted two long-time LaRouche enemies: "Dr. Arthur Shenfield of the Mont Pelerin Society and Stuart Butler, board member of the NRWC and board member of the Heritage Foundation"—both fairly obscure targets of LaRouche's wrath. "Of course, it's a phony letter," Larson snorted, adding that TDU had refused even to sell literature to the National Right to Work Committee. "They don't even want to talk with us," Larson adds. "We wouldn't object to talking to them."

These widely circulated forgeries are just two representative cases of the sort of campaign LaRouche sympathizers often conduct. (Labor Party publications have even taken on the protective coloring of official union periodicals. The *Beacon* is visually similar to *The Teamster;* and *New Solidarity,* the Labor Party newspaper, once emphasized the word *Solidarity* in its logo in an effort, claimed the United Auto Workers' general counsel, "to palm itself off as our newspaper," *Solidarity.* A UAW lawsuit against the Labor Party for trademark and copyright infringement eventually provoked changes in the Labor Party publication.) And according to several sources, LaRouche's people have hounded reformers, sneaking into meetings, posing as reporters and turning over names of those who attend reform meetings to union higher-ups.

But LaRouche's plumbers have *not* always enjoyed the active support of top union officials. LaRouche's first flirtation with Teamster brass occurred back in 1975, when operatives reportedly set up New Rule, a group ostensibly organized to address Teamster Union problems. In 1978, LaRouche's U.S. Labor Party produced its first broadside designed to curry favor among union chieftains. The exposé, entitled "The Plot to Destroy the Teamsters," reported a conspiracy by the "Rockefeller Lower Manhattan Group" and others, including the Trilateral Commission, the Institute for Policy Studies and the Stern Fund, to crush the Teamsters.

At first blush, LaRouche must have seemed too incredibly strange even for then Teamster President Frank Fitzsimmons. What changed? The never-ending support for Fitzsimmons' policies worked away at the Teamster inner circle's resistance, and Teamster International officials learned how useful La-Rouche's people could be in crushing growing dissent from below.

Listening to dissent is a relatively new experience for Teamster brass. Before 1976, the overwhelming challenge of battling antiunion employers largely spent the energies of the rank and file, and reform movements were short-lived affairs. But by 1976, the routinized convention steamroller changed forever. Top Teamster ranks had splintered in 1974, when Jimmy Hoffa left prison and threatened to oust Fitzsimmons and "clean out" former allies from the Mob. Hoffa disappeared and was permanently silenced before the 1976 convention, but a burly, open-faced dockworker named Peter Camarata —elected as a delegate from Detroit, Hoffa's home local— showed up to complain from the floor about overpaid union officials and undemocratic procedures.

Camarata was a radical rank-and-filer, unlike Hoffa, but he drew attention because his radicalism was rooted in his family history. He could speak softly about the human side of economic hardship, since his father had been an autoworker at Packard when that line was discontinued in 1958. And he knew about job grievances firsthand, from his experience as a dockworker in Detroit.

Camarata and a group of rank-and-file Teamster militants, a few associated with the Trotskyist International Socialists, met and founded Teamsters for a Democratic Union. Although their organization failed to catch instant fire among the two million Teamsters across the country, the past five years have marked notable successes. TDU merged with another reform group, the Professional Driver's Organization (PROD), and increased in membership to 8,000. From one end of the Teamster empire to the other, from New York to Los Angeles, the progressive group made steady progress, electing local union officers and delegates to the 1981 convention—no small task in an operation in which 90 percent of the delegates are union officials beholden to their headquarters.

In a 1981 TDU report, "Who Runs the Teamsters Union," the group revealed that 38 top union officials held a combination of union posts at more than $100,000 a year each. The report also raised uncomfortable reminders of top officials' career histories, including new president Roy L. Williams' four criminal indictments—two for embezzlement, one for a false entry on a government report and the last for conspiracy to bribe Nevada Senator Howard Cannon.

Though even Camarata admits TDU is no real threat to established Teamster power yet, its role as a bothersome public conscience and its steady growth and persistence probably panicked the Teamster top leadership, leading them to reach out to LaRouche's fanatics.

LaRouche's presence can be low-key; but reformers also report that in heated election campaigns pitting reformers against incumbents, LaRouche followers plunge right in, often with the active support of International Teamster officers. "[The union] has a general organizer named Larry McHenry. He is a full-time organizer to disorganize TDU. He works side by side with them [LaRouche's people]. They're the ones who put out the leaflets. They do barn distribution for

McHenry," Camarata says. (McHenry could not be reached for comment.)

Some of the LaRouche "intelligence" distributed to union officials is laughably unreliable. In the material Fitzsimmons sent to his high command, for example, radical journalist Paul Jacobs was identified as a "Controller of the Berkeley Free Speech Movement and later a controller of the Maoist Revolutionary Communist Party and the Eldridge Cleaver-Black Panther terrorists." The outline of his activities concludes: "Today Jacobs works at *Mother Jones,* a magazine which features slanders on the Teamsters and the Laborers." Jacobs left *Mother Jones* in 1977; he died of cancer one year later.

Whether accurate or not, LaRouche propaganda has had a brutal effect in some locals, however. When California recording secretary Jim Rush ran for re-election on a reform ticket in 1977, for example, he and his fellow candidates were buried by a tide of literature accusing them of drug selling and terrorism. It was produced by the U.S. Labor Party, paid for by an employer, then distributed by establishment candidates in the union hall. "It's hard to fight against that kind of thing," Rush says now. "The members pick up the material because they think it's the union newspaper. It's hard to go out afterward and find every member of a large local and explain the situation."

Rush has been offered a libel settlement by LaRouche's organization, but he lost the election and was never able to return to his local union. He now works as an investigator at the law firm that brought his libel suit in San Francisco. Rush claims that Labor Party involvement in the Teamsters is more widespread than this investigation shows. "Wherever you find local union officials who have titles with the International Teamsters, you'll find Labor Party people," Rush says.

Long-time Teamster militant Ted Katsaros of New York, where Labor Party staff members have been intensely active in Teamster politics, says that LaRouche's people have been successful in turning the tide against reform in close election contests. "The Labor Party's real purpose is to disenchant the critics, [to convince] people who are cynical already that nothing can change, that it's a stacked deck," Katsaros adds.

LaRouche and Jackie Presser

By 1980, LaRouche could count as allies Teamster Union Vice President Jackie Presser and two international general organizers, Larry McHenry and Rolland McMaster, who are appointed by the general president. Relations grew so warm that McMaster even publicly endorsed LaRouche for president when he ran as a Democrat in the 1980 primaries.

Teamster Vice President Jackie Presser is the director of the union's core strength in the Central Conference. He heads the union's communications department, and he runs the Ohio chapter of DRIVE, the Teamster political arm. He is a savvy political operator and has been largely responsible for the Teamsters' cozy ties with President Reagan, serving last year as a key advisor on the Reagan transition team.

Access to Presser for LaRouche is a prized possession, of course, because Presser is a high-level link to the Teamsters *and* to the White House. The ties between Presser's operations in the Teamsters and LaRouche's organization are sometimes circuitous, however. For example, Mitchell WerBell III, a blustery former member of the Office of Strategic Services and one-time international arms merchant, provides an interesting link between LaRouche and Presser. Although WerBell refused to be interviewed for this story, it is a matter of public record that he was an associate of Cleveland mobster John Nardi. Nardi was, in turn, Presser's right-hand man until 1977. In 1977, Nardi was blasted away by a 16-stick dynamite bomb placed in his car in the parking lot of Presser's home local— a yet unsolved murder. Nardi's friend WerBell is also an important figure in LaRouche's circle, having trained U.S. Labor Party bodyguards in guerrilla warfare techniques on his Georgia farm.

Since Nardi's murder, Presser has maintained his own discreet ties with LaRouche's followers. His articles in the Ohio Teamster newspaper mirror LaRouche "intelligence" and parrot the Labor Party's *American Labor Beacon* stories, but Presser never credits LaRouche directly. While the *Beacon* promises to defend "labor from its enemies within and without," Presser pledges, "We Must Get Ready to Take on Foes Within and Without"; the *Beacon* blames a conspiracy between government and the media for persecution of the union and warns of a "Get the Teamsters network," while Presser decries the "baseless, unjustified attacks from Communist Socialist-orchestrated media, newspapers, TV or radio—organized by the captive political spokesmen who are and have been the advocates of 'Get the Teamsters.' "

Presser is a glib speaker with the heavy gait of a fat man confident of power, and he is a steady source of quips for LaRouche's followers. When Presser began referring to Peter Camarata as "Commie-Rat-A" during last year's Teamster convention, for example, the *Beacon* quickly picked up the slur. When Presser is annoyed, he shakes the large gold bracelet inscribed with big letters, J-A-C-K-I-E, and clenches his jaw, as the folds of fat vibrate.

Presser denies close contact with LaRouche just as he denies contact with organized crime elements. Asked by *Mother Jones* about Jimmy "The Weasel" Fratianno's statements identifying Presser as a tool of an alleged organized crime figure in Chicago, Presser snapped, "Forget about Fratianno. . . . He's a pathological liar and killer and that's all he is." In another interview, this one with ABC News, Presser waxed more eloquently: "We've been the media's meat, and you boys continue to write about us as the stepchild of the labor movement. . . . I wouldn't know organized crime if they were filming this program."

If Presser cannot recognize mobsters, he needs an ophthalmologist. Jackie's father, "Big Bill" Presser—a key old-timer who brought Jackie into the union, showed him the ropes and protected him until he died of a heart attack in late July—was repeatedly identified during his lifetime as a central link between blue-chip criminals and the Teamsters Union. Big Bill Presser was twice jailed during the 1960s, once for contempt of Congress and later for obstruction of justice. A Labor Department probe of Jackie Presser's own base of operations,

Joint Council 41 in Ohio, found that the list of officials "read
like a Who's Who of organized crime."

Could Presser Become Top Man?

No organization is a monolith, and a small band of Teamster
officials led by the union's liberal gray eminence, Second Vice
President Harold Gibbons, has grown concerned about Presser's ties to organized crime, his continuing relationship with
LaRouche and the possibility that he will make a run for
the top union spot if Roy Williams is convicted on his conspiracy to bribe indictment and removed from office. The prospect
that Presser could win the presidency, bringing his seamy connections with LaRouche into the Teamsters' Marble Palace
in Washington, D.C., is a bit more than Gibbons can stomach.
"There will be a lot of meetings if this guy makes a grab for
the top spot," Gibbons says.

Gibbons blames Presser for the steady inroads made by La-
Rouche staff members into the Teamster community. "They
came out with some pretty snazzy material. And it probably
impresses him. That's why he associates with them. He seems
to admire the literature they put out. The more I see, the
more suspicious I become," Gibbons says.

Gibbons' conversation is sprinkled with nostalgic memories:
of desegregation drives in St. Louis; of actions in support of
civil rights, such as the time he shut down Missouri's largest
construction project in support of Martin Luther King, Jr.;
and of the social service centers set up under his direction
to care for the poor of East St. Louis. Gibbons also muses
publicly about a different vision of the Teamsters Union, a
vision that might reignite a coalition between labor and the
poor and reach out to European unions for mutual support
abroad.

While Gibbons dutifully echoes the official line about TDU,
calling Camarata and his allies a "crackpot, lunatic fringe,"
he also emphasizes that he has repeatedly counseled against
overreaction in the face of dissent, vigorously opposing any
alliance—public or secret—with LaRouche. For his efforts,

Gibbons has been targeted by LaRouche devotees as an "agent" for the "Second Socialist International."

The Beacon Brand of Unionism

Success with the Teamsters has led to recent expansion of LaRouche's labor campaign, featuring the Labor Party's Committee Against Brilab and Abscam, set up to defend union chieftains accused of taking bribes. In early 1981 he launched the high-gloss tabloid, *American Labor Beacon.* The *Beacon* has used the Teamsters as its centerpiece but reaches out to other union officials, such as Laborers Union President Angelo Fosco, recently indicted on criminal charges and reputed to have ties to organized crime, and International Longshoremen's Association President Tommy Gleason.

In a recent issue of the *Beacon,* an Operating Engineers Union local president from Wisconsin parroted the LaRouche conspiracy theory about "big money czars" supplying cash to the "association for Union Democracy, Ralph Nader's Public Citizen, Inc. etc."

"Dissidents in the ranks are only tools of the czars working to eventually bring about total control as in Russia," the local president was quoted as saying, a concise reflection of LaRouche's philosophy. Why the "big money czars" are so frantically intent on transforming the U.S. into a Russian satellite is never quite adequately explained.

It would seem that even the Teamsters would want to put some distance between LaRouche's brand of lunatic fringe politics and their own philosophy. Yet, at the Teamsters' convention in Las Vegas, Jackie Presser himself left the speakers' platform to cozy up to the *Beacon's* publisher, Allan Friedman, and its editor, Larry Sherman. In addition, local Teamster officials have been flooded recently with letters from well-known union officials and ex-officials urging them to support the *Beacon* with bulk subscription orders for their membership.

One typical letter was sent out on *Beacon* letterhead and signed by Jack Goldberger, a retired San Francisco-based

Teamster official with a reputation as a progressive. "Every day, people hear lies, half-truths and slanders coming out of the press," the letter read. "The *American Labor Beacon* has finally given an effective voice back to labor. I would particularly stress the importance of getting this publication out to the membership."

Goldberger confirms that he did, in fact, sign the *Beacon* solicitation letter. He says, now, that he does not "know who Mr. LaRouche is or who the U.S. Labor Party is" but that he still supports the *Beacon*. Teamster Second Vice President Harold Gibbons says the solicitation drive has been successful in drawing bulk subscription orders for the *Beacon* from across the country.

The latest issues of the *Beacon* are stuffed with such high-gloss praise for Teamster leaders that the paper resembles an official union publication. A catalog of other stories sketch coming battles for unions against:

- a federal strike force in Miami, which pursued an investigation resulting in the indictment of Laborers Union President Angelo Fosco;
- the "pro-terrorist rag" *Mother Jones, The Village Voice* and mass media on the whole; and
- "Socialist" labor leaders such as International Association of Machinists President William Winpisinger, Douglas Fraser of the United Auto Workers and Jerry Wurf from AFSCME, who, according to one headline, "Plan Government Disruption. . . ."

This is not a record that should go without comment. With influence in the Teamsters, the Operating Engineers, the Laborers and the Longshoremen's Association already, the *Beacon* could become an effective tool for indoctrinating labor into LaRouche's own brand of right-wing fringe politics. Access to the rank and file is LaRouche's best hope for converting a segment of the country's working people to the Labor Party analysis. That is, perhaps, its greatest danger.

Local union officials are drawn to the *Beacon* for its labor coverage in a nation where there is generally little media attention given to labor at all. They are not told of the *Beacon's* ties to LaRouche or the Labor Party. In fact the U.S. Labor Party no longer technically exists. It has dissolved itself, like the National Caucus of Labor Committees before it, into the National Democratic Policy Committee, the Fusion Energy Foundation and, now, the *Beacon* itself. But no matter what LaRouche calls it, the party line remains essentially the same, and the *Beacon* is rife with it. One recent story linked the Trilateral Commission, the Italian Communist Party and Alexander Haig in a plot to overthrow the Italian government; and even the *Beacon's* labor stories are filled with LaRouchianisms like "big money czars" or "international socialists" conspiring to attack trade-unionism.

Despite all of this evidence, the *Beacon* is still often mistaken for an independent, labor-oriented publication and not the LaRouche house organ that it is. Some union members interviewed during the research for this story stated that the *Beacon* had no affiliation with the U.S. Labor Party or Lyndon LaRouche. Bruce Wood, a *Beacon* staffer in Detroit denied any affiliation with the Labor Party. "We operate as a business," Wood said. "We're not a cause. We run it as a totally separate business." Perhaps the most overwhelming evidence to the contrary is simply in the backgrounds of the two men who are instrumental in producing the *Beacon:* editor Larry Sherman and publisher Allan Friedman.

Sherman's record speaks loudly. In 1973, he ran for the Boston school board on the U.S. Labor Party ticket. In 1974, he was a Labor Party candidate for the Ninth Congressional District in Boston. Also that year, he was a candidate for governor on the Labor Party ticket.

In 1976, he was a member of the executive committee of the National Caucus of Labor Committees.

In 1977, Sherman, as a representative of the U.S. Labor Party, met with the New Hampshire state police to give "intelligence information" on Seabrook demonstrators. The Labor Party is one of the nation's largest compilers of intelligence dossiers on antinuke and peace activists and has voluntarily turned over this information to police and federal investigative agencies like the FBI.

In 1979, Sherman ran in the Boston mayor's race as the

U.S. Labor Party candidate. That same year, *New Solidarity,* the Labor Party paper, reported that Sherman was the New Hampshire coordinator for Citizens for LaRouche during La-Rouche's presidential bid.

By the end of 1980, Sherman had become the editor of the *American Labor Beacon.*

For his part, *Beacon* publisher Allan Friedman ran for office only once. That was in 1976 in the 17th Congressional district in Harrisburg, Pennsylvania. He was the U.S. Labor Party candidate.

Is LaRouche Truly Dangerous?

One union president who finds LaRouche's penetration of labor disconcerting is Machinist chief William Winpisinger, a progressive who hopes to revitalize labor by building new coalitions with unorganized workers, minorities, women and the poor. Winpisinger was a key supporter of the AFL-CIO's "Solidarity Day" rally, which drew nearly 400,000 to Washington, D.C. last September. "I find it very disturbing to learn that these people have got a foothold in the labor movement," Winpisinger says. "If I ever have to resort to [using them] to get elected, I would withdraw from the race."

Even conservative unionists have spurned LaRouche's entreaties, refusing to stoop to an alliance with him, however convenient. When reform candidate Ed Sadlowski challenged stodgy Lloyd MacBride for the presidency of the United Steelworkers of America in 1976, for example, the establishment team received repeated offers of help from LaRouche. "They would send us enormously long messages about things they thought we should be doing," reports Steelworkers Secretary-Treasurer Lin Williams, who ran on the MacBride ticket. "They looked to us like long letters from fanatics."

For rank-and-file reformers who have been victimized by Labor Party smear tactics, the Teamster-LaRouche alliance is more than an abstract problem. In New York—where union officials subscribe, to the tune of $400, to the *Executive Intelli-*

gence Review and LaRouche followers have regularly picketed against reformers—activist Ted Katsaros is concerned about a "circle, a pattern hooking up the Mob, crooked labor officials and the U.S. Labor Party."

Several long-time observers of American labor history, with all its twists and turns, were shocked when briefed about this investigation. One of the most respected labor writers in the country, A. H. Raskin, now retired from *The New York Times,* says he considers it historically unprecedented for a group of such certifiable extremists to make headway inside the labor movement.

When all is considered, what is the real danger of this emerging alliance, beyond the unpleasant suppression of Teamster dissent? Is not Jackie Presser simply an anomaly, and are not Lyndon LaRouche's followers simply marginal, though dramatic, kooks? Not really. Union leaders like Presser use LaRouche propaganda to bolster their grip on the union. Their day of reckoning is postponed, and they avoid coming to terms with legitimate protests by the membership they claim to represent.

Where union members are taken in by the Labor Party material, because it comes to them masked as trade-union information, their attention is turned from the serious economic and political problems that confront them. Their energy is dissipated by worthless hatreds of nonexistent conspiracies. The possibility of a new, creative role for labor in confronting the nation's deepening economic crisis fades.

American labor has traditionally been torn by contentious impulses, to defend capitalism but demand reform of it. Even representatives of conservative "business unionism" have normally felt a deeply sown sense of social responsibility. Samuel Gompers, first president of the American Federation of Labor, said in 1893, "We want more schoolhouses and less jails; more books and less arsenals; more learning and less vice; more constant work and less crime; more leisure and less greed; more justice and less revenge."

LaRouche, it seems quite clear, would give us more revenge and less justice, more greed and less responsibility, more fanaticism and less thought. Never before have top American labor leaders forged an alliance with cryptofascists such as La-Rouche.

It is especially dangerous for labor to be sidetracked by LaRouche now, at a time of economic contraction and rising unemployment. Those hardest hit by the economy begin to look for ideological scapegoats. LaRouche and the Labor Party point out those scapegoats to organized labor at the same time that they offer to eliminate them, allegedly "solving" the complicated problems through simple means.

The U.S. Labor Party—with all its "conspiracies," "big money czars" and "enemies of labor"—provides a perfect smoke screen for overaged, hidebound, intransigent union leadership. The fanaticism of the Labor Party allows unions to *not* address the truly fundamental problems organized labor faces: how should income be redistributed; how can the unorganized be unionized; and how can the economy be revitalized to create new jobs?

Behind the Story

Las Vegas is a mecca for gamblers, entertainers, mobsters—and investigative reporters. It provides the backdrop for endless stories about the seamy side of America and how it prospers. The challenge for a journalist is to pierce the city's garish facade and expose the illicit activity. Doug Foster arrived in June 1981, on assignment for *Mother Jones* magazine, to report about one of the bulwarks of the Las Vegas power structure—the International Brotherhood of Teamsters. No place could have been more appropriate for the union's annual convention than Las Vegas, where the Teamsters have invested millions of dollars of their members' earnings in the casinos that line the strip.

During two and a half years as an aggressive reporter for the Salinas *Californian,* Foster often covered labor issues. He had recently moved to San Francisco to try freelance magazine writing on national issues, and he considered the Teamsters convention an opportunity for a major story. In preparation Foster had collected everything he could find about the union, including articles and books like Steven Brill's *The Teamsters* and Walter Sheridan's *The Fall and Rise of Jimmy Hoffa.* The *Mother Jones* editors were interested in the turmoil between the union's old guard and the small group of militant reformers known as Teamsters for Democratic Union (TDU). In addition, the recent death of Teamster president Frank Fitzsimmons had reportedly put the leadership of the union up for grabs. Still, since these aspects of the convention were likely to be well covered by the national media, Foster felt he was essentially on a "fishing expedition."

From the Las Vegas airport, Foster rode into town in a limousine and started a conversation with the driver. Two years before, the driver told him, all limo drivers in town were Teamsters. Now, in the city where they were holding their convention, the drivers had voted to decertify the union because they didn't feel it was helping them. Foster pondered the complexities of a union whose members were driven to a convention by nonunion drivers in a city where nonunion casinos had been built largely with union pension funds.

The contradictions were familiar to Foster. While a student at
the University of California at Santa Cruz, he had worked in a
nearby cannery as a member of the Teamsters. "That cannery had
been under Teamster contract for years and none of the workers
had ever seen a copy of the contract. During my years there, we
organized a worker committee. For the first time, the Teamster
business agent started coming around.

"The Teamsters' involvement in the cannery had been just a
dues checkoff, not real representation. Some of the left political
sects had begun to organize, and the Teamsters were pretty sensitive
to rumblings where they'd never had any trouble before. From
that involvement, I developed a special feeling about the way
workers experience outrage when unions take their money and don't
deliver representation."

Outside the convention hall the first morning of the proceedings,
a group of pickets from TDU were passing out leaflets protesting
the high salaries of the union leadership. Even though they were
members, the TDU activists were denied entrance to the hall because
high union officials considered them troublemakers. Most of the
convention attendees were appointed officials who owed their
allegiance to the union hierarchy, and therefore they were hostile
to the TDU picketers. So far, everything was as Foster had expected.

Once he had passed through the phalanx of security guards at
the entrance, however, Foster was confronted with a surprising
scene. Two well-dressed, clean-cut men were passing out copies
of a slick magazine. It was similar in appearance to official Teamster
periodicals but was called the *American Labor Beacon.*

"I knew from living in San Francisco and knowing about extremist
political sects that the *Beacon* was started and run by supporters
of Lyndon LaRouche," Foster explains. "I was struck to see
outsiders from an extremist right-wing sect allowed free rein of
the convention hall to pass out their publication. Meanwhile, dues-
paying union members who opposed official policies were kept
outside and excoriated as extremists. I wondered who had given
them permission to come inside the hall, but at first I didn't spend
too much time thinking about it. I figured it would be picked up
by the daily newspaper reporters."

Over the next few days, as he realized that the daily press was *not* going to cover the LaRouche group's activity, Foster decided to make it an important part of his story. He knew that the Labor Party members had attempted to infiltrate other unions in the past, but he was unaware of the extent to which they had ingratiated themselves with the Teamster hierarchy.

By the middle of the second day of the convention, Foster had begun a systematic search to locate a possible source on the Teamster national executive board. He wanted to learn more about the Labor Party's involvement with the Teamsters. Since board members had been the targets of numerous government and press investigations over the years, they routinely brushed off his and other reporters' requests for interviews. So Foster's persistent attempts to question the board members as they emerged from meetings earned him only hostility at first. An opening resolution denouncing the press in general and celebrating a recent libel judgment against *The National Enquirer* had set an antipress tone for the convention.

Foster decided to concentrate on finding those board members most likely to oppose the Labor Party. He knew who they were from the reading he had done prior to the convention. "In a convention situation," he explains, "you can save many months of later work by simply developing some rapport with possible sources. I'd never met any of these officials before. I just wanted to get close to them and establish some kind of rapport so I could call later with questions."

Here Foster's freelance status worked both for and against him. The labor reporters for national newspapers and the television networks were covering the daily events on the convention floor. Unlike them, Foster was free from daily deadline pressure and could develop his story thoroughly; he didn't face the risk of offending union sources with stories he had filed the day before. On the other hand, Foster was unknown and lacked the clout of a big-name media connection.

Foster focused his attention on second vice-president Harold Gibbons, a progressive member of the inner circle who had been stripped of most of his powers under Fitzsimmons's regime. Circumventing the union's communications director, whose job was to shield board members from reporters, Foster buttonholed

Gibbons at the noon recess on the second day and insisted that
they meet over drinks that evening. Gibbons agreed to a brief
interview, but Foster was able to stretch the meeting into an hour-
and-a-half discussion. Gibbons, who had been singled out for
criticism by the Labor party in the past, was especially angered
and frustrated by the board's decision to allow the sect's members
free access to the convention floor.

Having established Gibbons as a sympathetic source, Foster set
out to find other union officials who could corroborate information.
Again he hovered about the union members as they entered and
left sessions, trying to persuade them to talk to him. Finally, after
repeated failures, he convinced some officials to cooperate. Unlike
Gibbons, these sources were extremely nervous and insisted that
they remain unnamed in the story. These sources agreed only to
provide confirmation for any part of Gibbons's story that Foster
felt needed multiple sources. With the subsequent addition of a
surprise source *inside* the Labor Party, Foster had now laid the
groundwork for writing "Teamster Madness."

Meanwhile, the reporter was busily trying to research other
aspects of his assignment. He still considered the Labor party angle
only one part of an overall feature on the union's problems. Despite
the general antipathy toward him as a reporter on the convention
floor, eventually he was able to fill six notebooks with interviews
about attempts at union busting, deregulation of the trucking
industry, renewed attempts to organize farm workers, and the
involvement of organized-crime figures in the union. In the midst
of the convention excitement, it was difficult to determine whether
the Labor Party activity was a better story than the appearance
of notorious figures like Allen Dorfman* or board member Salvatore
"Sammy Pro" Provenzano, whose brother Tony was a prime suspect
in the disappearance of Jimmy Hoffa.

For Foster, the convention turned into five days of nonstop
reporting. From breakfast meetings with TDU dissidents, to hallway
interviews with executive board members, to late-night readings
of the convention transcripts, Foster probed for the issues and people
around which to build his story. By the end of the week he was

---

* Dorfman was murdered, gangland-style, in early 1983 amid suspicions that his conviction
in a bribery case would lead him to "snitch" to the authorities.

exhausted and not yet sure which theme to concentrate on for *Mother Jones.*

He spent the next month reviewing and organizing his notes for follow-up interviews. He realized that the Labor Party issue would be the major investigative angle for his story, but he still wanted to include much of the other material he had gathered in Las Vegas. *Mother Jones* wanted the story fast—in six weeks—so Foster decided that there wasn't time for Freedom of Information Act (FOIA) requests on the union or the Labor Party. These requests often take months or even years to produce results. Instead he began a round of telephone calls to his various sources and to the new names he collected as the investigation progressed.

He also got a few lucky breaks. A friendly Teamster from his reporting days in Salinas called to ask him about the *American Labor Beacon* that was being distributed in his local. This call led Foster to probe Labor Party activities at the local level and to see how they tied in with what he had witnessed at the national convention. Another chance phone conversation located a researcher who had made a hobby of collecting Labor Party documents and newsletters for years, ever since LaRouche had become active in the late 1960s. Later, a call to a freelance writer who had written about LaRouche produced a comprehensive card file on Labor Party personnel based on names listed in party publications.

Foster's most useful source on the party, however, was the insider he had met at the convention. "I got to know him well enough to say hello," Foster explains. "Once I was back from the convention I began a campaign of regular phone calls." Foster was performing the delicate operation of "baptizing" his source. "I kept calling him to show I was serious, to get a tidbit here and a tidbit there rather than push for it all. In my experience, with this kind of hesitant source in an organization like the Labor Party, you could get him to say a lot if you didn't push him, if you didn't make him say it all at once. You didn't make him feel like a traitor for laying out the whole scheme if he could say a small piece, and when he got embarrassed or uncomfortable, let him hang up. I wasn't worried about getting the whole story every time."

This type of interview was the opposite of the work Foster had been doing in Las Vegas. "It's the flip side of dealing with a Roy

Williams or a Jackie Presser in a situation like the convention where
you've got one shot for the next couple of years to ask them a
question. There, you insist on asking a follow-up question, making
them stand there, getting it all. They're experienced and they know
how to deal with the press."

Foster's sensitivity with his Labor Party source eventually paid
off. "He gave me a lot: the whole story of the party moving in
and running the campaign against trucking deregulation and
organizing demonstrations on behalf of the Teamsters against Ted
Kennedy; the information on Labor Party publications on the
Teamsters, the number of publications, the amount of money it
cost; the way in which general Teamster organizers had endorsed
LaRouche for president in 1980. He told me small things that added
up to a lot. It showed a pattern."

There was little written documentation of the Labor Party's
relationship with the union, so Foster's sources were vital to the
story. His careful interviewing techniques, patience in developing
the sources, and background in labor issues all contributed to his
success.

"The only union I'd ever belonged to was the Teamsters," he
says. "That was useful with some of the hostile officials. I'd say
things like 'Listen, I've been a Teamster; you can't bullshit me.'
That would have some effect. Labor people tend to see reporters
as part of an elite that oppresses them. When it becomes clear
that you're a worker too, there's more opportunity for creating
rapport."

His initial deadline was delayed, so Foster's research stretched
into August before he began to write. Just before ending his
investigation, he requested interviews with LaRouche and his
supporters in San Francisco, Los Angeles, New York, and Boston.
All were declined.

Foster's first draft was an overview that placed his new
information about the Labor Party as only one of several important
issues facing the Teamsters union. The editors responded by
identifying the Labor Party as the focus they wanted. He reluctantly
returned to his typewriter to pare the story down. Although he
agreed that the Labor Party alliance was an important aspect of
the current state of the Teamsters, he wanted to write about the

dissidents, the leadership fight, and organized crime as well.

"In some ways, the emphasis solely on the Labor Party material missed the point by shifting the onus of responsibility from Teamster officials to LaRouche," Foster feels. "LaRouche and his supporters are not a powerful force either politically or economically, but the willingness of the Teamster brass to engage in this alliance made the LaRouche people dangerous. The focus of the story was something reasonable people could disagree about, and the *Mother Jones* editors and I did disagree."

Foster used what was now an extensive interview file to redraft the story. "I had a master interview file with all the interviews in it. I went through it and highlighted the parts of each that I wanted to make sure were included because they had either important information or good colorful transitions. Then I went to my day-to-day diary of the convention and did the same thing. Then I pulled every piece of major documentation I had and stacked them in roughly the order I thought I would need them. Next, I did an outline with a couple of lines for each major category. Finally, I sat down and wrote."

For encouragement, Foster recalled a saying from the late investigative reporter Paul Jacobs. "Whenever I think I've got writer's block, I always remember what Jacobs used to say: 'Don't give me that bullshit. A plumber doesn't get up in the morning and say, "Ah, I can't work, I've got plumber's block." ' Put your ass in the chair and start typing."

After numerous rewrites, Foster arrived at a final draft. He remembers how difficult it was to change his writing style after several years on a newspaper. "Compared to a newspaper reader, a magazine reader wants something that's artfully done. The writing must have some attention paid to it and the story should unfold in an interesting way. A magazine reader is going to take more time to get the subtlety and complexity of the story." Although "Teamster Madness" had an investigative tone, Foster believes magazine writers need to take a softer approach generally. "The magazine writer should have the story unfold in a way that enlightens and changes readers by the process of reading, rather than hitting them over the head with the information."

The story finally appeared in the January 1982 issue amid

concerns of a Teamster lawsuit to halt distribution. "I hoped they would [file a suit]," Foster remembers, "because of the attention it would have caused. They said they were going to have a point-by-point response. They never did."

When no demand for a retraction or correction came from the union, Foster knew that "the work I'd done and the month-long fact-checking work of the magazine had all paid off."

There was some internal reaction among the Teamsters. Harold Gibbons introduced a motion against any affiliation between the executive board and the *American Labor Beacon.* Several local labor councils reproduced the story for dissemination to their membership. Foster appeared on numerous radio and television talk shows and received many calls from concerned local union presidents and business agents both in and outside the Teamsters, who wanted to know more about LaRouche and his hold over the *American Labor Beacon.* Several union officials promised to halt bulk subscriptions paid for by union dues.

Beacon staffers also sought to distance themselves from LaRouche. In a *Beacon* statement, the publication's editor and publisher insisted that "there is no existing relationship between the *American Labor Beacon* and LaRouche." Within a year and a half of the article's publication, the *Beacon* reportedly ceased publication.

In April 1983, Teamster president Roy Williams was convicted of federal fraud and bribery charges and resigned his post to avoid prison. Harold Gibbons had pledged in his final interview with Foster to lead a protracted battle to keep Jackie Presser, his longtime foe, out of the top position if Williams was convicted. But by the time that battle came, Gibbons was dead from a heart attack. Vice-president Jackie Presser, of all top union officials the most closely linked to LaRouche's followers, was elected to replace Roy Williams.

4

Let Them Eat est

by Suzanne Gordon

An evening at the White House is not an unusual event for Enud McGiffert. As the wife of Assistant Secretary of Defense David McGiffert, she has been there many times. But one particular evening, May 1, 1978, stands out in her mind. Mrs. McGiffert had gone to the majestic building on Pennsylvania Avenue to attend a performance of a play presented by her daughter's elementary school, whose students included Amy Carter. Before the performance, President and Mrs. Carter greeted children and parents on an informal reception line. It was then that Mrs. McGiffert drew open the curtain on her own personal drama. She stopped, said hello, and then she simply could not refrain. She had to convince Jimmy Carter of the significance of a new "experience" in her life—the Hunger Project, the latest venture of Werner Erhard's est. For est, or Erhard Seminars Training, which began as one of the evangelistic human potential movements of the '70s, had recently expanded its horizons from the self to the world. Werner Erhard had inaugurated a campaign that, he promises, will end hunger on the planet within the next two decades.

As Jimmy shook Enud McGiffert's hand, she smiled and began her tale. "I just want you to know," she told him, "about the Hunger Project. There are 100,000 people out there who really just want to totally serve you and do anything you want them to do to end hunger and starvation on the planet in the next 20 years." The people standing behind her pressed her on. She could not decipher Carter's reaction.

All through the play, anxiety ate at her. Had she done the right thing? Poor man, she thought, he can't even stand on a reception line without someone pestering him. After the play, as the parents gathered in the White House dining room for refreshments, the President walked up to her. "Now, where were we?" he asked, smiling his famous smile.

Enud McGiffert was thrilled. "I want you to know," Carter went on, "that I know about your group and will call upon you when we have our plans ready."

Mrs. McGiffert, an est graduate and enrollee in the Hunger Project, was not the only one pleased with Carter's response. Upon hearing of the incident, est Public-Relations Manager Brian Van der Horst beamed. It was nothing short of a miracle, a miracle that would delight Werner Erhard. For if one man will spark America's movement to end hunger, many loyal est supporters believe, it is Werner Erhard, founder of est— a man who has transformed thousands of Americans' experience of themselves, has "made it work," and who has not only now gone on to forge a campaign to end hunger on the planet but also, in the process, will show us how to "complete" our lives and make the world our "context rather than our condition."

Until 1977, Erhard's activity was based on a training system where some 250 people sit in a hotel ballroom for two weekends to hear Erhard or one of his trainers combine techniques as varied as Eastern mysticism, Dale Carnegie and behavior modification so that they can heal their souls. The going price for this is $300. The training takes place in a distinctive upbeat estian language whose phrases pepper the statements of both Erhard and his disciples. Est's expansion into the field of hunger is significant not only because Erhard has initiated it, but also because it is one of the first attempts so far by one of the "self"-oriented movements of the '70s to address social or political issues.

To assure the eradication of hunger and starvation within the next two decades, est created the Hunger Project as an independent, nonprofit organization and gave it a $400,000 interest-free loan. Est's tax-deductible arm, the est Foundation, bestowed on the Project a $100,000 grant. This money financed a series of 12 "presentations" in urban centers across the nation, where Erhard "presented" the idea of ending hunger to 40,000 Americans. In a slide show and lecture, he and his resident hunger expert, Roy Prosterman, tried to "get at" the first principles of hunger and starvation. He then "gave" the Project to those Americans who, after paying $6 to attend the show, demonstrated that they wanted to take "personal responsibility for being the source of the Project and ending hunger and starvation on the planet in the next two decades."

Who Gets the Money?

What, precisely, does the Hunger Project plan to do to end famine and starvation? The Hunger Project does not, you see, *do* anything about ending hunger. That's why, Erhard tells anyone who asks, it is a difficult idea to grasp. The Hunger Project does not advocate any particular solution to hunger—like land reform, food self-sufficiency or the wresting of power from landowners by peasants. Nor does it ask its enrollees to make "dehumanizing gestures"—like sending money to anti-hunger organizations. Above all, the Project does not want its members to feel guilty about the deplorable situation that causes, each year, the death of some 15 million people all over the world. Rather, it asks them to view hunger and starvation as a "wonderful opportunity," an opportunity to "make a difference in the world."

To create such optimism, Erhard counsels us to examine our "positions" about hunger and starvation. This is the first step in "getting" the Project. Once we examine our attitudes, we will discover that two prevail: one, we think hunger and starvation are inevitable; two, we think that to end it, we have to "do" something, support a particular "position." But these things, Erhard assures us, are not the case. Hunger and starvation are not inevitable. We have the technology to eradicate them. And positions merely make matters worse—by engendering opposing positions.

What the Hunger Project literature—a slick collection of Werner Erhard's sayings, photographs and aphorisms gleaned from hunger experts and their writings—counsels is a process of de-education. For anyone confused by the complex issues of the day, this has enoromous appeal. "Rather than knowing more and then more as you go along," Erhard counsels, "you will need, instead, to be willing to know less and then less— that is to say, to become somewhat confused as you go along. Finally, you will have struggled enough to be clear that you don't know. In the state of knowing that you don't know, you get, as a flash of insight, the principle out of which the answer comes."

What forces caused hunger in the first place? Erhard is vague about this. "Call them political forces, if you like," he advises generously. "Study the political forces and you will see that hunger and starvation on the planet are the inevitable result of those forces. . . . If you don't like the politics, do it with economic forces. If you don't like the economics, do it with sociological forces. Psychological forces. Philosophical forces. Or if you prefer, a combination of them."

So far, 180,000 people have enrolled in this project to make the world "work"; they have made more than 30,000 tax-deductible contributions, which have totaled $883,800. Almost none of this money goes into the mouths of hungry people, for that would, remember, contribute to the "dehumanization" of the world's hungry. This money goes, instead, toward the continued communication of the Hunger Project to an ever-expanding sector of the American public: it produces the Hunger Project quarterly newspaper, *A Shift in the Wind;* it helps pay for office space and slide shows and films. Less than one percent of the Project's money, $2,500, went to a well-known British hunger organization called Oxfam. But the essence of the Hunger Project is workability, alignment, communication and more communication.

And here he is now, Werner Erhard, founder of the Hunger

Project. Here he is on the stage of the San Francisco Cow Palace, or that of the Felt Forum in New York, communicating the Hunger Project to thousands of Americans. The auditoriums are enormous, so we have two Werners before us—the man on stage, and above him, bigger than life, a videotaped image on a huge screen. Or here he is in Washington, gathering hunger experts together to convince them that ending hunger is an idea whose time has come. Or there he is in India, talking with Prime Minister Morarji Desai, and then quick, we have to catch up with him as he jets to the Franklin House, his Victorian mini-mansion on Franklin Street in San Francisco. Wherever he is these days, the Hunger Project is on his lips, for it's a project that comes from his very intimate experience of the souls of the thousands and thousands of Americans with whom he has had, he says, a very meaningful personal relationship.

The est staff, the Hunger Project staff, the Hunger Project Council, the est Advisory Board, the Hunger Project Advisory Board, est assistants and volunteers all echo Werner's language when "communicating" the Project. And they all claim that, except for the seed money, the Project has nothing organizationally to do with est and that Werner Erhard has magnanimously taken months off his busy schedule to help Americans end world hunger.

A six-month investigation by *Mother Jones* and the Center for Investigative Reporting, however, has revealed a far different set of goals for the Hunger Project:

- Werner Erhard is using the Hunger Project not only for self-aggrandizement but for promoting the for-profit corporation he founded, as well. The Hunger Project is a thinly veiled recruitment arm for est. Hunger Project volunteers have said that est-trained Hunger Project staffers have pressured them until they agreed to do the $300-a-shot est training. Others told of being asked to lend their cars or provide other services to est.

- The Hunger Project has nonprofit status—which gives it the ability to receive tax-deductible contributions. But this use of a nonprofit organization to recruit customers for a for-profit one is in violation of the spirit, if not the letter, of Internal Revenue Service laws.

- In various cities across the country, Erhard's disciples have organized a "Hunger Project Seminar Series" at $30 per enrollment. Yet the proceeds go, not to the Hunger Project, but directly to est.

- The official claim that est and the Hunger Project are organizationally separate is a fabrication. Careful examination reveals that top personnel pass through a revolving door from est to the Hunger Project. In many cities, the Hunger Project is housed in est offices. Est graduate bulletins advertise Hunger Project events. The three initial directors of the Hunger Project, Michael Chatzky, Robert Dunnett and Mark Schiavenza, all work out of the law firm of est lawyer and offshore tax-haven expert, Harry Margolis. In addition, Dunnett was vice president of Erhard Seminars Training, Inc., when that was est's corporate name, and Chatzky was one of the directors of California Aesthetics, which was once the sole shareholder in est. The Hunger Project's current vice president, John Emery, and the secretary-treasurer, Helen Nahm, are both on the est Advisory Board. The Project's resident hunger expert, Roy Prosterman, the man who does the traveling hunger road show with Erhard, receives a grant from an est foundation, which helps support his own hunger consulting work.

As we shall see, Erhard will deny some of these charges in his uniquely estian way in an interview.

No More Struggle

Erhard's founding of the Hunger Project, a little over a year ago, was a stroke of genius. Though the est movement has been growing rapidly, Erhard had been getting increasingly bad reviews. There had been a number of newspaper and magazine articles criticizing his movement's obvious authoritarianism and its devaluation of independent thought. There were also questions about whether, with tens of thousands of people paying up to $300 a crack for est training, Erhard was using the consciousness movement to make himself a tidy personal fortune. Erhard needed a good promotional weapon to fight back with and, in the Hunger Project, he found it.

Examined carefully, of course, the Hunger Project is not a new departure for Erhard, but merely an application of the familiar est approach. Consciousness is everything; distribution of wealth and power, nothing. The Hunger Project takes one of the most potent political issues of the day and totally depoliticizes it. The persistence of hunger, Erhard says, is not primarily due to an economic system in which rich get richer and poor get poorer (of which Erhard is a part, as est money finds its way to offshore tax havens). Rather, it is due to the lack of will, to attitudes, to bad intentions.

The emphasis is on the positive. Don't think about the depressing facts of hunger or the causes of starvation, think of the hunger issue as the chance of a lifetime—a way to have an impact on the world. All this talk of impact neatly brackets the starving and the dying. They appear in beautiful color pictures in Hunger Project brochures—but the needs of middle-class Americans eclipse their reality. The people who flock to est, the Hunger Project and the other consciousness movements have just escaped a decade of disillusionment where political action promised social transformation. This promise was not fulfilled. Similarly, the '60s and early '70s were an era of journalistic exposés that revealed widespread corruption: Watergate, the CIA, FBI provocateurs, the list is endless. But again, information has not led to transformation. The more people learn about how bad things are, the more powerless they feel. Erhard realizes that his fans want to feel both powerful and needed. "The idea [of the Hunger Project] germinated itself from my experience of people with whom I was interacting, primarily people who had been through the training," he explains. So Erhard creates a way for them to *feel* like they're having the impact they know they've lost.

"Brenda, Brenda, I Just Got Manifested!"

What attracts a talented, busy and hitherto sensible person to Werner Erhard and his Hunger Project? Mother Jones' Mark Schapiro called Valerie Harper, star of TV's Rhoda, to ask her a few questions, and found her so eager to talk he could barely get a word in edgewise. Here is a condensation of her response:

Well, first of all, the Hunger Project is each one of us. It's not like I joined an organization and now I'm a member of this group called the Hunger Project. In our world you have to say, 'What is the organization?' And of course there is an organization, but the actual work of the Hunger Project is individual responsibility. It does manifest and it's not a solid thing, it's not an object, as human beings are not objects. So the Hunger Project lives in each person who chooses to have it be there. And so, since I've been participating in the Hunger Project, a lot of things in my life have altered and my own personal power has expanded.

"What the Hunger Project is, is affording one that opportunity to create an idea's time coming. You see, there's only one way that an idea's time comes, and that is not through organization or money or political action or group stuff. It comes through the individual. So what the Hunger Project is, is an alignment of individuals, each doing their particular, individual thing. Now Wilbur and Orville Wright created the airplane. Now, what it looks to us—and now we'll talk physics for a minute—it looks to us like Wilbur and Orville built a plane and then flight occurred. So that's the Hunger Project. The way an idea's time comes is individuals create it. Individuals create—again physics—a critical mass of agreement about an idea, and then out of that, things manifest. You got that? You don't have to believe it or understand it, but just kind of get the sense of what I'm saying.

"Werner Erhard has formulated the Project. He has . . . I'll tell you what he did, literally. He personally took responsibility for ending world hunger. He said to the Advisory Board, and I was at the meeting, 'That's what I want to do.' And there was tremendous static, and we all said, 'Now wait a minute, Werner, what are you doing? What are you talking about?' He said, 'This is an est organization, our organization will continue, will fill trainings, will keep giving people a chance to nurture, expand their lives, etc. If the training's something they want to do, fine.

If it isn't, they don't, and we'll keep providing it. That's our work as an est Advisory Board. I'm just telling you that I am personally taking responsibility to end the starvation on this planet by 1997.' And I remember standing up and saying, 'But Werner, listen, I was taught as a child, and I believed, that it will always be with us. There will always be the starving throngs because it's part of the world, the Middle Ages, for all time—much further back than the Middle Ages people have starved.' And he said, 'I would put to you, Valerie, that you holding that is contributing to hunger. Your responsibility is not if you ate pizza this afternoon.' And I *got* it so clearly, and I began to see.

"The clearer I get about starvation, the more I can take responsibility for it. So, in one sentence, the Hunger Project is a project of communication and enrollment, and by enrollment that does not mean that you pay a fee and you're in and you have a card. It means that you enroll and then you enroll to enroll. You enroll people yourself. I'm sure you'll speak to other people about this. I'll send you material and I think you'll like it. I have exactly the person for you to call to get some material. Brian Van der Horst is the public information office, the office of public information for the Hunger Project. Well, now wait a second, I'm giving you the wrong thing, honey, hold it, he's with est, that's not right. . . .

SOIPs

Hunger is one of the sexier issues in Washington, D.C., this year. No one is for it, and everyone is against it. Hunger is consequently a perfect issue around which a President with lagging popularity can mobilize public support. Recently, Carter appointed a Presidential commission on the subject. Like all Presidential commissions, it includes a "non-partisan" assortment of college presidents (Steve Muller of Johns Hopkins), millionaires (Sol Linowitz), scientists (Jean Mayer), Republican and Democratic senators and representatives, and, among others, entertainer Harry Chapin and singer John Denver—the latter, an enthusiastic backer of est.

Denver is unfailingly helpful. His greatest contribution, aside from his coming role in the Presidential Hunger Commission, was a film he financed and narrated called *I Want to Live.* He sang the theme song, which centered around the lines: "I want to share/I want to give/I want to live." The film also included the opinions of such luminaries as Hubert Humphrey, U.N. Representative Andrew Young and various hunger experts, who spoke about the possible solutions to the hunger problem. Ending on a rather vulgar note of self-celebration, Vice President Walter Mondale congratulated Denver on his great personal commitment. This film is a staple of Hunger Project promotion.

Werner Erhard has promptly gone to work trying to propagate his ideas to the Presidential Commission's members and others in the White House. President Carter's son Chip, for example, represented his father at a three-day Hunger Project symposium at the Tarrytown, New York, Executive Conference Center in September. Chip Carter seems to have swallowed Erhard's pablum undiluted: "If my father can go from being almost unknown to being President in four years," he was quoted as saying by *The Washington Post,* "we can certainly end hunger in 20 years."

Harry Chapin and est regulars John Denver and Valerie Harper (TV's Rhoda) were also among the 100 guests at the Tarrytown symposium. Harper has also been active in the Hunger Project. She has served on the est Advisory Board and is a member of the Hunger Project Council. Her public effusions about est have been innumerable. On national television and in magazine articles, she has thanked Werner for transforming her life. Now, she enthuses about the Hunger Project. She participates in events to promote the Project—a soccer game here, a speech there, a gathering at her house— or to help Werner meet the important people.

Because of hunger's non-partisan appeal and President Carter's interest, a campaign to end hunger is a natural way in which Erhard can appear to be "doing good" while cultivating powerful connections. A number of key people have paved Erhard's road from San Francisco. These people are known in est lingo as "Sphere of Influence People" or "SOIPs"— types who have taken the training and are later courted to help aggrandize Erhard. Although est would not admit whether or not it had constructed such a category as SOIP, internal documents prove that it has. ("New York SOIP Participants," begins one of them. "The following people have responded and *will* attend the Reception: 1. Paul Albano, Asst. V.P., Chemical Bank. 2. Dave Andrews, V.P., Chase Manhattan Bank. 3. Dick Aurelio, heads Daniel Edelman. 4. Polly Bergen, Actress. 5. Josh Reynolds, Guest of Polly Bergen. . . ." This list of 33 names is followed by a list of those who *"will not* attend the Reception," and finally a list of people who haven't answered yet, identified by connection to SOIPs if they are not ones in their own right: "Senator and Mrs. [Jacob] Javits, Mrs. Javits is a grad . . . Edith Rivera, Daughter of Kurt Vonnegut. . . ." and so on.)

John Denver and his manager, Jerry Weintraub, as well as Valerie Harper, have given Erhard an SOIP entrée into Hollywood. Est enthusiasts Buckminster Fuller and Dick Gregory provide other ties. But the real help comes from people with government connections.

For example, take Roger Sant, former Assistant Administrator of the Federal Energy Administration under President Ford. Sant has also been a member of the prestigious San Francisco businessman's group, the Bay Area Council, a director of the National Security Bank and a frozen-food supplier. His wife, Vicki Sant, is Regional Director of the Hunger Project in Washington. The Sants introduced Erhard to former Carter administration drug and food policy adviser Dr. Peter Bourne, before Bourne's sudden fall from power last July.

As we talk in Sant's Arlington, Virginia, office on the top floor of a building that overlooks the Potomac and Washington beyond, Sant radiates enthusiasm about Erhard and his latest undertaking. Currently a director of the Energy Productivity Center of the Carnegie-Mellon Institute of Research, an organization funded by, among others, Gulf Oil and Atlantic Richfield, Sant is a member of the Hunger Project Council and speaks officially for the Project. He admits that he has not "read enough to be even informed about the problem." But since Werner says that to know less is to know more, this doesn't matter. "In effect," he says of the Hunger Project, bouncing with enthusiasm, "it's the world working. That's the exciting part of that. . . . So if you can handle hunger, you sort of get to go on to everything else. If you can get rid of hunger, my gosh," he trills, "we might even be able to get rid of mental illness."

Besides Sant, Erhard has on his team another well-connected Washington executive—Greg Votaw, the former director of World Bank programs in East Asia and the Pacific. Votaw provided introductions for Erhard's trip to India and has introduced him to various hunger experts in Washington. And, finally, there is Roy Prosterman, a truly non-partisan hunger expert who has worked as a consultant in land development for such diverse nations as Brazil, the Socialist regime in Portugal, and South Vietnam (in 1967).

Roy Prosterman attended some of the first meetings between Erhard and former Presidential adviser Bourne. Prosterman and Erhard were able, Prosterman says, "to communicate a real sense of what the Hunger Project is about and *the kind of support that that might mean is waiting in the wings for the President. I'm persuaded that this is a thing that could greatly add to Carter's political capital to do lots of other things* [emphasis added], that if Carter showed himself to be someone with the vision and leadership and the sense of the future that would allow him to make a commitment to join with others on the planet to end hunger by the year 2000, *I think he would be seen as a person of greater stature than he is now seen as being.*"

The Hunger Project is every politician's dream: a huge block of voters who have nothing to advocate and who will contribute their time and, although no one explicitly mentions it, their votes to the President and his programs. Erhard knows this, and Hunger Project staffers are quite open about their plans to go straight to the top. No matter who replaces Bourne on hunger issues, says Ellis Deull, president of the Hunger Project, "we'll be talking to him."

The Washington connection shows another side of Erhard's ingenuity in creating the Hunger Project. The Project manages to give Erhard a legitimate issue through which he can reach people in government (he could never, for example, have gotten Carter to provide direct governmental support to est), while providing his followers with a program that will both occupy their time and assure their continued allegiance. This latter result is no mean thing. Although Erhard has put more than 150,000 people through his training and retained the loyalty of many est graduates, there is always the risk that without ongoing programs, they will move on to another of the many new consciousness gurus who have come after him. The Hunger Project minimizes this risk. Est graduates can become obsessed wth hunger. And, when Erhard goes to Washington, est graduates all over the country can feel that they, too, have Jimmy Carter's ear.

"Werner Says . . ."

Any new volunteer to the Hunger Project coming to est headquarters in San Francisco is ushered into a huge, thickly carpeted room with large potted plants strategically placed next to partitions and walls. Overhead pipes and vents, painted various tones of orange and rust, crisscross the high ceilings. Partitions section off offices, without, however, actually dividing the area into private, soundproof rooms. Walking through the large, fragmented room, one has the uncanny feeling of people being together, occupying the same space, but never connecting. It's the same feeling one has at an est training session. There are 250 people in the same room, but they do not relate. In proximity one practices not intimacy, but the ability to maintain a discreet distance.

Proximity within distance, distance at the heart of intimacy, the same play operates in the Hunger Project's relationship to est. The volunteer has been told, upon calling the Hunger Project, that est and the Project are totally different organizations. Never mind that the Hunger Project caller's inquiry is answered with the familiar estian "Hello, this is Grace, how may I assist you?" It's not est. Never mind the fact that its offices are at est Central, that it uses est's phones, that est started it, that Werner Erhard is its chief spokesperson and that his picture and aphorisms adorn the walls. Remember, it's not est.

Despite denials of any relationship, however, the two organizations are virtually one. Recently, for example, the Hunger Project purchased $1,200 worth of tickets for a San Francisco World Affairs Council luncheon at which India's Prime Minister Desai was to speak. When the Indian consulate was distressed that the word "hunger" would appear on tables and programs, the Project conveniently switched identities. After purchasing the tickets with Hunger Project funds, they used est's name on its place cards at the tables (laden with crêpes Argenteuil, grilled mango and apple tart).

The Hunger Project is technically a separate legal entity, but in fact it functions as a recruitment arm for est. The experience of Hunger Project volunteers confirms this. From the moment she first went to the Project's offices in San Francisco as a volunteer, reported Lori Lieberman of the Center for Investigative Reporting, members of the Project staff concentrated on recruiting her to est. "I was greeted by Tracy Apple [a local Hunger Project staffer and est graduate]," she recounts, "who immediately asked me whether or not I had undergone the est training. When I said I had not, she reassured me that that was okay, but that it 'would be easier for you to work around the office if you do take the training because we use a different language and different ways of communicating around esties.' Pressure to take the est training continued throughout my five-hour stay. I discovered only one other person among the 20 or 30 people that I encountered to be a non-est graduate. She was an office worker. And as I was sitting in the bathroom, I heard two other women office workers harassing her because she had worked at the Hunger Project for a month and still refused to take the training. They said she was 'uncooperative, closed-minded and had a narrow perspective.' I was later asked to provide my car to chauffeur some out-of-town est officials around the city several days later.

"I was also struck," Lieberman adds, "by the emphasis on Werner Erhard. Everything was 'Werner says.' When I expressed confusion to someone about the way the Xerox machine worked, she explained that I 'really ought to study this machine because Werner says we all ought to get clear about how machinery works so that it doesn't control us.'"

Another Center for Investigative Reporting staffer volunteering at the Hunger Project described a similar experience. The effort to pressure him into taking the est training, says Dan Noyes, was as important as Hunger Project business: "When I asked Tracy Apple if est was important, she said 'I personally recommend it, but it's not essential. It will help you understand the Hunger Project and the man who created it. It's the greatest thing that ever happened to me.' Although she was careful to say that est was not essential to the Hunger Project, she then proceeded to pressure me to sign up for the two-weekend seminar, saying it cost $300. She asked me when I had a free weekend and sat down to call and find out when the dates of the next Bay Area sessions were. I said I would think about it.

"The next time I came in, I saw Tracy Apple. After saying hello, the first thing she asked was 'Have you decided about your training yet?' She told me that I had to have the $300 enrollment fee by the next day. She called to arrange for me to go down and enroll. When I went to a special est guest seminar the next week, I was surprised to see that it began jointly with a Hunger Project seminar, which then split up into an est seminar and a Hunger Project seminar. My general impression was that there was no difference between the two." Hunger Project staffers expended so much energy trying to get Noyes to join est that they neglected to collect his Hunger Project enrollment card or to convince him to contribute time or money to the Project.

Such pressure in recruiting new est members comes as no surprise to anyone familiar with the organization. Est has monthly enrollment quotas and staffers are put under enormous pressure to fill them. "Werner once put out a list of ways to recruit people to est," explains one disillusioned former est staffer. "You would not believe the lengths staffers were asked to go to get people in the training. If someone called est by mistake, you know, a wrong number, you were supposed to not hang up but to try to recruit him. You were supposed to recruit your lover, your mate, your friends, your family, the milkman or paper boy. It was incredible." According to another former staff member, Werner explained the purpose of the Hunger Project as that of increasing enrollments in the est training.

One has only to do some minor arithmetic to determine how potentially lucrative a recruitment arm the Hunger Project is. There are, so far, about 180,000 enrollees in the Project. About two-thirds of them have not done est. This means est has more than 100,000 potential students in close reach. If only half of these people take est, that is $15 million which Erhard can funnel into his offshore tax shelters.

Even when Erhard can't manage to recruit Hunger Project enrollees into est, est still has managed to get their ear and sometimes their money. Cleverly benefiting from the whole confusion between est and the Hunger Project, est officials recently mounted around the country a series of seminars on hunger, whose proceeds went directly to est. It worked this way: in a number of cities, the est organization held a seven-session "Hunger Project Seminar Series." Both est graduates and non-graduates were eligible to come. The purpose of the seminars, in typically estian language, was advertised as being to "support you in realizing your intention in making a difference in the world, in making the world a place that nurtures and enlightens human beings." The advertisement adds, "to register, call the est Center in the city where you want to take the series." Forty-two hundred people enrolled at $30 apiece. The money, both Brian Van der Horst and Ellis Deull of the Hunger Project admit, went directly to est.

Where Erhard Launders the Money

Trying to trace the flow of money through Werner Erhard's est operation is a bit like watching the flight of a golf ball on television. The commentator excitedly shouts "There it goes!" but all you can see is an endless fairway and trees waving in the wind.

In Erhard's case, the grass and trees that have swallowed up the golf ball are provided chiefly by Harry Margolis, a skillful California lawyer who has improbably combined a leftist past, an enthusiasm for est and an expertise in the arcane and lucrative field of offshore tax shelters.

After examining many documents and interviewing many

sources, *Mother Jones* has pieced together the following picture of the complex financial shell Margolis has built for est:

Erhard Seminars Training, Inc. (EST—the use of the lower case came later) was born late in 1971, when Margolis changed the name of Saratoga Restaurant Equipment, a corporation in his office, to EST.

As EST was being formed, Erhard sold, for a promise of $1 million, what he called his "body of knowledge" to Presentaciones Musicales, S.A. (PMSA), a Panamanian corporation, whose nature, musical or otherwise, remains hidden behind the Panamanian secrecy-in-business laws designed to attract U.S. investors. EST then turned around and paid PMSA $1.2 million for the license to that body of knowledge for ten years.

What's known of PMSA's recent history leads to Margolis. Everyone *Mother Jones* could find who was associated with recent PMSA activities was a Margolis employee.

Another oddity: EST originally had no money to pay PMSA for the license on the body of knowledge. To get the money, EST borrowed $1 million from a Nevada corporation named International Aesthetics Limited (IAL), and sold IAL $200,000 worth of EST stock.

What kind of a company would loan $1 million and invest $200,000 in EST, a then brand-new firm with no success record, no money, no assets and no collateral except an intention to buy a license to use Erhard's knowledge? Again, the answer leads back to Harry Margolis. All IAL officers and directors worked out of Margolis' office.

This complicated series of paper shuffles created important tax benefits for Erhard. In selling the body of knowledge to PMSA as a capital asset, Erhard could claim that PMSA's million-dollar promise was "capital gain," rather than ordinary income. Under U.S. tax laws of the time, only half of the $1 million would be taxable as capital gain. And by receiving a promise to be paid over ten years instead of $1 million cash, Erhard could have the money trickle in slowly enough to avoid placing himself in higher tax brackets.

Did that $1 million really exist somewhere, or did Margolis construct an empty prefabricated tax shelter for a million dollars Erhard hoped to collect in future years from people who took his training?

That is one question the IRS tried to answer when the government, in 1975, indicted Margolis on 23 counts of tax fraud and

one count of conspiracy. Mentioned in connection with the indictment were EST, IAL and the two million-dollar deals, which,
the government charged, had never really taken place.

Federal lawyers argued that all the paperwork had been drawn
up and shuffled by Margolis employees. But in 1977, a jury acquitted him. Court observers say that too many companies hid behind
their status as foreign corporations, and ambiguities in tax law
confused the jury.

Meanwhile, back to Erhard and the million dollars that may
or may not have existed. Prior to the Margolis indictment, the
IRS had disallowed Erhard's claim that the sale of his knowledge
brought him capital gain. Furthermore, PMSA's word that it
would pay up sometime during the next ten years wasn't good
enough, in the government's view, to qualify for taxation on the
installment plan.

So the feds slapped Erhard with an income-tax bill on the million
dollars, amounting to nearly half that amount. Currently, six tax
cases against est and Werner Erhard, dealing with different aspects
of their income, are lined up in U.S. Tax Court while Margolis
and the IRS counsel conduct pre-trial negotiations.

Now, our invisible golf ball suddenly bounces off in a different
direction. Perhaps Margolis felt shaky about his prospects of winning a case involving a body of knowledge no one could see,
touch, patent or copyright. Or, perhaps, EST income had just
outgrown the million-dollar shelter. Whatever the reason, Margolis has created a brand-new set of corporations to house Erhard's
empire. Four months after the IRS began asking for back taxes,
public documents recorded the creation of "est, an Educational
Corporation"—a for-profit California business, owned by the Werner Erhard Charitable Settlement—a tax-exempt trust on the Isle
of Jersey. Any est profits flow to Jersey, after the government
diverts 30 percent to the U.S. treasury.

But 30 percent is a big dip. So est the second, like EST the
first, shows a paltry profit, when it shows one at all. How can
est avoid showing a profit when we know 161,395 people have
taken Werner Erhard's training, now selling at $300 a shot? A
good question. The answer is that before reporting any income,
est pays for the use of Erhard's "knowledge." That knowledge
has now found its way from Panama to its current owner, Welbehagen, B.V., a Dutch corporation. Est pays royalties to Welbehagen for using the body of knowledge, while Welbehagen pays
only 7 percent in Dutch taxes. Then, all Welbehagen's after-tax

profits go to the Werner Erhard Foundation for est, which is headquartered in Switzerland.

Just how much may be piling up in Switzerland is hard to say, since Swiss tax returns are private. Available documents show that through April 30, 1973, EST, in its first corporate incarnation, paid out nearly $300,000 in "interest" and "amortization." How much of that—or whether all of that—went to Welbehagen, the Swiss foundation or Erhard, no one knows.

During the first six months of est's reborn corporate existence, revenues through February of 1976 totaled almost $6 million. Nearly one-fourth was reported to have been paid out in "interest" and "amortization."

Income and expense figures since March of 1976 are unavailable.

What of Erhard's first million? PMSA no longer owes it, since Erhard cancelled the contract without payment in 1975. Last year, at Margolis' trial, Erhard couldn't remember whether he was still owed the million dollars.   *—Arnold Levinson*

Like a Temperance Union?

Erhard claims that the Hunger Project has the support of other organizations that have been working for years to eradicate hunger. In February of 1978, he met in Washington, D.C., with representatives of those organizations to explain the Project to them. Erhard, Prosterman, Van der Horst—all insist the meeting was a fantastic success. Ellis Deull, the New York attorney who is president of the Hunger Project, optimistically explains that people from hunger organizations are thrilled about the Project. "They're delighted to have us aboard," he enthused.

This positive reaction is contradicted by the facts. The *San Francisco Chronicle* reported a skeptical-to-hostile reception of Erhard at that February meeting. Many of the most influential people in anti-hunger organizations are quite critical of the Hunger Project.

Lester Brown, for example. Vicki Sant was evasive when asked why Brown, who heads the Worldwatch Institute and is a widely respected expert in the field of world food problems, failed to appear at the Washington meeting. Mrs. Sant explained that he was absent from the dinner because he was "out of town." Yet internal Hunger Project memos state very clearly that Brown did not attend because he was, in principle, against the Project. When pressed again about Brown's lack of involvement, Mrs. Sant replied that Brown was not involved "because he just isn't." Brown, however, says he has repeatedly explained to Vicki Sant his objections to the Hunger Project, and that he is quite outspoken about why he just isn't involved. "You have to do more than just collect pledge cards to end hunger. They [the Hunger Project] remind me of when I was a boy, and they used to pass out cards for the Women's Christian Temperance Union in church," Brown elaborates. "I can't speak for the others who signed up, but they didn't work all that well for me.

"I have serious doubts about the social value of the Hunger Project," Brown continues, "about its real contribution to the alleviation of hunger. It's probably collected more money in the name of hunger and done the least about hunger than any group I can think of. Anyone who has a real concern about hunger has to have some understanding and concern for social justice in developing countries, about existing inequitable structures, about rapid population growth. I can't see the Hunger Project doing anything about this."

The Man in the Mobile Chair

The Hunger Project staffers, who busily recruit Project volunteers into est, insist that to understand the Hunger Project, you must understand Werner. If you want to understand Werner, take the training. That is Werner. They are right; the Hunger Project is Werner's. Whatever it does leads right up to his front door, then inside the hallways, through the thickly decorated rooms and the extraordinarily invasive comfort of his Franklin Street Victorian mansion in San Francisco.

Any experience of Werner Erhard is orchestrated in advance. The environment in which he lives is as much a part of an interview with him as the words he purrs out—thousands of them, wending their way past logical intervention—or the warm handshake of greeting, or the obligatory parting hug.

The interior of the Franklin House is overwhelming, opulent, dripping good taste and prosperity. Plants—perfectly watered and tended so that not the slightest brown curls the end of leaf—protrude from enormous wicker baskets. In the midst of this modern decor is a collection of African and Oriental gods and goddesses, among them an ancient Buddha. Puzzled, or in impassable resignation, he tends to his inner life while above him, from the midst of a clutter of ferns, a single rocket-shaped sculpture juts out from the wall. The tip is whittled to a sharp point. Lethal, phallic, primitive, it seems a reminder that no matter how carefully assembled is this collection of dormant divinity, the primary theme is power—hard, driving, alive, spikelike, nailed through the trappings of aesthetics.

I am told, as I walk in, where the interview will take place. "Here is your chair," a young man points to a thick, overstuffed armchair. "Put your tape recorder here," he points to a table, "and here is where Werner will sit." Erhard's chair, unlike any other in the room, is a comfortable office chair on casters, apparently out of place in this well-decorated living room/library.

After a half-hour delay, Erhard finally appears. He is better-looking than his stage or screen image. He is filled with charm. From his perfectly coiffed head to perfectly shod toe, the effect is deliberate and immaculate. Clean-shaven, white-shirted—several buttons, but not too many, open from the collar—he is a blend of browns that match the beiges and browns of the room in which we sit.

He smiles, shakes my hand, tells me how much he appreciates all the work I've put into this article. A rare thing, he compliments, to do so much work. Then, after the preliminary flattery, he begins to tell me the Hunger Project line. Word for word he goes on and on. When he is not intent on seduction, he is haranguing. And suddenly, the role of the chairs becomes clear. I am stationary, sitting back from him some six or eight feet. But he moves. He rolls in and back, intense and then relaxed, close and far. In control, while I am immobile.

The Hunger Project, he says, is about one thing and one thing only. "The Hunger Project represents a significant opportunity for us to learn what the principles of things working are. If we can discover the principles by which you end hunger and starvation," he explains, his eyes monitoring my every gesture, "we can discover the principles by which you handle . . . prejudice, by which you handle . . . violence." The pauses around the words are deliberate.

Because of its political and social value, the Hunger Project, Erhard declaims as if addressing 10,000 people at the Coliseum, is immune to the bad publicity est has received. "I don't think that est's relationship to the Hunger Project is really very much of a detriment. I think you can make a case for its being a detriment, but I don't think that it is," Erhard continues. "In fact, it's proven that it's not. The enrollments in the Hunger Project are an absolute statement that est is not a problem for people. That doesn't mean that it's not a problem for some people."

The main person for whom est is not a problem is, of course, Erhard himself. Despite the fact that the law makes distinctions between for-profit and nonprofit corporations, Erhard seems to think that a "really big" person does not occupy himself with such pettiness. "For me," he explains, "the whole issue of what's est and what isn't est had disappeared. I know that is not true for most of the rest of the world, but, for me, the boundaries have kind of washed away. I'm fairly clear that whatever's happening in est is really happening in the world, so how can you call it est? It's what's happening, and I'm very clear that it's what's happened. I used to be clear about that when nobody was clear about it. And therefore I didn't see much use in saying it very often, although I did from time to time. But now I don't think it's my clarity any more. I think that people are pretty clear it's what's happening."

Struggling to find a way out of this extraordinary, overwhelming maze of language, I ask Erhard about his connection with the controversial tax attorney Harry Margolis, one of the IRS's prime targets in its attempt to close offshore tax loopholes. Erhard's continuing relationship to Margolis—whom he says he would never abandon because it's simply not his policy to "sacrifice" people, even if they were indicted for tax fraud (of which, he cautions, Margolis has been acquitted)—seems particularly ironic. For here is a Project that

Jimmy Carter feels he will be able to support, but that is rooted in est, an organization heavily tied into the offshore tax havens Carter constantly rails against. But Erhard has never been troubled with irony, either on the score of Margolis or his own efforts to pay as little taxes as possible. "It's incumbent on a person to be responsible within the system in which they function to function in a way that's most workable. For instance, in my personal tax return, I pay the maximum amount of taxes that I can pay," Erhard outlines his generosity. "I just take a standard deduction, whatever it is. I don't even understand what I'm saying, totally," says the man who is responsible for everything in the world, trying to wiggle out of responsibility for this particular issue, "because I don't know all the words to use. But I don't make up deductions for my tax return. [But for est] you maximize your assets in an organization by paying the least amount of taxes."

If Erhard did take the standard deduction on this year's tax form, it was a radical departure from his past practices; the IRS is now questioning a series of Margolis-engineered deductions that Erhard made in the early '70s on interest payments to paper corporations overseas, as well as Erhard's personal expense deductions that the IRS claims are invalid. Ironically, if the IRS has its way on one of the cases and disallows his deductions, they will grant him just that: the standard deduction.

Erhard does not like my line of questioning. He acknowledges that it is my job, my responsibility, but it was not what he had in mind. Nor is my response to him, it seems, a part of his symphony. At our initial greeting, he was thrilled by my efforts. Now, as we part, he dismisses me. "See, I don't really give a damn what you write because that's none of my business. That's your job, and not my job. And I don't want you telling me how to do my job, so I'm not going to presume to tell you how to do your job. You might even be a jerk and write something stupid, which would really be all right with me," he says, giving me permission to be an idiot, encompassing my potential stupidity in his world, "because God must have loved us jerks, he put a lot of us around. . . . I don't think this story is going to make any difference one way or the other. I have very little concern about one day's output. But, it's kind of a shame that you had to put so much time in for one output. But that's the way the business is."

True, Erhard says, he appreciates me—his experience of my experience of the Hunger Project. As for my story, well, it's a pity so much effort for nothing. Or, as he tells someone several days later when speaking of our meeting, "You know what happens to magazine articles, they're used to wrap fish in the next day."

Behind the Story

Sunday, October 10, 1981. It is the final night of the American Writers Congress in New York City. Two thousand people are jammed into the ancient ballroom of the Roosevelt Hotel in midtown Manhattan. On stage, under floodlights, sit famous writers like E. L. Doctorow and Toni Morrison. Across the floor, under slowly rising swirls of cigarette smoke, row upon row of writers argue loudly over whether to create a National Writers Union.

The moderator announces that it is time for the final arguments. A tall, black-haired woman in her mid-thirties pushes her way to a microphone. As Suzanne Gordon begins to speak, a mood of excitement sweeps the room. When she finishes, the crowd erupts in cheers. A vote is taken: a lopsided majority in favor of supporting the formation of a National Writers Union.

Suzanne Gordon is an author, an activist, a union organizer, an intellectual. One thing she is not, in her opinion, is an investigative journalist. She doesn't like to go through records or to read reports. And although she tends to "overresearch" her stories, it is not the facts per se that she is concerned with, but her ability to interpret those facts. She feels that journalistic "objectivity" is a myth and that readers want to know the writer's point of view. Underlying all of her work is a powerful belief in understanding the important role psychology plays in people's public and private lives. With considerable writing skill, she concentrates on unusual people and organizations in order to present portraits of the abuse of power.

The daughter of a famous ophthalmologist and educated both in the United States and in Europe, Gordon combines a radical's sense of outrage at injustice with an intellectual's appreciation of history, the arts, and language. Her writing is strengthened by her fluency in French, Italian, Spanish, and Yiddish and her working grasp of Russian. She has authored books as diverse as a photojournalistic exposé of strip mining on Indian lands in the Southwest (*Black Mesa, the Angel of Death*), a portrait of loneliness as a social problem (*Lonely in America*), and a study of dependence and authority in ballet (*Off Balance: The Real World of Ballet*).

It was a reference in a newspaper article that set her off on the trail of the Hunger Project. She had written about the self-improvement organization est (for Erhard Seminars Training) in *Lonely in America.* Her interest focused on Erhard's use of the ideology of obedience as a tool for psychological manipulation. As an advocate of social change, she perceived Erhard's work as a "justification of the status quo." Est was, in her view, not an "ideology of change" but an "ideology of acceptance, particularly acceptance of authority which basically makes people feel that anything they are doing is fine as long as they accept full 'responsibility' for it."

When she read that est, with a certain degree of hoopla, had announced the creation of something called the Hunger Project, "it was" she says, "like a crick in the neck. I knew there was something interesting to explore. I suspected that their motives were not altruistic. But I also recognized that it would take a lot of digging to find that out."

Gordon called Adam Hochschild, an editor at *Mother Jones,* for advice. Hochschild assigned the story and sent Gordon to the Center for Investigative Reporting. At the Center, staff members agreed to help and research interns Lori Lieberman and Arnold Levinson were assigned to the project.

The team decided to divide the investigation into three sections. Gordon remembers the first part as "me being out there, interviewing people in the Hunger Project and est and finding out their motives."

The second part of the investigation would be to send Center researchers into the Hunger Project itself—to see the operation from the inside and check whether the "official" version Gordon was getting was accurate.

Finally, it was necessary to put one researcher—Arnold Levinson—on the trail of the money. In the story's earliest stages, the team turned up public records that included a number of complicated Tax Court cases involving Erhard and est; these demanded closer scrutiny if the Hunger Project's finances were to be understood.

As a first step the team gathered the Hunger Project's promotional literature, catalogued the names of the people involved, and noted which public events seemed worth attending. Erhard announced a series of large public meetings in various cities across the country to launch the project. Gordon attended one of these rallies, a huge event held in San Francisco's Cow Palace.

"Everybody had a little name tag, hair perfectly coiffed, trousers with noticeable creases, dresses all sleek. They looked like they never sat down, and they all looked like clones, with duplicate smiles. There was a mammoth video screen on the stage, and then suddenly there was Werner at the microphone, and above him was an image of Werner, larger than life."

Erhard's speech contained no plan for giving money to hungry people, nor was there a discussion of the political causes of hunger in Third World countries. Instead Erhard announced the Hunger Project's "line"—that hunger was a problem because everybody *thought* it was a problem. It was all in our minds. And if we could all just decide that "ending world hunger by 1997 was an idea whose time had come," that would in effect end the problem.

The group's seminars and slick brochures represented a major financial outlay—the kind of expenditures by a nonprofit enterprise that raise an investigative reporter's suspicions, especially if they are purportedly in the pursuit of feeding the world's hungry. After all, what was in this for est—and Erhard? Investigative reporters have come to expect that things are usually more than they seem.

The U.S. Tax Court in Washington, D.C., contains details and documents to excite the most jaded of investigative minds. Here is where the IRS disputes the tax returns of the wealthy and powerful, and figures on income and holdings for individuals and corporations are open to public scrutiny. The Tax Court had become the resting place for numerous documents on the operation of the Erhard empire.

"The combination, I think, of the three strands of investigation was really central," says Gordon. "I don't think any one of us working alone could have produced the story.

"We had three different ways of proceeding with our work— me going in the front door, others going almost undercover, and Arnold looking at records and tracing the money."

Gordon began her work by meeting with Brian Van der Horst, who was public relations representative for est at the time. "With Brian, I concentrated on being very charming. I dressed up and tried to look nice and so forth. He was a bit wary of me in the beginning, because of previous articles I'd written critical of est, but instead of being confrontational, I simply told him the truth, which was that I was fascinated by est's move into the social change business. What I didn't say was that I suspected it was a fake. But, in fact, I didn't *know* at the time it was a fake, or how it was a fake." If she had found the Hunger Project to be a genuine effort at alleviating world hunger, Gordon would have dropped her investigation.

Meanwhile, Dan Noyes and Lori Lieberman from the Center volunteered to work at the Hunger Project. They used their real names and addresses and did the work they were assigned. In addition, they carefully observed the operation and reported back on their experiences. Both reporters wrote frequent memos about their work, noting what they had done, whom they had met, and what they had overheard or seen.

The ethics of undercover work are debated energetically throughout the field of journalism. Many observers are concerned that overeager reporters may become participants in stories and influence the information and events they want to describe. Like the undercover FBI or police agent who goes awry proving loyalty to an organization in order to gain its trust, reporters may trip over their own stealth and alter a story significantly. Overzealous deception or unfair methods may harm the public trust in journalists. This is an area of journalism that demands the most thoughtful consideration and should be used only when its benefits seem to outweigh its drawbacks.

In the case of the Hunger Project, Noyes and Lieberman did not attempt to infiltrate the organization or gain the trust and confidence of its leaders for "inside" information. They went as volunteers into a program open to the general public, and they tried to observe and ask questions, not influence events. Noyes set a rule for himself: he would not mention the word *est* until someone else said it first. In this way, he would try to avoid making a possibly nonexistent connection between the two organizations.

The undercover work turned out to be vital in making the direct link between est and the Hunger Project. As Gordon explains, "We had no idea at first that one of the purposes of the HP was to pressure people to take the est training, which cost three hundred dollars. We found this out because both Noyes and Lieberman were pressured repeatedly to take est. And furthermore, one day in the bathroom, Lori overheard another HP volunteer being accosted by several Hunger Project staff members who insisted she take est. Then, as a final corroboration, I myself was pressured to do est by Ellis Duell, who was the president of the Hunger Project. He even said he'd pay for the training. I got numerous phone calls from a woman in the HP office who tried to get me to take the training."

Noyes and Lieberman's discovery of the use of the HP to channel volunteers into est was a pivotal moment in the investigation. Internal Revenue Service rules governing tax-exempt organizations restrict financial benefits for individuals. This made the question of where est's money was going all the more critical.

Arnold Levinson had been asked to trace the financial transactions. He first assembled whatever corporate records were available from the federal and state agencies that regulate businesses. "I had to learn the hard way to find the shortcuts," he remembers. "For instance, I found a bored secretary in the state government who began to give me information it had taken me days to find on my own. Clerical workers were not accustomed to reporters digging out documents on their own. They were used to businesses demanding to be helped. So I figured the best attitude to assume was that of a businessman."

Soon he found that "the more I dug, the more trails there were." To help him understand where all the footprints led, he pieced together a chronology of est's corporate history, relying heavily on est's own rebuttal to a critical magazine article by Jesse Kornbluth in *New Times* in 1976.

Still, tracking the convolutions of est's money demanded great persistence when Levinson began to uncover a complex scheme of shifting money overseas to tax havens. This arcane world of blind trusts, nameless accounts, and faceless money is understood by only a handful of lawyers who study the intricacies of the tax code as though it were a page-turning thriller. In the case of est, all the money trails led back to one man—Harry Margolis, the tax lawyer who appeared to be the mastermind behind Erhard's international empire.

Therefore, a crucial goal was to obtain an interview with Margolis. Levinson learned of some lawyers who had worked with Margolis in the past and contacted them first. He spoke with reporters who had interviewed Margolis and with government prosecutors who had fought him in court. From these sources, Levinson pieced together a portrait of a competitive man "who likes to match wits with people."

By persevering when early attempts to obtain an interview failed, Levinson eventually got Margolis on the telephone. "Margolis said his partners advised him not to talk to me but then he went ahead and did anyway," which seemed to fit his reputation. During the ensuing interview, Margolis confirmed and explained many details of est's financial scheme, enabling Levinson to outline the complicated financial dealings in an instructive sidebar to Gordon's feature.

Meeting with U.S. government attorneys proved every bit as tricky as the Margolis interview. Not wanting to endanger their various tax cases against Margolis, these officials declined any interviews for the record, but eventually agreed to meet Levinson on a "background" basis only. Luckily for the story, they had recently lost a tax case to Margolis and were more than eager to explain what they had been trying to prove to the judge in that particular case. "In the end, I probably understood the operation almost as well as the U.S. attorneys," Levinson says—largely because he had conducted a thorough investigation when the government attorneys were strapped for time and resources.

Levinson's use of background sources points out a tricky relationship in journalism: the reporter and the source. Journalists need to discern when they can let an interview be on-the-record (for direct attribution), off-the-record (no quotation or attribution), or for quotation but no attribution. Reporters must determine when they need to go off-the-record to get someone to talk, but also how to keep someone on-the-record to ensure that readers will know their involvement in the story. The only rule of this relationship is that there are no rules.

While Levinson pursued his financial sleuthing, Gordon was meeting numerous new people—members of the so-called hunger community introduced to her by the est PR man. One of these was Roy Prosterman, whose past included a "land reform" job in Vietnam. The background checks of Prosterman and other Hunger Project "experts" were supplied by Center researchers.

"Prosterman, we discovered, had been talking about hunger for years, but he and his issue had never made it big," Gordon remembers. "He was a very self-conscious kind of guy, who had been going to basement meetings for years. Suddenly, Erhard was taking him seriously in return for Prosterman giving Erhard legitimacy. Now Prosterman was talking to five thousand and ten thousand people at a time."

The Center's research identified a list of "legitimizers" like Prosterman—somewhat successful people in and around the government, recruited by est to promote the Hunger Project to press and public. "Roger Sant was another," Gordon explains. "He had been in and out of government. He was the assistant administrator of the Federal Energy Administration under President Ford. Now he was director of another energy agency. Sant's wife, Vicki Sant, was regional director of the Hunger Project in Washington; the couple used their connections to generate new SOIPs [Sphere of Influence People, in est's internal language] for the Hunger Project's use." The Sants introduced Erhard to White House drug and food policy adviser Dr. Peter Bourne, who became interested in the Hunger Project.

During a trip to Washington, Gordon went to the White House and interviewed Bourne. "He was an Australian, and while interviewing him I realized that he had no political constituency whatsoever. He had gotten to where he was, basically, because he catered to Roslyn Carter's interest in mental health and drugs." Bourne later left the Carter administration in disgrace after it was revealed he had issued a phony drug prescription for a White House staff member.

"My analysis of the people in and around the Hunger Project was that they were marginal people," Gordon explains. When she was drafting the piece, before Bourne fell from power, she described him as "someone who could be gone if he did anything to offend anyone"—a phrase that was deleted when it proved itself accurate before the story was published.

Gordon's interest in understanding the people in this story and their motives was rooted in her analysis that "Erhard wanted to get into Washington, and he had to have an 'issue' to get there, and this was his issue—world hunger." To pave the way, he needed people like Prosterman, Sant, and Bourne.

The culmination of Gordon's investigation was an interview with Erhard himself. Getting an interview with the key figure can help to make or break an investigative story. A flat denial or an unrevealing discussion can lead editors, or producers in the electronic media, to kill what is otherwise a good story. Gordon was able to meet Erhard in his headquarters in San Francisco. In preparation, Gordon met with Center staff members many times to plan strategy. "We decided in the end that I am not a confrontational reporter and that Erhard would smell me out if I tried that approach. Instead, I decided to play it 'laid back' and let Werner do the talking."

While Erhard kept her waiting, Gordon tried to relax and think about how she wanted *him* to perceive *her*. "I decided I was going to be the absolute model of an interested and open-minded reporter." Once the meeting had begun, Gordon noted the little details of their mutual situation, or "context" as Erhard would put it. Gordon's chair was stationary. Erhard's had wheels—and he made use of them. He rolled away and then toward her, coming close enough to rest his hand on her knee, then rolling back again. "It was as though he would completely lose contact with me. He was in his own 'space,' as he was always saying, and he had just completely lost contact with the subject at hand. It was important to him, though, to show how important he was. At various points in our discussion, he turned to the people he had there with him and asked them to remind him what it was he had said at a particular time. At another point he wanted to quote from something, so he sent someone to get the book. This person returned briskly with the book and Erhard read it to me."

After letting the show go on for a time, Gordon injected several of her prepared questions into the discussion—questions about where the Hunger Project's money was going and what the connection between the HP and est was. Erhard began to show displeasure at this turn of events. And Gordon realized that despite his seeming "loss of contact" with her, Erhard had in fact been "trying to play directly to me" all along.

"Now, from a psychological point of view, this really became interesting," Gordon explains. "I had never seen anybody put so much energy into trying to manipulate before. It was fascinating to watch somebody whose total being was involved in trying to seduce you and convince you. It certainly was not the way most of us function. I mean, you either win or lose an argument."

Gordon's questions about Margolis and the IRS made Erhard visibly nervous. He denied that anything wrong had been done and then abruptly ended the interview session. Before he left the room, though, he put in what Gordon called a "parting shot," what became the final two paragraphs in her story.

At this stage of her investigation, Gordon felt she had everything she needed to write her story: the HP was not sending the money it raised to help alleviate world hunger; HP staff members were pressuring volunteers to take the est training; Erhard and est had constructed an intricate financial structure that included offshore tax shelters; and finally, Erhard, the man who had created this strange empire in the first place, had given a revealing interview.

But the key to Gordon's story was her analysis that Erhard had created the HP partly as a way to gain legitimacy in the corridors of power, especially Washington, D.C. And by a stroke of luck, in the final weeks before her *Mother Jones* deadline, Gordon uncovered two sources who were in positions to corroborate her analysis. A friend introduced her to someone who had previously worked at a high level in the est organization and who had become disenchanted with Erhard's ambitions. The source agreed to meet with Gordon on a confidential basis. "This person confirmed an enormous amount of my analytical, psychological, and financial findings about Erhard and est and the HP," Gordon says. The source, however, was very nervous at first about talking to a reporter. "To get my foot in the door, I had to say I wasn't going to use anything, that this was a very preliminary conversation, that I was just interested in understanding the phenomena. In this case we liked each other and it went quite well. We met several times."

Gordon's confidential source did not supply any new information but rather served to confirm the findings of the team's investigation, thereby strengthening Gordon's confidence in the material she was about to write. A second person with access to est's internal operations also confirmed her analysis.

Gordon says she has found this kind of "end confirmation source" on other occasions as well and draws a lesson from the experience: "I think that sometimes you're tempted as a reporter to stop interviewing new people at the point when you feel that you've essentially heard it all already. But even if that turns out to be the case, the discovery of a 'rubber-stamper' really helps the writing process. So it's important to follow that last lead even though you might feel, 'I already know everything there is to know about this story.'"

In October 1978, *Mother Jones* held a press conference to announce the release of the story in the magazine's December issue. At the door to the magazine's office on the day of the press conference, neatly dressed leafleteers handed out a not-so-veiled threat to the reporters who attended. The leaflet stated that the Hunger Project was going to sue *Mother Jones,* and any publication that republished the magazine's information, for libel. This lawsuit was never filed, but the Hunger Project's tactic appeared to limit press coverage of the story—for a while. Later, however, *Newsweek* magazine reported the group's action against *Mother Jones* as an attempt to intimidate the press, and several publications around the country published follow-up articles similar to Gordon's story.

Gordon herself wrote a psychological portrait of Erhard in the *Village Voice* and then had a final, brief encounter with Erhard in Washington, D.C.

Erhard was in Washington to lead seminars on the topic "Completing Your Relationships," and his press agent had arranged for him to be interviewed by National Public Radio (NPR). NPR, which had aired several commentaries by Gordon on various subjects, asked her to do the interview. When Erhard was introduced to Gordon he "looked startled," Gordon recalls. "We got into the interview booth, and he said to me, 'Are you *the* Suzanne Gordon?' And I said, 'Well, I'm Suzanne Gordon.' And Erhard said: 'This is a setup. I'm not going to do this interview. Once burned, shame on you. Twice burned, shame on me.' And he walked out."

The team also received reports that at est public meetings up to ten minutes were devoted to sending "bad vibes" toward *Mother Jones* and Suzanne Gordon. Later, a *Mother Jones* editor discovered that est trainers were shown a videotape of Gordon's original interview with Erhard as an exercise in "how to handle hostile press." Gordon was outraged that she had been secretly videotaped, but in reconstructing the scene she realized she probably did not have a legal basis for seeking redress. "I remembered that before the interview they asked, 'Is it okay if we tape this?' They had a tape recorder and so did I and I said, 'Sure.' I had no idea they were videotaping me. But they kept the shades tightly closed, which seemed odd in the middle of the afternoon. . . ."

Today Gordon is an associate editor at *Modern Times* magazine in Boston and continues to write books and occasional magazine articles. She believes that "journalists are the documenters of our age, so it's important to not just be a journalist. I think journalists should know about psychology, sociology, anthropology, history, and politics. It's important not just to say something, but to have something to say. All too often, investigative reporters have been like private detectives, which is helpful on a certain level, but they need also to develop a perspective on the information they lay out to people."

Assessing her own strength as an interviewer, Gordon feels it is due to her attempt to have "conversations," not interviews. And she transcribes the tapes herself, a "painful and boring process" but one that forces her to review each source. "That reminds me of the person, and as I'm listening to the tape, I make notes to myself of what I thought of the person or of what they were saying."

She feels comfortable, she says, only when she has too much information for the assignment in question. "If I've been assigned four thousand words, then I'll invariably write six thousand and let the editors cut it down. It's sort of like psychoanalysis, you know. Freud used to say, 'Don't censor yourself, just say what comes into your mind and that will be productive and interesting.' It's the same way with writing. If you begin to censor yourself, you might leave out something important. I prefer to let the magazine editors be the censor because I find it just works out better that way."

Five years after "Let Them Eat est" was published, the Hunger Project apparently is still thriving. According to the group's publicity, there are now 2.4 million people enrolled in the project— a fivefold increase since 1978. Roy Prosterman and Peter Bourne are still active in the organization, and Werner Erhard remains on the board of directors. A brochure boasts that the Hunger Project distributes the "world's largest-circulation publication on hunger" and financed an advertising campaign that "raised one million dollars in direct donations to organizations providing relief in Cambodia and Thailand."

After the article appeared, the Hunger Project tried "to establish its own credibility and viability in the hunger community," according to an organization official. Headquarters were moved out of est's offices to a luxurious two-story building in San Francisco. Although the busy office was no longer physically part of est, the language and grooming styles present there revealed to the casual visitor that Erhard's influence was still strong.

Besides the threatened lawsuit against *Mother Jones,* the Hunger Project has reacted strongly against other reporters who have attempted to cover the group's activities. Pat Lynch, then an NBC News reporter, stated that the Hunger Project carried out a four-month campaign to discredit her while she was preparing what eventually became an *NBC Evening News* segment in 1980. And when Dan Noyes was asked by a radio station in 1983 to participate in a program with a Hunger Project spokesperson, the organization refused to appear. Instead they requested a tape of the program with Noyes alone for review by the group's lawyer.

Meanwhile, Werner Erhard has taken on new social issues: the physically and mentally disabled, refugees, and development in the Third World. One project, called the Community Workshop, is similar to the Hunger Project in both its approach and its tax-exempt structure. It attempts to end another global problem: juvenile delinquency.

The Corporate
CRIME
of the
CENTURY

When Maria Aguirrez woke up, she was too
drenched with sweat to feel the blood. Soon
she would be one of this crime's countless victims.

5

The Boomerang Crime

by David Weir, with Mark Schapiro and Terry Jacobs

Once or twice every working day a sealed semi-trailer winds through a grimy industrial section of the Los Angeles basin called the City of Commerce. The truck moves slowly up Pacific Street past a row of dingy warehouses to the loading dock at the rear of Amvac Chemical Corporation's pesticide plant. There, from a storage area labeled "RESTRICTED AREA/ AUTHORIZED PERSONNEL ONLY BEYOND THIS POINT," pallets of light-blue 30-gallon drums stacked three high are loaded into the huge truck-trailer.

When it's full, the rig heads for Interstate 10 and moves into the stream of traffic flowing back and forth across the country 24 hours a day. The driver carries emergency telephone numbers and special instructions in case the colorless, odorless fluid in the drums somehow spills or is released. No unloading or transfer of the toxic cargo is permitted enroute.

A few days and most of the continent later, the same truck rolls into the bustling coastal city of Gulfport, Mississippi, and up to the automated loading docks of Standard Fruit & Steamship Company. There, the light-blue drums labeled "Re-

stricted Use Pesticides" are lifted onto the deck of one of
the 30 vessels owned or leased by Standard's parent company,
the U.S.-based Castle & Cooke Inc.—largest importer of bananas to the United States.

The ship retraces its route, out of Gulfport, into the balmy
waters of the Gulf of Mexico. The light-blue drums will stay
above-deck to lessen dangers to the crew in case of a spill.
The banana ship's destination is one of the romantic-sounding
ports of Central or South America—Puerto Limón in Costa
Rica, La Ceiba in Honduras, Guayaquil in Ecuador—a journey
that can take from four to seven days.

When it docks at one of these ports in the tropics, the pesticide drums will be unloaded and taken to their ultimate stop—
the vast banana and pineapple plantations of Castle & Cooke.
C&C is one of the largest foreign corporate landholders in
Central America. The workers on the company plantations
are mostly illiterate peasants and Indians. They are the people
who will use this pesticide to kill the soil-dwelling worms that
attack bananas and other crops destined for U.S. kitchens.

What is the pesticide in the light-blue drums? DBCP. One
of many pesticides that are banned or severely restricted in
the U.S., but which American companies buy, sell and dump
freely on the Third World. Use of DBCP (the acronym for
its cumbersome chemical name 1,2-Dibromo-3-chloropropane)
was banned in California in August 1977, because it makes
humans sterile and causes cancer. The Environmental Protection Agency (EPA) has imposed stringent limits on DBCP
use in the other 49 states and has instituted procedures which
may result, within the next few months, in a total ban of
DBCP here.

But even if the EPA does ban all use of DBCP, the action
will not interrupt the flow of the chemical from Amvac to
Castle & Cooke's overseas fruit plantations. It would still be
legal to manufacture DBCP here and sell it abroad. "There
is absolutely no control over the worldwide distribution of
hazardous pesticides," says Dr. Harold Hubbard of the World
Health Organization (WHO). A provision of U.S. law governing pesticides explicitly states that pesticides banned in the
U.S. may be exported to other nations. The foreign buyers,

in turn, either do not know or do not care that the chemicals have been found too dangerous for use in the U.S., the country where they are usually made. In this way, millions of pounds of banned and restricted pesticides are dumped each year on the Third World.

The Boomerang Dump

Dumping pesticides is a little different than selling Dalkon Shields or Tris-soaked pajamas to unsuspecting consumers. Heinous as those dumps might be, the injury or death inflicted as a result happens on an individual basis, in distinct tragedies, one body at a time. Not so with pesticides. Most of the peasants applying the poisons to crops can read neither the English nor the Spanish instructions printed on the labels of the chemical containers. Pesticides are often poured on crops in excessive amounts. Many people, in addition to the pests, are poisoned by the chemicals—about 500,000 yearly, according to the World Health Organization. Some victims die immediately; the long-term effects on the rest are unknown.

"The people who work in the fields of Central America are treated like half-humans," says Dr. Lou Falcon, a University of California entomologist who visits the region often. "When an airplane flies over to spray, they can leave if they want, but they won't be paid their seven cents a day, or whatever. They often live in huts in the middle of the fields. Their homes, their children and their food get contaminated."

Pesticide poisoning is only one aspect of the massive dumping of these chemicals. A three-month investigation by *Mother Jones* and the Center for Investigative Reporting shows that U.S. companies—while not the worst offenders, since that distinction belongs to firms headquartered in Europe—have an enormous stake in exporting these chemicals. Uncontrolled, the worldwide pesticide trade is on its way to becoming a scandal of international proportions:

• Nearly 40 percent of the 1.6 billion pounds of pesticides sold annually in this country is sold to export buyers. It

appears that *every* pesticide banned or restricted by the federal government here has been exported. A full 15 percent
of U.S. pesticide exports are "unregistered." They are chemicals that were never licensed, tested or reviewed by the EPA
at all.

- Pesticides are sold throughout the Third World without con-
trols to people who usually do not know how the chemicals
should be safely used. Leptophos, a nerve-damaging pesticide
that brings on paralysis in its victims, was never approved
for sale in the U.S. In Indonesia, according to an official
of that country's Food and Agriculture Organization, leptophos was sold "alongside the potatoes and rice . . . people
just collect it in sugar sacks, milk cartons, Coke bottles. . . ."

- Both farmworkers themselves and those who eat food grown
throughout the developing world with the aid of pesticides
run a high risk of pesticide poisoning. One Central American
farm survey found the levels of the pesticide aldrin on cab-
bage to be nearly 2,000 times the level allowed in food sold
in the U.S. The average content of DDT in the blood of
people in Guatemala and Nicaragua is over 30 times the
U.S. average.

- Not only are U.S.-based companies selling pesticides overseas, they also are *buying* them there. In Costa Rica the
main importer for seven heavily restricted U.S. pesticides
(DDT, aldrin, dieldrin, heptachlor, chlordane, endrin and
BHC) is not a local farming operation, but Ortho, a division
of Chevron Chemical Co.—an arm of Standard Oil of California. This way, the multinational companies circumvent
U.S. regulations and continue using hazardous chemicals
for food production.

- The "vast majority" of the nearly one billion pounds of
pesticides used each year in the Third World is applied to
crops that are then exported *back* to the U.S. and other
rich countries, according to WHO. This fact undercuts the
industry's main argument defending pesticide dumping. "We
see nothing wrong with helping the hungry world eat," is
the way a Velsicol Chemical Company executive puts it.

Yet, the entire dumping process bypasses the local population's need for food. The example in which DBCP manufactured by Amvac is imported into Central America by Castle & Cooke to grow fruit destined for U.S. dinner tables is a case in point.

Pesticides are, of course, considered a useful tool in combating the loss, due to pests, of an estimated 40 percent of each year's global food crop. But the record on pesticide use has been, at best, mixed. Insects have great genetic plasticity. They can adapt quickly to poisons and outlive them. In India and Central America, DDT was believed to eradicate malaria-carrying mosquitoes. For many years it did. But recently, malaria epidemics broke out in those areas that have aggressive DDT spraying programs, signaling that the mosquitoes have become resistant to the poison.

The hazards of dumping pesticides overseas are many, but it would be inaccurate to believe they are the Third World's alone. Pesticides, once dumped, have a way of coming back, like a boomerang. U.S. government spot checks have found that approximately 10 percent of imported food is contaminated with illegal levels of pesticides. The Food and Drug Administration (FDA) reports that nearly half of the green coffee beans imported by this country are contaminated with pesticides that have been previously banned in the U.S. At least 20 pesticides, potential carcinogens, are undetectable with FDA tests used to find residues in food. In many other cases, the FDA simply does not know what the substances are that *do* show up in its tests.

There are, for example, 94 different pesticides used by the six coffee-growing countries in Central and South America. Studies by the General Accounting Office, Congress' investigative arm, found that, of those, 64 are not detectable by FDA multiresidue tests. Of those that are detectable, only 18 have tolerance levels set for restricting the sale of coffee contaminated with them. This means that imported coffee can be sold in the U.S. with the residues of 76 pesticides that are either undetectable or completely unregulated.

The Case of Phosvel

The Velsicol Chemical Corporation of Chicago is not the largest pesticide dumper in the world, but it is known as one of the most shameless. Financially, Velsicol is dwarfed by giants like Dow, DuPont or Shell. But despite its size, the company has been implicated in more environmental disasters than nearly any other. In the U.S., Velsicol was the company that brought us PBB poisoning, the Tris baby clothes case and the Tennessee leaky pesticide drums, to name three. Internationally, Velsicol's record has been no less extraordinary. The company earned its notorious reputation through the global sale of the pesticide leptophos, trade-named Phosvel.

Phosvel is an organophosphate nerve toxin that attacks the human body like rattlesnake venom. The EPA never allowed Velsicol to sell the stuff in this country, although it did issue an experimental use permit (EUP) for one year. According to Robert Chambers of the General Accounting Office, "Velsicol used its EUP to mislead countries overseas about the status of leptophos." Third World nations had the impression the pesticide had been approved for use in this country. It had not. Perhaps lack of EPA approval gave Velsicol the incentive to massively dump leptophos in the developing world. The company looked to the government for the dump.

The "arranger" for this dump was the U.S. Agency for International Development. AID spent $5 million in taxpayers' funds to send Phosvel—as well as other restricted pesticides, including heptachlor, chlordane and endrin—overseas in 1974. Recipient countries included India, Pakistan, Brazil, Colombia, Vietnam, Indonesia and Israel. In Egypt, Phosvel exposure killed more than a thousand water buffalo and an unrevealed number of humans.

Although Velsicol says it no longer manufactures Phosvel anywhere in the world, documents obtained from the government of Costa Rica reveal that the company has continued selling the chemical on world markets. As recently as July 1978, in three different shipments originating in Panama and Mexico, Velsicol imported Phosvel into Costa Rica. In addition, the company continues to manufacture three highly persistent, carcinogenic pesticides—chlordane, heptachlor and endrin—for export to the Third World. Under terms of a legal settlement with EPA, Velsicol will have to phase out all U.S. sales of heptachlor and chlordane by 1983. The company bitterly contested this EPA action, initiated in 1975, since at that time it was selling nearly $45 million worth per year of the two banned pesticides—25 percent of its total sales.

The giants of the U.S. chemical industry, as much as they might like, cannot insulate themselves from the scandals of small firms like Velsicol or Amvac. The industry is so interconnected, through licensing and patent arrangements, that virtually every company is profiting from every other's activities. Dow, for instance, receives three cents on every gallon of DBCP sold by Amvac. (Dow stopped making DBCP after the sterility scandal made headlines, but Amvac must produce its DBCP under Dow's patent.) The export product Velsicol substituted for Phosvel in its Texas plant is EPN. That poison, now under government review for possible cancellation, is twice as neurotoxic as Phosvel and is produced under a similar patent arrangement with DuPont.

Conflicts of Interest

The leaders of many Third World nations are themselves deeply enmeshed in the pesticide trade. "One of the reasons the LDC [less-developed countries] governments don't do anything about the pesticides problem," says Hubbard of the WHO, "is that the people who use pesticides, the people who import pesticides and the people who 'regulate' pesticides are the same people. It's a tight little group in each developing country."

Entomologist Lou Falcon says that a previous minister of agriculture in Nicaragua also had investments in a company importing pesticides. "In Nicaragua," he added, "pesticide importing has been a $20 million-a-year business in a country with an entire operating budget of only $90 million. The important people are simply not interested in pesticides becoming a controversy."

Pesticide promotion abroad is also big business. "Whenever a new pesticide hits a country, every farmer knows about it right away," Falcon says. "There is heavy publicity by the companies."

One of the issues discussed at a recent State Department conference on pesticides was what kind of notification officials should give LDCs when a pesticide is banned in the U.S. Sam Gitonga, an official in Kenya's Ministry of Irrigation, complained that the "information received from the U.S. now is quite inadequate—usually just a photocopy of a telex to the American attaché that something has been banned." Gitonga pointed out the contrast between this haphazard official notice and the "pesticide salesman who comes to our office with a bulk of papers. It is very difficult for us to check and cross-check whether this particular product is actually registered in the 50 countries where the seller claims his pesticide is registered."

EPA officials unveiled a new notification procedure at the State Department conference, which, once adopted, will require exporters to obtain written acknowledgment from importers that they know they are buying a hazardous pesticide. But as Frances Miley, a former official who helped write the new provision, told *Mother Jones,* "If the companies don't do it, there is no penalty."

Of course, in a country like Costa Rica, where U.S.-owned Ortho is the major pesticide purchaser, notification will accomplish nothing. In any event, it is difficult to imagine how notifying purchasers that they are buying banned pesticides is going to improve the lot of the workers who have to apply the poisons in the fields.

Global Leech

The new EPA notification procedure will undoubtedly bring on more cries from industry of "over-regulation" by U.S. government agencies. To make its point, the industry cites statistics like those in a 1974 survey by the trade magazine *Chemical Week,* which reported that U.S. chemical firms spend 44 percent *less* on pollution control at their overseas plants than at those inside the country.

Accordingly, there has been a tendency in recent years for

producers of pesticides or other banned and heavily restricted products to move their production facilities abroad. For years, Hercules Inc. has produced toxaphene in Nicaragua, and American Cyanamid Co. announced it has built a pesticide plant in Brazil, where Dow already has one making the herbicide 2,4-D. Two DBCP plants operating in Mexico are closely allied with foreign chemical giants; since Mexican law generally prohibits foreigners from legally owning more than 49 percent of any company inside its borders, the plants' actual equity relationships are closely guarded secrets. Velsicol also has a plant in Mexico, which is producing what the company has identified only as "agricultural chemicals."

"We are getting to the point where we might have all the restrictions in the world on pesticide exports," says Jacob Scherr, staff attorney for the Natural Resources Defense Council, "but then the companies just move their plants to the LDCs."

"These global companies have subsidiaries and formulation plants all over the world." says Hubbard of the WHO. "You've got to take them all on—not just the American companies. Call them the bad-ass operators they really are. The multinationals simply go into the LDCs, give a banned pesticide a local name and then turn around and sell it all over the world under that new name. It's a real Mafia-type operation."

Through all the charges and countercharges of over-regulation or under-regulation, beneath the statistics thrown around at high-level conferences, there is one blantant fact that cannot—must not—be overlooked when discussing pesticide dumping in the Third World. The uninformed use of banned pesticides is killing people. Just that. Stories like the following from the village of Bahia, in Brazil, are too common.

Thirteen children in Bahia died in the summer of 1975. They lived not only in the same village, but on the same street. The oldest child was only eight. When they became ill, the children broke into severe sweats, foamed at the mouth, vomited and went into convulsions. Most died within a few days. The eight-year-old, a girl, survived her first bout with the illness and then, more than three weeks later, suffered the same symptoms again, and died.

The medical examiner found that samples of the little girl's blood and liver showed extremely high levels of the pesticide aldrin and its breakdown product, dieldrin. Aldrin and dieldrin were banned in the U.S. a year *before* these deaths. But Shell— the company holding the exclusive patent on aldrin—simply switched production of the poison from a plant in California to another in the Netherlands. Shell then continued to dump aldrin on the Third World, including sales to Brazil.

In Brazil, as in too many other developing nations, banned pesticides are sold over the counter, like flour. Anyone can buy them. Those who investigated the case of the 13 children believed the aldrin was bought by a well-to-do landowner. The landowner used the aldrin on fresh meat to kill hungry dogs in his district. He killed 13 hungry children with the pesticide instead.

Selected List of Chemical Companies Producing, Buying, and/or Selling Hazardous Pesticides in the Third World

| | Pesticides | | |
| | A | B | C |
Company (*U.S. unless* *otherwise noted*)	*Banned or* *Heavily* *Restricted*	*Under* *Review*	*Unre-* *stricted*
Allied Chemical	Kepone, Mirex	—	—
Amvac	DBCP	—	—
American Cyanamid	Kepone, Mirex	Toxaphene, 2,4-D	Malathion Parathion
BASF (W. Germ.)	2,4,5-T	2,4-D	—
Bayer (W. Germ.)	DDT, Heptachlor, Lindane	Toxaphene	Parathion
Celamerck (W. Germ.)	Aldrin, Dieldrin, DDT, Endrin, Hep- tachlor, Chlordane, Lindane, 2,4,5-T	Toxaphene, 2,4-D	Parathion
Chevron	DDT, Aldrin, Diel- drin, Heptachlor, Chlordane, Endrin, Lindane, BHC, Silvex	Toxaphene, Paraquat	Malathion

Selected List of Chemical Companies Producing, Buying, and/or Selling Hazardous Pesticides in the Third World (*Cont.*)

Company (*U.S. unless otherwise noted*)	Pesticides		
	A *Banned or Heavily Restricted*	**B** *Under Review*	**C** *Unre-stricted*
Ciba-Geigy (Swiss)	—	2,4-D	—
Dow	2,4,5-T, Silvex, DBCP	2,4-D	—
Dupont	—	EPN	Parathion
FMC	Heptachlor	—	Malathion
W. R. Grace	—	Toxaphene	—
Hercules	—	Toxaphene	—
Hoechst (W. Germ.)	DDT	—	Parathion Malathion
Hooker	BHC, Lindane, Mirex	—	—
Imperial Chemicals (UK)	BHC, Aldrin	Paraquat	—
Kerr-McGee Chem.	—	—	Parathion
Monsanto	—	2,4-D	Parathion
Montrose	DDT, Endrin	—	Parathion
Nissan (Jap.)	—	EPN	—
Pfizer	—	—	Malathion
Rohm & Haas	Silvex	Toxaphene	Parathion
Schering (W. Germ.)	Aldrin, BHC, Hep-tachlor	—	Parathion
Shell (UK-Neth.)	Aldrin, Dieldrin, DDT, DBCP, Endrin, 2,4,5-T	2,4-D	Parathion
Stauffer	DDT, Dieldrin	EPN,2,4-D	Malathion, Parathion
Sumitomo (Japan)	—	—	Malathion
Union Carbide	DDT, Mirex, Hep-tachlor, Chlordane, Endrin	EPN	Parathion
Velsicol	Chlordane, Hepta-chlor, Phosvel, Endrin	EPN	Parathion

Note: Category A: Those which are banned or heavily restricted inside the U.S. Most uses for these products have been outlawed,

Selected List of Chemical Companies Producing, Buying, and/or Selling Hazardous Pesticides in the Third World (*Cont.*)

but important uses for some remain, such as termite control for Chlordane. Certain pesticides have recently been discontinued, including DBCP (Dow) and Kepone (Allied Chemical), but are included because they were important products for the companies involved.

Category B: Those which are under review for future regulatory action. Toxaphene, Paraquat and EPN are termed "suspect chemicals" by EPA.

Category C: Those which are unrestricted in the U.S. but which have caused human deaths in the Third World. Parathion is reportedly the number one killer among all hazardous pesticides, banned or not.

Sources: This table was compiled from a variety of official and unofficial sources, including the EPA publication "Suspended and Cancelled Pesticides"; EPA production reports; company records and advertisements; personal interviews and observations; and government import statistics for seven Third World countries.

Behind the Story

Some stories start with an urgent telephone call late at night; others begin over a cup of coffee in a restaurant. "The Boomerang Crime" had an even more humble origin—a packet of Kool-Aid.

The location, at least, was exotic. In 1970 David and Alison Weir were English teachers for the Peace Corps in a remote town in northern Afghanistan. On one of their periodic trips to the mountain nation's capital city, Kabul, the couple visited a row of bazaar stalls known for selling Western goods. There they bought a packet of Kool-Aid. Once back at their remote home, Alison happened to read the list of ingredients on the product's label and was startled to see cyclamates listed. She remembered reading that cyclamates recently had been banned as a cancer risk by the U.S. Food and Drug Administration. That Kool-Aid packet launched a lengthy series of inquiries into hazardous exports, culminating in "The Boomerang Crime" and *Circle of Poison.* *

In 1972, while editors of a small San Francisco publication, *SunDance* magazine, the couple researched the problem of banned products sold in the Third World. Then David continued looking into the subject while working at another small West Coast publication, *Pacific Basin Reports,* in 1973 and 1974. Limited resources precluded much work on the story at the time, but they did gather valuable files for later use.

Then, while an editor at *Rolling Stone* in 1975 and 1976, David had access to three of the critical tools investigative reporters need most: a long-distance telephone line, a photocopy machine, and postage. Early in his research he learned the story behind that Kool-Aid packet, when he discovered a *Wall Street Journal* exposé by Stan Sesser which documented the wide-scale export of cyclamate products overseas after the FDA ban. Through interviews with public interest activists in New York and Washington, Weir developed sources in South America. Those sources sent him evidence of banned drugs and pesticides sold locally by U.S.

* In 1981 Center staff writers David Weir and Mark Schapiro co-authored *Circle of Poison,* a book published by the Institute for Food and Development Policy in San Francisco. The book expanded on the work done for "The Boomerang Crime."

corporations. His article "For Export Only: Poisons and Dangerous Drugs" was written in late 1975, but it did not appear in *Rolling Stone* for almost a year and a half.

The long time lag between writing and publishing is one of the common frustrations magazine journalists face. In this case, the reason for the delay was that *Rolling Stone* was in a transition period, deemphasizing in-depth reporting on "political" subjects in favor of expanded coverage of music and entertainment figures. The "Export" piece simply fell between the cracks.

In February 1977, after he left the magazine's staff, Weir learned that *Rolling Stone* had suddenly decided to publish the piece when another article was rejected just before deadline. The check of the editor's inventory list found that "Export" was the only piece available of the right length to take its place. Thus the first major magazine article detailing the role of U.S. corporations in selling hazardous products in the Third World appeared in *Rolling Stone* in February 1977.

When articles of this sort are well promoted, they can attract considerable attention. However, since *Rolling Stone* did not promote this piece, it was overlooked by the rest of the U.S. press. But it *was* noticed in some of the countries most affected by the problem and was translated and reprinted in Mexico and Colombia. Equally important, someone on President Jimmy Carter's White House staff spotted the article. Carter's weekly magazine summary included a five-paragraph abstract of the piece.

Later that year, Weir published two stories through Pacific News Service, a San Francisco–based news service, exposing the contamination of U.S. coffee imports by banned pesticides. In addition, he repeatedly proposed to various publications a long investigative story about pesticide exports to the Third World. His proposals were continually turned down. Finally, in early 1979 an assignment came through.

Mother Jones magazine decided to devote an entire issue to "dumping," a new term for hazardous exports coined by editor Mark Dowie.* There was a story behind that decision, too.

---

* *Dumping* had been a term used solely by economists to describe the practice of companies based in one country which undersell those in another to gain an unfair advantage. Dowie appropriated the term for this new usage concerning hazardous exports.

A woman (who requested anonymity) had been a victim of dumping. While vacationing in the Caribbean, she had visited a medical clinic to have an IUD inserted. Only later did she discover that the device was a Dalkon Shield, the infamous IUD that had injured and killed hundreds of American women and that Mark Dowie and Tracy Johnston had exposed in *Mother Jones* in 1976. She then came to the magazine and offered financial support for further work on investigating the practice of exporting hazardous products. Her financial backing was critical to the project's completion.

Dowie asked the Center staff to provide research for the dumping issue and to write an individual article on pesticides. Other reporters, including Dowie himself, went to work on drugs, IUDs, and other consumer products. As the investigation got under way in January 1979, the Center put together a team of David Weir, Mark Schapiro, and Terry Jacobs. The eventual success of the pesticide story depended on the teamwork among these three, but most directly on the quick development of reporting skills by Schapiro and Jacobs.

For Terry Jacobs, this assignment was her first chance to work on a major magazine story. A recent graduate of the journalism program at San Francisco State University, Jacobs was facing the desperate scramble to locate a reporting job. There were few good prospects in the Bay Area for someone just out of college. So she jumped at this chance to do investigative journalism, even though the pay as a Center intern was only $100 a month and the hours were long.

Mark Schapiro had become an intern at the Center while finishing his senior thesis at the University of California at Santa Cruz on the loan policies of the U.S. Export-Import Bank. He had put this academic work to journalistic use in a Center story about the bank's loan to the Philippines to build a nuclear reactor near an active earthquake region in that country. He quickly became fascinated by the intricacies of whatever story he was working on, and he now immersed himself enthusiastically in the dumping investigation.

In his initial checks with old sources, Weir had been told that pesticide dumping was mainly a problem of the past. His contacts in the public interest community in Washington said they felt that the adverse publicity about dumping had caused all but a few small companies to abandon the practice. If this was true, there could be no major exposé.

Nevertheless, the team started its work with the *investigative hypothesis* that pesticide dumping was still going on. What they sought was proof. "We had to think like prosecutors," Weir explained. "In the end if we couldn't prove our case, we would have to drop it—and not publish the story. But we just couldn't believe, in the light of what we'd found in the past, that the companies had simply ceased what had been an extremely lucrative practice."

An important clue to the likelihood that pesticide dumping was still occurring was the law. The Federal Insecticide, Fungicide and Rodenticide Act—the most important legislation governing pesticides in the U.S.—specifically exempted exports from any restrictions imposed by agencies of the U.S. government. Therefore dumping was, and is, entirely legal.

The only solid leads the team had to start with were the poisonings of thirteen children in Brazil and the Phosvel case. Both were old stories by 1979. The challenge was to uncover something new.

Jacobs and Schapiro funneled daily memos to Weir, who decided which leads they should pursue. There was, in Jacobs's words, "a huge exchange of paper."

The editors at *Mother Jones* had requested a list of all products banned in the United States. Armed with a copy of the *U.S. Government Manual,* Jacobs plunged into the alphabet soup of acronym upon acronym of federal departments and agencies. She found that each government agency has its own procedure for reviewing, restricting, registering, banning, or removing products from the marketplace. Nobody, however, seemed to have the job of compiling a list of such actions by the different agencies. After scores of telephone calls and letters and Freedom of Information Act requests, Jacobs reported to Weir that there were no simple lists of banned products to be found anywhere in the U.S. government.

Mother Jones wanted a neat chart of banned products. But as Jacobs discovered, "regulatory agencies shy away from the term *banned.* They use a totally different language." The Environmental Protection Agency (EPA) had so many different levels of limitations that it was not possible to lump them all together. And, in fact, the EPA claimed never to have "banned" a pesticide, despite numerous press reports to the contrary.

In addition, regulatory officials frequently cited the "trade secret" barrier, claiming that information Jacobs requested had to remain confidential in order to protect companies' proprietary interests. By persisting, Jacobs managed to compile what was probably a better list of banned and restricted products than the government itself maintained, but the magazine's editors eventually decided not to use it.

The frustrations of working on narrow parts of the investigation caused Jacobs and Schapiro to wonder how or when the overall story was going to emerge. For Weir, however, who had been pursuing the story in one form or another for eight years now, the frustration and delays were commonplace.

Schapiro then became interested in DBCP, a sterility-inducing, cancer-causing pesticide that had been banned for all uses in California in 1977 and was under review by the EPA. Through a friend he discovered that he casually knew an official affiliated with the Amvac Chemical Corporation, the only company producing DBCP in the world. Schapiro approached the official cautiously and developed him as a background source. The official was never identified in the article.

Schapiro's source was able to corroborate key pieces of information the team was uncovering in other ways. By collecting Amvac's 10-K Reports—forms that large publicly traded companies must file with the U.S. Securities and Exchange Commission (SEC)—the team learned what was behind Amvac's decision to make DBCP when other companies had abandoned the chemical.

"Management believes that because of the extensive publicity and notoriety that has arisen over the sterility of workers and the suspected mutagenic and carcinogenic nature of DBCP, the principal manufacturers and distributors of the product (Dow, Occidental, and Shell Chemical) have, temporarily at least, decided to remove themselves from the domestic marketplace and possibly from the world marketplace.

"Notwithstanding all the publicity and notoriety surrounding DBCP," Amvac's report continued, "it was [our] opinion that a vacuum existed in the marketplace that [we] could temporarily occupy. . . . [We] further believed that with the addition of DBCP, sales might be sufficient to reach a profitable level."

Schapiro's source elaborated: "They're not really for spreading cancer or 'no-production' growth [a reference to the chemical's sterility link]. But DBCP is very important to them. Quite frankly, without DBCP, Amvac would go bankrupt."*

Learning Amvac's motivation for selling DBCP overseas was an important part of the Center team's investigation. The threesome hoped to present a sampling of the different points of view on the issue—victims, activists, government officials, and corporate officials—in the final story. (The article's readers did not read these quotes, however. *Mother Jones* edited Amvac's 10-K quotations out of the manuscript because of space considerations.)

At this point in the investigation, Schapiro's work resembled that of a private detective. He started following the trail of DBCP leaving the country, much as other investigative reporters "follow the money" when probing organized crime. The "front-door" approach—calling Amvac on the phone—had already failed, so Schapiro went under cover (see "Let Them Eat est" for a discussion of the ethics of undercover reporting). During a trip to Los Angeles, Schapiro visited Amvac's production plant in the City of Commerce and applied for a job. He approached workers lounging around the factory gates during lunch breaks and asked them questions about how the DBCP was being manufactured inside, what the working conditions were like, and whether anyone knew where the chemical was being shipped.

Schapiro checked back with the personnel office to see about a job, but none was available. So he confined himself to walking along the plant's perimeter and noting the comings and goings of a number of trucking rigs. After several days of this kind of behavior, Schapiro aroused the suspicion of Amvac's security official. But by then he had the evidence he had come for. Through the fence he was able to photograph barrels of DBCP on Amvac's loading docks, as well as the sign reading "RESTRICTED AREA." He also jotted down the name of the trucking company and the times of

---

* The source's statements are now quotable, since he has ended his affiliation with the firm.

its visits. In addition, he spotted a pollution-control-district truck monitoring air emissions from the plant.

Once back at the Center's office, Schapiro confirmed that DBCP was indeed being trucked from the plant (the name of the trucking firm was later removed from the *Mother Jones* story for libel considerations). The trucking company itself would not cooperate, so Schapiro went to the California Department of Occupational Safety and Health (commonly called "Cal-OSHA"), which was responsible for keeping records of the transportation of dangerous substances throughout the state. The growth of toxic and hazardous substances has sprouted numerous governmental regulatory agencies. An alert investigative reporter is always pondering which of these might be collecting information about a business or individual in a story. By checking with a source inside Cal-OSHA, Schapiro was also able to document the next stage of DBCP's particular "circle of poison." The chemical was being trucked to a major point for trade with Central America: Gulfport, Mississippi.

Schapiro's next step was to find out who was buying the DBCP from Amvac and precisely where it was going from Gulfport. Through Directory Assistance in Gulfport he obtained the number of the port agency; calling there, he asked for the official in charge of coordinating cargo in and out of the port. He was put through to a man whose title was "dockmaster."

"This man was almost stunned that I was even interested in calling him," Schapiro remembers. "My biggest problem was overcoming his own sense of astonishment at being called by a reporter in California."

Schapiro explained to the dockmaster that he was writing "something about chemicals used in agricultural development." He asked the dockmaster to explain how the port operated.

"It turned out that the port had just installed a new automated loading system which the dockmaster was really excited about," Schapiro recalls, "so we talked about that for a long time, far longer than necessary for our story per se. But it allowed me to establish a rapport with him before we got to what I was really interested in."

By the time Schapiro shifted the discussion around to the name of the company purchasing the DBCP from Amvac's truckers, the dockmaster readily revealed that it was Standard Fruit & Steamship Company, a subsidiary of San Francisco–based Castle & Cooke. He described the loading of DBCP onto Standard's "banana ships," which made regular round trips between Gulfport and ports in Central and South America—bringing bananas to the United States and returning with the chemicals.

This was a major break in the investigation. Dumping was clearly occurring. Next, Schapiro checked with the regional office of the U.S. Occupational Safety and Health Administration (OSHA) to confirm Standard's role in buying and shipping DBCP out of Gulfport. He was able to locate an OSHA inspector who had recently inspected Standard's DBCP loading procedures. From him Schapiro obtained key descriptive details that were used later in writing the story.

By now all three members of the team were convinced that the DBCP narrative was central to their story. They mounted an all-out effort to learn how the DBCP was being used at the other end of the shipping routes. The dockmaster and the OSHA inspector had already given them a major clue—bananas—but they did not yet have documentation.

In their search for such proof, the team dashed off letters to the ministries of agriculture or their equivalents in the respective Central and South American countries, asking for official records on pesticide sales. In addition, they contacted public interest groups, churches, and overseas organizations that might have people working in the countries using DBCP.

And, as always, they tried getting the information the easiest way, through the "front door." In this case, that meant calling Castle & Cooke. No cooperation there, so they decided to go in the back door. By doing a little long-distance rummaging through the EPA's Administrative Law files in Washington (via cooperative officials they'd developed as sources during the months of the investigation), the team unearthed a document filed by Castle & Cooke. The papers verified that the company was using the chemical on its vast banana plantations in Central America. Further research documented that the company was the largest banana importer in the United States (under the Dole label) and that it was fighting the EPA's efforts to restrict the chemical's use inside the United

States itself. (The EPA removed DBCP from the continental U.S. market in the fall of 1979.)

Before long, one of the team's queries to Third World governments was answered. A large, tattered manila envelope arrived from Costa Rica containing month-by-month export/import records for pesticides in 1978. It came to the Center's office only a few weeks before the July 1, 1979, deadline at *Mother Jones.*

These records were a godsend. They not only documented Standard's role as the importer of DBCP to Costa Rica, but gave the amounts and value of its shipments. Of course, the records were in Spanish, and many of the chemicals were listed under trade names that were unfamiliar to the U.S.-based researchers. But by using U.S. government guides to chemicals,* the team was able to match DBCP and several other chemicals with those the EPA recognized as hazardous enough to warrant some sort of restrictive action.

In addition to Costa Rica, six of the other fourteen Third World governments eventually supplied import/export records to the Center team. This response came as a surprise to people accustomed to the idea that information is more freely available in the United States than overseas. It also illustrated the value in persistence. Regardless of how many governments refused to cooperate, the team kept sending inquiries.

A similar method yielded important research information for the overall *Mother Jones* package of stories. President Carter had formed an Interagency Task Force on Hazardous Exports. By spring 1979 the task force had prepared a draft report, but the White House official coordinating the effort refused to release it. At Dowie's request, Jacobs systematically queried every agency taking part in the study with Freedom of Information Act requests. Although most agencies checked with the White House first and then refused her request, several honored their responsibility under the FOIA and mailed a copy of the draft report in its entirety. In this way the team circumvented the White House's attempt to withhold critical information for what the reporters considered an unjustified reason—that it was not yet a "final" draft.

* From the National Institute for Occupational Safety and Health (NIOSH).

The team also hoped to document other examples of pesticide dumping as effectively as the DBCP case. Toward this goal, Jacobs and Weir chased the Phosvel story. Although widely covered by the press in earlier years, several sources rumored that Velsicol Chemical Company's controversial pesticide was still available in Third World markets. In scrutinizing the documents from the government of Costa Rica, they saw that Velsicol had imported Phosvel into that country several times in 1978.

In addition, during a brief trip to Washington near the end of the investigation, Weir attended a special conference on pesticide exports sponsored by the State Department. There he interviewed officials from Third World governments about Phosvel, DBCP, and other pesticides the team was studying. Officials from Colombia, the Philippines, and Guatemala all told him of approaches by Velsicol to sell Phosvel in their countries after the U.S. ban. (These incidents were cut by *Mother Jones* for space considerations.) Weir also interviewed a number of agricultural experts attending the conference, obtaining background information, corroboration, and quotes used in the writing of the story.

"As at most conferences," Weir remembers, "the actual papers delivered were deadly boring, dealing with policy questions and so forth. But meeting people is what makes conferences like this so valuable for reporters. There, in one place, were scientists, environmentalists, corporate officials, international experts, and government bureaucrats. I spent most of my time running from person to person, notebook in hand."

Getting the corporate point of view was important to the team, and it was Jacobs who achieved one of their best corporate interviews. She prodded a Velsicol PR official into indirectly acknowledging the company's past dumping practices when he argued, "We see nothing wrong with helping the hungry world eat." This reasoning was contradicted by research showing that from half to three-quarters of all pesticides used in the underdeveloped world are not applied to local food crops. The pesticides are used on export foods destined for dinner tables in the developed world.

Further checking of every investigative lead led them to some obscure tidbits useful to the story. Schapiro checked the civil court index during his trip to Los Angeles and discovered a lawsuit against Amvac by Dow Chemical Corporation. Included in the terms of the settlement of this suit was an arrangement whereby Amvac had to pay Dow a royalty on every gallon of DBCP sold. Further checking revealed similar examples of the interlocking financial relationships between small chemical producers and the industry's giants. This put to rest once and for all the original claim that only small companies were profiting from pesticide dumping. By the time Weir and Schapiro had compiled a table of pesticide dumpers for *Circle of Poison,* they had evidence against a virtual "Who's Who" of the global chemical industry.

To make sure their investigation was thorough, the team pursued many diverse types of research. By checking trade journals—the magazines and newsletters of the chemical industry—they found useful statistics and an explanation of the economics of the pesticide dumping issue. According to one industry publication, the U.S. pesticide market was "approaching saturation"; therefore pesticide manufacturers were expanding sales overseas.

By checking foreign agriculture journals in nearby university libraries, the reporters found direct evidence of which companies were selling which hazardous pesticides in which countries—in the form of glossy four-color advertisements. And by studying government reports, they learned of the official concern inside the State Department and other offices of the Carter administration that a Love Canal–type incident overseas might endanger U.S. foreign policy interests. Also, by interviewing United Nations officials, they were able to sketch out the weak beginnings of international regulation of what one UN official labeled the "chaotic pesticide export trade."

The final vignette in "The Boomerang Crime," a description of the tragic deaths of the thirteen Brazilian children from aldrin poisoning, required a special effort at verification. The original source for the story was a newspaper clipping sent by a Brazilian contact to Weir at *Rolling Stone.* The clipping mentioned that tissue from one of the children's bodies had been sent to a "biological research institution" in São Paulo to determine the cause of death. By checking a World Health Organization publication listing medical facilities in the Third World, Weir happened upon the name of the Instituto Biologico in São Paulo and the name of an official there. He wrote a letter to the official asking for confirmation of the newspaper account. Weir received not only a full explanation of the poisoning incident, but a summary of all known pesticide poisonings in Brazil over several years. It was a piece of good luck—the official Weir had contacted turned out to be the expert who had examined the child's tissue.

In order to confirm that the aldrin in the incident had indeed been manufactured by the Royal Dutch/Shell group, Weir wrote to the company headquarters in The Hague. The company replied by Telex, denying any blame for the deaths but admitting that it had sent an official to the village to investigate the incident soon after it had happened. Weir Telexed back that he would like some further information about the company's investigation. But Shell replied, again by Telex, "MUCH REGRET THERE IS NO ADDITIONAL INFORMATION WE CAN PROVIDE."

During the process of putting together "The Boomerang Crime," the team had interviewed well over a hundred people, from workers to company officials to government bureaucrats to scientists. The techniques used in the interviews varied according to the person on the other end of the telephone line.

By late June, just before their *Mother Jones* deadline, the team determined that they had enough information to produce a manuscript. Weir sorted through the piles of memos and documents and interview summaries from six months of investigation and reread everything that seemed critical to the story. In addition to the new sources uncovered during the investigation, Weir checked with many of his old sources from the *Rolling Stone* and Pacific News Service stories. They gave him many of the quotes that appeared in the final story.

Once he felt that he had "sufficiently mastered the details of the investigation," Weir sat at a typewriter and wrote for three days. At the end of that time he had a draft manuscript, which was edited by *Mother Jones* editor Amanda Spake into the version that appeared in the magazine and is reprinted here.

"We had so much information that most of it had to go," Weir says. "Our original hypothesis had been corroborated by our investigation, with only minor adjustments. So we felt comfortable alleging that pesticide dumping was a major problem. In addition to DBCP and Phosvel, we had uncovered evidence that *every* banned or restricted pesticide was being sold in the Third World."

Spake remembers the magazine's approach to the story. "We were all interested in dumping for some time before the stories appeared. I personally felt that pesticide dumping was the most important story of all because it affects more people."

While editing the article, Spake had to remember the marketplace for the magazine—the United States—and bring out what was new and unusual about the story so that the other editors at the magazine would approve it. "Some of the information had appeared before about poisonings in the Third World, so what was unusual and new was the fact it was coming back to us in our food. Otherwise people's eyes start to glaze over when you mention the Third World or pesticides."

"The Boomerang Crime," more than all other Center stories, has had a visible impact. Much of the initial attention the story received, as part of a November 1979 *Mother Jones* cover package of stories collectively entitled "Corporate Crime of the Century," can be attributed to a strong promotion effort mounted by the magazine's staff. Press releases were issued in San Francisco and Washington upon publication, and issues of the magazine were hand-delivered to every Third World embassy in Washington.

Meanwhile, the issue of banned pesticide exports exploded into the public arena. Congress held hearings and issued reports, and both network and public television aired prime-time treatments of the issue. The United Nations passed resolutions; and Third World advocates started speaking out, demanding, in the words of one, to "stop using us as a dumping ground."

"The Corporate Crime of the Century," including "The Boomerang Crime," was awarded the National Magazine Award for Reporting Excellence in 1980. In addition, the package also was named the Best Censored Story by a national panel of judges selecting the most important articles ignored or underplayed by the press.

The pesticide dumping scandal did not long remain ignored by the world's press, however. The Associated Press assigned a senior reporter to do a worldwide survey of the hazardous export issue; so did *Newsday.* In 1981 the Public Broadcasting System aired a two-part documentary, "For Export Only: Pesticides and Pills," by Bob Richter, an independent filmmaker who relied on the Center for a significant portion of the content of the pesticide portion of his program. In 1983 this film won the Alfred I. duPont–Columbia University Award in Broadcast Journalism.

Dozens of other reporters around the country called the Center offices asking for assistance in pursuing the story on their own. Later, when *Circle of Poison* was published, all three national radio networks, as well as NBC-TV's *Nightly News,* covered the story. Newspapers around the world, including the *New York Times, Los Angeles Times,* and *Chicago Tribune,* reviewed the book or carried excerpts or stories about it and the issue of pesticide exports. Many magazines, including *The Nation, Multinational Monitor,* and *The Ecologist,* ran excerpts. Weir and Schapiro appeared on NBC-TV's *Today* show, as well as numerous other radio and television talk shows around the country. Weir also spoke to a United Nations forum on World Environment Day in 1981.

During 1982 the issue continued to gather steam here and overseas. In May Weir traveled to Penang, Malaysia, to attend the founding meeting of Pesticide Action Network International (PAN), a coalition of public interest organizations formed to stop pesticide dumping in the Third World. PAN is similar to the infant-formula campaign that has made Nestle's and other multinational corporations' marketing practices in the underdeveloped world a matter of global concern. Since the formation of PAN, Weir and Schapiro have spoken in Australia, Switzerland, and Japan about pesticide dumping.

Following the publication of *Circle of Poison* in 1981, several books on hazardous exports, especially pesticides, have appeared. David Bull of Oxfam, Britain's largest charity, wrote *A Growing Problem,* a systematic study of the pesticide export issue. Jacob Scherr, a key public interest attorney with the Natural Resources Defense Council, and virtually the only activist who fought pesticide dumping in the years before it became a national issue, helped co-author a study. The days when Weir and others at the Center had tried in vain to find a book publisher for a study of hazardous exports seemed long ago.

One packet of Kool-Aid with cyclamates went a long way to provide grist for the Center's investigative reporting mill. But investigative reporters know that a wheel is also a circle. In September 1982 Abbott Laboratories asked the Food and Drug Administration to overturn its 1970 ban of cyclamates and to once again approve the substance as a sweetener for beverages and other foods in the United States.

The Bechtel File

How The Master Builders Protect Their Beachheads

6

The Bechtel File

by Mark Dowie

In the course of researching this article on the Bechtel Corporation, I met about a dozen reporters who had looked at the company over the years. Most of them found out very little of interest. One reporter told me, "Bechtel will never talk to you. You'll have to get it all on your own." He was right.

When I had compiled enough information on Bechtel to ask intelligent questions, I called its public-relations department to request an interview. I was routed to Tom Flynn, whose name I recognized as the crack reporter who covered Vietnam for the Oakland Tribune. *Flynn returned from the war to take a job as press secretary to San Francisco's Mayor Joseph Alioto. At the time Alioto was beleaguered by charges of Mafia involvement, and it was while working for him that Flynn learned, in his own words, "how to stonewall."*

I met Flynn once, but he asked all the questions: Whom was I writing for? With what angle? What questions did I have for company officials? After that, Tom Flynn promised to meet with me again. Three separate appointments were postponed for various reasons. The last postponement turned out to be a cancellation.

"We will not cooperate," Flynn announced through tight lips.

"You mean no press releases, no brochures, no interviews? You're stonewalling us."

"That's right."

And that's the way it has been with Bechtel. This story is based mostly on documents, sources outside the Bechtel Corporation itself and interviews with nervous Bechtel employees who talked only after I assured them total and permanent anonymity. I was surprised how little they knew about their company— even some who had worked there for many years. The stone walls are not just around Bechtel. They are inside the company, too.

Today, Jubail is a sleepy little fishing village on the Persian Gulf. Sixteen years from now it will be a major industrial city the size of Toledo, Ohio, with oil refineries, steel mills, a deep-water port, hotels, hospitals, an international airport, several power plants and the world's largest desalinization complex. This mammoth engineering feat is at the heart of Saudi Arabia's plan to transform itself from a nation of desert nomads into a major industrial state. Jubail is far and away the largest single construction project in history. The entire city is being built by a secretive family-owned business in San Francisco whose name is familiar to prime ministers and presidents around the world but is unknown to most Americans: the Bechtel Corporation.

Bechtel would be important if for no other reason than its sheer size. If privately held firms were listed among the Fortune 500, Bechtel would rank about 25th—bigger than Coca-Cola, Lockheed or American Motors. Bechtel, however, is far more than just another large corporation. It is an empire that hires its executives right out of the President's Cabinet at huge salary increases, receives billion-dollar government contracts, maintains close ties with the powerful elites of most major countries and harbors the secrets of uranium enrichment (although they deny this knowledge).

If Bechtel manufactured musical instruments or beer, its complete lack of public accountability would not be so alarming. But a company that has designed or built almost half of our nuclear power plants, traded technological information with the Soviet Union and written three major sections of the Ford Administration's energy plan must, in the words of one of its own top executives, "be able to stand the light of day." Yet not only does the company refuse to talk to reporters; as a privately owned firm, it does not even publish an annual report. With this article, then, we're publishing that report for Bechtel—and we hope this will be just the beginning of a process of public inquiry into the effects this corporation has had on our lives and our environment.

Few unnatural forces have altered the face of this planet more than the Bechtel Corporation. Following its terse slogan, "Bechtel Builds," the company has undertaken as projects the world's first nuclear power plant (Arco Idaho, 1951), the Hoover Dam, the San Francisco Bay Bridge, the Alaska Pipeline, the Washington, D.C., Metro, the San Francisco Bay Area Rapid Transit system and the 1,100-mile Trans-Arabian Pipeline. Bechtel has built the world's tallest earth-filled dam (Swift Dam in Oregon), Central America's first oil refinery (in Panama), the biggest copper complex in the world (Bougainville, Papua New Guinea), the first and biggest coal-slurry pipelines, the planet's largest hydroelectric project (Labrador) and this country's largest nuclear power plant (San Onofre, California). With one major construction project, Bechtel doubled the energy output of South Korea.

Started by an immigrant muleskinner named Warren "Dad" Bechtel in 1898, this "little family business" has grown to be the largest engineering and construction company in the world. All three of Dad's sons, Warren, Steve and Ken, have worked with the company over the years; but during the '30s the gregarious and resolute Steve emerged as the leader of the three brothers and, at 77, remains the senior director of the Bechtel domain. Ken and Warren both died recently. Steve's 53-year-old son, Stephen Jr., who, in contrast to his father, is highly educated, reserved and calculating, is now chief executive officer, a position he assumed at 35 after "working his way up through the ranks" in a short 13 years after graduating from the Stanford business school.

Steve Sr. is now one of the five richest men in the United States, with personal wealth exceeding $700 million. He and Steve Jr. own and control about 40 percent of the company's common stock and an undisclosed percentage of the preferred stock, and both have multi-million-dollar investments in land and other corporations. When old Steve dies he will most likely pass most of his wealth on to his son, making him the family's first billionaire. Financial experts believe that only one other living American—oil-tanker tycoon Daniel Ludwig—is worth a billion dollars. When Ludwig dies, Steve Bechtel, Jr., stands a good chance of becoming the wealthiest man in America.

A Confidential Memo

To build the city of Jubail, billions of cubic yards of earth and sand must first be moved—in an enterprise reminiscent of the company's humble beginnings, when Dad Bechtel leased his mule team to grade a railbed through Oklahoma Indian territory. Dad later sold his mules and made construction history by being the first person to use a steam shovel in road construction.

Today, teams of another sort—hundreds of architects, engineers and computer specialists—travel back and forth from San Francisco to Jubail, drafting a totally planned community. They bring to the project a myriad of closely held secrets developed, traded or brought to the company in the brains and files of more than 1,000 scientists raided from competitors and foreign countries.

When Bechtel is ready to begin building Saudi Arabia's new city, 42,000 laborers will move into a temporary city that Bechtel will construct before beginning Jubail. Most of them will travel thousands of miles from countries like Korea, the Philippines, India, Taiwan and Algeria, where wages are lower than in oil-rich Saudi Arabia.

Although Bechtel's original price tag for Jubail was $9 billion, estimates in the engineering press began running as high as $20 billion shortly after the contract was signed. A recent *New York Times* article alluded to rumored adjustments running as high as $45 billion. Having been badly burned on one or two fixed-price jobs in the past, Bechtel will sign only cost-plus contracts on projects like Jubail. So the total bill will not be seen until the key is turned and the city is running.

If the final prices of the San Francisco Bay Area Rapid Transit system, the Alaska Pipeline and the Washington Metro are fair examples of Bechtel's recent work, the cost of building Jubail should come in just under $55 billion. That's about three percent of this year's U.S. Gross National Product.

Jubail is Bechtel's largest current project, but far from its only one. More than 26,000 full-time employees in about 21 permanent offices and 30-odd subsidiaries are busy at work on elaborate oil and gas pipelines in Indonesia, a pet-food plant in Missouri, a trade center in Moscow, a copper complex in South Africa and a harbor for nuclear-powered submarines that will extract oil directly from the ocean floor and pump it ashore.

As if it didn't have enough to do, Bechtel has salesmen out hunting for new business. Unlike other construction companies, however, which seek out single-item projects—a $2 billion nuclear plant here, a $70 million shopping center there—Bechtel has taken to proposing the building of entire cities, like Jubail, or the installation of industrial infrastructures for entire nations.

Jubail is only a sample of what the company has in store for countries like Nigeria, another oil-rich country that today stands on the brink of industrialization. "Using criteria starting with oil," begins a March 4, 1977, company memo on "International Job Strategy," "we have selected nine countries, including four where Bechtel could exploit good current positioning and five where we suggest business-development positioning should begin or be intensified. Heading the list of the latter five is Nigeria." (The others: Iraq, Malaysia, Algeria and Indonesia.)

This confidential memo goes on to say that Bechtel has learned from U.S. foreign-service intelligence sources (more on that point shortly) that Nigeria is planning to spend $50 billion on industrial development. The Bechtel memo then touches on Nigeria's enormous potential for construction in "irrigation, power, hydrocarbon installations, airports and oil refineries."

Bechtel's political clout in Nigeria is underlined in the memo by its reference to the ease with which a meeting can be arranged with Lieutenant General Obasanjo, chief of state, whom Bechtel's intelligence sources describe as "a very good man, competent and honest." Such intelligence is particularly vital to Steve Sr., who expounds eloquently and frequently on the virtues of honesty and competence. In fact, if he really trusts his sources, he will probably fly into Lagos after contract negotiations are completed and ink the deal with Obasanjo himself. Or he may send his energetic son, Steve Jr., who circles the globe more than ten times a year visiting Bechtel projects and signing contracts.

"There are great problems working in Nigeria," the memo concludes, "but profits are excellent, perhaps better—if care is taken in contract negotiations and appropriate positioning—than even in the Middle East."

You Scratch My Back

Although Bechtel seems like a true international corporation—with a polyglot work force, with most of its permanent offices overseas and with more than 50 percent of its revenues from foreign projects—it is *very* American. Despite valued contracts with the General Obasanjos of the world, the company's rise to power has been helped most by a key friend in Washington.

During its first 40 years in business Bechtel stayed in the United States, building mostly in the Western states. Railroads, irrigation systems, natural-gas lines and earth-filled dams all led to the first big break in 1931, when Dad Bechtel was asked to join a consortium called Six Companies that formed to build the Hoover Dam. Later voted president of the consortium, Dad committed the best and brightest of his growing company to work on the dam. Dad Bechtel died suddenly in 1933 in the Soviet Union while inspecting a dam similar to Hoover, and the three Bechtel sons finished the Hoover Dam. Left with an established membership in the construction fraternity and enough retained earnings to expand rapidly into new industries, Bechtel began to look beyond the American market. And expand it did, diversifying into power plants, mines, refineries and shipbuilding. In 1940 it accepted its first overseas challenge—the Mene Grande Pipeline in Venezuela.

When the Hoover Dam was being planned, an aggressive young steel salesman named John McCone came to call on Bechtel. Since the company needed literally miles of reinforcement bars for embedding in the dam's pre-stressed concrete, Bechtel was a natural customer for McCone's employer, Consolidated Steel. The cool, handsome, gray-eyed McCone was probably assigned the call because his old University of California pal Steve Bechtel was in charge of procurement for the project. McCone graduated from the U.C. engineering school in 1922, but Steve had dropped out earlier because "Dad needed me in the business." McCone and Bechtel rewarmed their old friendship and, after the dam was finished, formed a business partnership called Bechtel-McCone, of which McCone became president.

Although Bechtel-McCone was supposedly formed to build refineries, by 1940 the United States was tooling up for war, and McCone consequently landed contracts to build Liberty ships and tankers for the Pacific theater and an aircraft-modification center in Alabama. The company then formed a syndicate with major competitors Kaiser Industries, Brown and Root, and Parsons to build enormous shipyards in Los Angeles and in Sausalito, a town across the bay from San Francisco. McCone ran the Calship yards in Los Angeles, and Steve's younger brother Ken ran Marinship in Sausalito. Together they collected the bill for almost 600 ships built for the war effort.

After the war McCone left the company and went where so many government contractors have gone since: to the Defense Department. At his Senate confirmation hearing, General Accounting Office official Ralph Casey entered evidence that McCone and his associates had made a $44 million profit from Calship on a personal investment of $100,000.

"I daresay," Casey testified, "that at no time in the history of American business, whether in wartime or in peacetime, have so few men made so much money with so little risk and all at the expense of the taxpayers, not only of this generation but of generations to come."

McCone calmly denied being a war profiteer, pointing out that an additional $7 million in loans and bank credit had been invested in Calship. This absurd logic satisfied the Senate, and McCone was confirmed as Undersecretary of Defense. There, he became the center of a major conflict-of-interest scandal by giving out multi-million-dollar government contracts to companies like Standard Oil and Kaiser Industries, in which he retained large investments.

Although the Bechtel-McCone "corporation" was dissolved, the unofficial Bechtel-McCone partnership remained intact. As John McCone rose through the Washington bureaucracy—from his Defense job to that of chairman of the Atomic Energy Commission and ultimately to the post of director of the Central Intelligence Agency—he never forgot his old friend Steve Bechtel.

When the country's first commercial nuclear power plant in Dresden, Illinois, was dedicated on October 12, 1959, McCone, by then chairman of the AEC, showed up to praise it as "the largest, most efficient, most advanced" power plant in the world.

Although the Dresden facility has since been plagued with serious operational problems, it gave Bechtel an enormous head start in the nuclear business. Since 1959, Bechtel has participated as either engineer or builder or both in the completion of almost half of the United States' 68 commercial nuclear plants—thanks in large measure to John McCone.

. . . *And I'll Scratch Yours*

High-level back-scratching is a mutual affair. John McCone was appointed CIA director in the fall of 1961, at a time when the agency was expanding its arrangements with American corporations to provide cover to CIA operatives and to share in intelligence gathering, particularly in countries like Iran, Algeria and Libya, where Bechtel was constructing, designing or pursuing large projects.

In every respect, Bechtel is a CIA director's dream come true:

- The company's chief executive is an old and trusted friend. (Recent evidence indicates that the CIA prefers to deal from the top to the top in its relationships with corporations.)
- It is privately held and already secretive in style.
- The company operates in more than 100 countries.
- Many of its projects are out in the "boonies," where revolutionary activity often begins—and where it's usually hard to find cover for agents.
- Since its assets are not fixed in place, as are mines and factories, Bechtel is mobile and can leave projects quickly if things get too hot. (Company personnel don't often leave, though, electing instead to hole up in a hotel until the shooting stops and a new strongman emerges with whom they can negotiate a new contract.)
- The potential information exchange is mutually beneficial—industrial intelligence (the background for something like Bechtel's Nigeria plant) for political intelligence (the kind of information the CIA needed to successfully engineer coups in places like Iran and Guatemala).

Two organizations as security conscious as Bechtel and the CIA don't leave many visible traces of their relationship. And Bechtel employees are sworn to secrecy, both when the company hires them and when they leave. But the movement of men back and forth between the two institutions indicates more than mere coincidence.

Take John Lowrey Simpson, for example. His sudden employment as chair of Bechtel's high-level finance committee in 1952 surprised the company's old-timers. He was a distant relative of Steve Bechtel, but Bechtel has a strong tradition of internal promotion, and Simpson, whose prior job was as executive vice president of the obscure Schroder Bank in New York, seemed to come out of nowhere. What the old-timers didn't realize, though, was that Simpson had strong ties with the Office of Strategic Services through his friendship with Allen Dulles (a founding director of Schroder Bank as well as of the OSS), and that Simpson, who had access to military intelligence during the war, served as a Bechtel adviser during those years. After the war the OSS, of course, became the CIA, and the Schroder Bank, of which Simpson remained a director after joining Bechtel, was recently discovered to have been a bank for the CIA director's controversial discretionary fund.

Then there is C. Stribling Snodgrass (whose name is *not* an alias), who went the other way. As vice president at Bechtel, Snodgrass masterminded the company's near-monopolization of Saudi Arabian heavy construction, primarily through cordial relationships with influential State Department officials who sold Bechtel to King Faisal and his predecessor, Ibn Saud. Snodgrass retired early from his Bechtel vice presidency and set up a small energy-consulting firm called LSG Associates. While Snodgrass was alive, LSG Associates was one of many CIA proprietaries run out of the Washington law offices of Burwell, Hansen and Manley. Under the LSG cover, Snodgrass's assignment undoubtedly was to collect economic intelligence and pass it on to American companies that, like Bechtel, were in a position to profit from it. The companies in return would furnish voluminous political information on the countries in which they operated to Snodgrass, who would pass it on to the CIA.

Bechtel's links with the CIA through men like Simpson and Snodgrass gave the company an invaluable boost in its dealings with the Third World. Look, for instance, at Bechtel's operations in Libya. Few American companies were willing to operate in Libya during the volatile 1960s; yet, with the Suez Canal closed, Libyan oil was vital to the West.

In keeping with Steve Sr.'s proud claim, "We will build anything, anywhere, anytime," Bechtel constructed a pipeline from the Sahara Desert to the Mediterranean coast for Occidental Petroleum (estimated cost $43 million, final cost $147 million). Occidental, and other American oil companies, paid Bechtel an 18-percent handling charge to manage its affairs rather than send its own executives into Libya's explosive political climate. Occidental even arranged for Bechtel to conduit "payments" to Libyan officials so that it could continue working in the country. (A Bechtel lawyer recently warned us that the company would sue us if we used the word "bribe.")

Bechtel was able to stay in Libya without serious consequences by forming a joint venture with a corrupt ex-premier named Mustafa Ben Halim. Although Ben Halim was held in high disgrace by most Libyans, Bechtel was advised by the CIA that he was the man it would have to work with to build the pipeline.

In the Libyan case, as always, Bechtel's correspondence with the CIA went through the top. A company officer in Libya wrote to Jerome Komes, the pipeline project's home-office sponsor, asking whether or not he should deal with Ben Halim. Komes wrote a memo to president Steve Jr., asking him to ask his father to check with Undersecretary of State C. Douglas Dillon and Bechtel CIA sources for advice on Ben Halim. We have no record of what the actual advice was: it appears to have come verbally. But the results are clear. Ben Halim was paid a "retainer" of $2,500 a month not to obstruct the project. And in return for the "free advice," Bechtel provided cover for at least two CIA agents operating in Libya between 1965 and 1969.

Secrecy Pays

Besides helping its relationship with the CIA, secrecy has been a continuing theme for the Bechtel family. The company, like most of the other great American empires, could have gone public years ago. It undoubtedly could have had its stock listed on the New York Stock Exchange and would have done well in the capital market. New York analysts estimate that Bechtel shares would trade publicly at about nine times the current value now arbitrarily placed on each tightly held share by the family-dominated stock-evaluation committee.

But the Bechtel family has deliberately exchanged higher stock prices for greater advantages. They are happy not to be listed with the Fortune 500, or indexed in Standard and Poor's or registered with the Securities and Exchange Commission. In fact, if they had their way they would be known only by their customers, a few key Cabinet members and perhaps a dozen bankers. They rarely advertise, and when they do it's usually in trade publications.

What appears to an outsider as an almost paranoiac preoccupation with privacy is instead a strategic business policy with several motives:

- Privately held companies are not subject to SEC regulation. So Bechtel does not have to file lengthy and revealing financial reports with the government and is thus correspondingly immune from inquiring federal investigators. Unlike publicly traded companies like Lockheed and Ford, Bechtel has not been required to disclose any overseas bribes, slush funds or illegal payments. (One member of Congress is currently drafting a bill that would change this situation. He plans to use Bechtel as a prime argument for his legislation.)

- All Bechtel shareholders (about 56 at last count) are either company vice presidents or their wives (wives' shares are held in trust by their husbands, who retain voting power). Each shareholder agrees to sell his stock back when he leaves the company or dies, at a price determined by the owners of 66 percent of the company's stock. A Bechtel shareholder thus has less power than a shareholder has in, say, General Motors. If a Bechtel shareholder proposed a resolution calling for termination of company business with South Africa, as a Ford shareholder did at the company's 1977 annual meeting, he could be fired by the family and forced to sell his stock back to them at a price determined behind closed doors by the Bechtel family and two or three other shareholders.

- Most foreign governments and corporations would rather deal with a U.S. corporation than a government agency, and particularly with one that is immune from government surveillance. Bechtel is able to offer this feature to overseas customers. The Soviet Union, for instance, recently signed a technological-exchange agreement with Bechtel (a fact learned not from Bechtel's tight-lipped vice chairman, Jerome Komes, who refused to comment, but from the Soviet news agency, Tass).

The McCone of the '70s

Hiring people in high places to deal with others in high places is nothing new for American corporations. The revolving door between big business and government is well documented. But Bechtel seems to hire higher. When it needs financial connections it hires the Secretary of the Treasury. When it needs nuclear technology, it hires the general manager of the Atomic Energy Commission. When it needs international clout it hires an undersecretary of state. And when it needs expertise to run the bureaucracy it is becoming it hires the secretary of Health, Education and Welfare.

Names like George Shultz, Caspar Weinberger, Cordell Hull, Rear Admiral John Dillon and William Hollingsworth (former general manager of the AEC) are found sprinkled through the Bechtel directory. A look at one of Bechtel's strategic hires, George Shultz, reveals the advantages of this business practice. If John McCone was the key Bechtel-Washington link of the '40s, '50s and '60s, George Shultz clearly plays that role for the '70s.

While he was Secretary of Labor, director of the Office of Management and the Budget (OMB) and Secretary of the Treasury, Shultz played golf with Steve Bechtel, Jr., whenever Steve went to Washington. Steve Jr. was impressed with Shultz's mind and background. There were also a few minor entries on his résumé that made Shultz even more attractive to Bechtel—former chair of the Council of Economic Advisers, member of the President's Foreign Intelligence Advisory Board and member of the Cabinet Committees on Federal Credit and Construction.

Furthermore, as Secretary of the Treasury, Shultz had traveled to Russia in April of 1973 to arrange U.S. credit for a gigantic natural-gas project Bechtel was interested in. And as OMB director he pushed for the privatization of uranium enrichment, a Nixon-inspired boondoggle that eventually could have given Bechtel a world-wide monopoly on the sale of nuclear fuel.

Since leaving the Treasury Department for Bechtel, Shultz has joined the boards of Morgan Guaranty, J. P. Morgan Company, the World Bank and the InterAmerican Development Bank. These connections, combined with the occupation of other bank boards by members of the Bechtel family and other Bechtel directors (Crocker National, Wells Fargo), cover the financial markets fairly well. Today Bechtel is in a position to channel long- or short-term finance capital anywhere in the world.

Bechtel's access to capital has placed the company in a unique bargaining position. If it can assure a Third World country of U.S. financing of a major project, it doesn't have to worry much about competition. Since most developing nations can't afford to pay out billions for roads, power plants, ports or refineries, U.S. financing is the *sine qua non* of development. Bechtel arranges the financing, Bechtel gets the job. And because Bechtel is never the *direct* recipient of World Bank loans or IMF credit, George Shultz can use his influence without fearing the kind of conflict-of-interest allegations that plagued John McCone during his years in government.

The Politics of Profit

Although the Bechtels and most of their executives are conservative Republicans domestically, internationally they seem almost apolitical. Unlike many of the company's competitors, who patriotically refuse to work in hostile nations, Bechtel will work for anyone who has borrowed or can borrow large sums of money: socialists, tribal sheiks, fascist dictators and even alleged enemies of the United States. Bechtel, for example, was the first American company to resume doing business in Egypt after 1956, when John Foster Dulles forbade Americans to work on the Aswan Dam.

Beyond American shores, Bechtel's only publicly expressed concern is for the safety of its employees. Its unofficial ideology is that technology is apolitical and brings the progress and well-being that inevitably lead to democracy and freedom. The Bechtel philosophy, of course, ignores the fact that repressive military dictatorships arose in Iran, Indonesia, Brazil and Saudi Arabia following the introduction of centralized technology into those societies. Even when, as in the case of Indonesia, the technology is supposedly owned by "the people," a new elite class of technocrats, middlemen and business leaders— many of them trained by Bechtel—take control of the government. One of their first moves is often to apply for U.S. military aid to protect their new technology and institutions—not from foreign invasion but from peasants, poor city dwellers and students, who can't always discern the beneficial effects of industrial development. All too often the result has been bloodshed, although Bechtel has usually received enough advance notice from the CIA to keep clear of conflict.

Perhaps the best example of Bechtel's apolitical stance is its operations in Algeria. Even though in the '60s Bechtel's middle management, whose anti-Communist leanings superseded their profit motives, offered considerable resistance to working in Algeria, the family's "apolitical" policies prevailed, and in 1972 the company signed a $167-million contract to build a natural-gas pipeline for Sonatrach, Algeria's state-owned oil and gas complex.

Through close ties with the Export Import Bank, Bechtel was able to negotiate a $67-million line of credit for the project—no mean trick, given the bank's statutory position on lending to the "Communist bloc" and to countries that harbor exiled terrorists.

At a committee hearing, Congress member Les Aspin protested the loan, not because Algeria harbored the likes of Eldridge Cleaver, but because Steve Sr. was on the Eximbank's powerful advisory board. The bank simply denied any conflict of interest and the loan went through. Bechtel has since then stayed in Algeria, where it has also built a large liquefied-natural-gas facility and is proposing many new projects. Socialist Algeria is one of the top nine countries in Bechtel's previously mentioned "International Job Strategy" plan.

Bechtel's apolitical stance is also evident in its eagerness to participate in the reconstruction of Vietnam, a country whose destruction the family supported through generous gifts to Richard Nixon's election campaigns.

After the war Bechtel hired South Vietnam's exiled Minister of Industry Khuong Huu Dieu. Dieu, who was a close friend of Ellsworth Bunker when he was ambassador to South Vietnam, had discovered oil off the Vietnamese coast.

Using Bunker's friendship with Dieu as entrée, Bechtel's Washington consultant Parker Hart (retired ambassador to Saudi Arabia) met with Bunker in March of last year, ostensibly to discuss the forthcoming American (Mansfield-Woodcock) mission to Vietnam. Although the alleged purpose of the mission was to seek an accounting of Americans missing in action, Hart's memo to San Francisco reporting the meeting suggests that Bechtel had other interests. "Bunker felt that Bechtel's opportunities in Vietnam might depend on the outcome of the American special mission. . . . Bunker stated that he would keep me advised of the results and offered to be of any help he could."

Nuclear Power . . . and Beyond

Bechtel saw the profits in nuclear power early on and quickly moved to become a dominant company in the field. After John McCone gave Bechtel its nuclear head start in the '50s, Bechtel hired W. Kenneth Davis, head of reactor development at the AEC, along with a handful of his top aides. They began to push nuclear power as the salvation of the modern world. Bechtel pumped money into campaigns for this "clean and safe" source of energy, helped finance the opposition to antinuclear referenda and began building nuclear plants all over the world.

However, all has not gone smoothly for Bechtel's nuclear business in recent years. The directors of Consumers Power in Michigan sued the company for $300 million in 1974, when the Palisades nuclear generator broke down shortly after opening. The suit was filed when a number of metal steam-generator tubes corroded, allowing radioactive water to leak into the steam-generating system. Consumers Power claimed that Bechtel had not fulfilled its "duty and obligation to warn the company about potential operating problems and to prevent errors in design and manufacture of equipment and components." Bechtel recently settled with Consumers Power for $14 million in cash and a promise to fix the problem.

Another Bechtel nuclear trouble spot has been its Tarapur reactor in India, which has been plagued with breakdowns, radioactivity leaks and unexplained deaths among former employees. An AEC inspector called the plant "a prime candidate for nuclear disaster."

Such problems—and Bechtel is not the only firm in the nuclear field experiencing them—have put a damper on Bechtel's nuclear business in the last few years. But because the company doesn't own the plants it builds, it doesn't have to worry about being saddled with billions of dollars' worth of obsolete and dangerous machinery. Leaving that problem to its customers, Bechtel has quietly changed directions and set its sights where the smart new money in the energy business is: on coal.

Bechtel is "quick on its feet," one engineer from the company's Scientific Development Department told me. Bechtel has five-year plans, and the engineer was discussing the one that covers 1974 to 1979. It was in this confidential plan that the company spelled out its intention to increase its investment in coal technology while cutting back on nuclear. "Bechtel sometimes likes to pioneer a new construction technology," he explained, "and get as much profit as it can out of it while no one else is around. Then when the competition gets stiff, as it is in nuclear power, it moves on to something else."

Once Bechtel decided to move into coal, its first step was to join a consortium with Newmont Mining Company, Boeing and Bechtel's rival construction firm, the Fluor Corporation, to buy Peabody Coal Company from Kennecott Copper for $1.2 billion. Peabody owns by far the largest coal reserves in the United States.

The second step was to join with Lehman Brothers, the New York investment banking firm, and the Kansas Nebraska Gas company to form something called Energy Transport Systems, Inc. (ETSI). Bechtel initiated the joint venture, bought 40 percent of ETSI and made its own vice chairman, Jerome Komes, the chairman of ETSI.

After Bechtel pioneered slurry systems—pipelines that pump large quantities of pulverized ore or coal suspended in water from one point to another—ETSI proposed to build thousands of miles of coal-slurry pipelines criss-crossing the United States. To the present day, Bechtel has built 70 percent of the world's slurry lines—pipelines that service copper mines in Venezuela and Indonesia and carry coal from Black Mesa, Arizona, to the California border.

The slurry project that ETSI/Bechtel is now pushing hardest for is a 1,000-mile line that will move 25 million tons of coal a year from the huge strip-mining area along Wyoming's Powder River to White Bluffs, Arkansas, where Arkansas Power and Light wants to build a large coal-fired generator. ETSI estimates that the pipeline will cost $750 million, but Bechtel's recent history of cost overruns suggests it could cost twice that.

With formidable opposition from farmers (who fear dust bowls and cattle deaths from the loss of scarce groundwater), environmentalists (who claim that water that has been used for slurrying is toxic and pollutant) and the railroads (which will lose billions in freight revenue), ETSI/Bechtel faces an uphill battle for its proposed pipeline.

ETSI's tactics in the ongoing battle with the rails illustrate the determination and tenacity of its energetic backer, Bechtel. As a first step, Bechtel lobbyists persuaded friends in Congress to introduce legislation that would redefine federal eminent-domain law to give pipelines right-of-way over railroads. No hostile railroad could prevent the ETSI pipeline from being built over or under its tracks. The Coal Slurry Pipeline Act, containing this giveaway, is now one of the most hotly contested bills on Capitol Hill. Bechtel helped form a front group to lobby for the bill. Ex-Clerk of the House Pat Jennings has been put in charge of maneuvering the bill through the committees.

If the Coal Slurry Act passes (and even its opponents are predicting it will), ETSI/Bechtel will still have to face the farmers and the environmentalists. And, assuming they persuade or defeat these adversaries, they still have to prove to various state and federal agencies that coal slurry is more economical than rail transport. In that effort Bechtel has shown extraordinary *chutzpah*.

The day after ETSI was incorporated, Bechtel wrote an unsolicited letter to the Interior Department's Office of Coal Research proposing to do a study of different coal-transportation methods. Bechtel did not mention its ETSI partnership in the letter. By sane standards, the recipient of a $418,000 government research contract should have been examined for any possible conflict of interest. Bechtel somehow persuaded the Interior Department to skip that process. Bechtel was granted the contract and promptly began its coal-transportation study. The study concluded that of all possible coal-transportation methods, the most economical was . . . you guessed it—slurry pipelines.

While Bechtel was arriving at its $418,000, taxpayer-supported pro-slurry conclusion, however, the University of Illinois Center for Advanced Computation Research was also studying the economics of coal transportation. Its research was funded by the National Science Foundation. Rumor had it the Illinois study would conclude that, where railroads existed, transporting coal by rail was far more efficient than building a new slurry pipeline.

Shortly before the study's release, the National Science Foundation issued an unexpected statement disavowing any endorsement of the study it had financed. No reason was given.

Paying the Piper

After Congressional hearings on the coal-slurry battle, Bechtel Vice President Jerome Komes commented: "To stay in this game you have to be stubborn as hell, and be willing to spend some money."

Although many cash-stuffed envelopes have reportedly been passed under tables in Wyoming and South Dakota to smooth the way for coal slurry, it is unlikely that Bechtel people have actually passed any of them. Within the United States, at least, the Bechtel family has a strict policy against cash bribes.

This policy appears to be due less to ethical considerations than to the fact that past cases of bribery have brought the

secretive company too much unwanted publicity. In 1972, felony convictions were given to four Bechtel executives who
bribed the mayor of Woodbridge, New Jersey, with $50,000
to gain a pipeline right-of-way through the town to a tank
farm Bechtel was building nearby. Bechtel appealed. Its
grounds—quite ironically, in view of the company's own abys-
mal record in hiring women—were that the jury selection in
Woodbridge discriminated against women because no women
were on the jury panel. The Bechtel Four won a new trial
but were reconvicted.

These infractions, along with recent publicity surrounding
corporate bribery, have made Bechtel more circumspect in
its irregular payments.

Perhaps the cleverest cover for questionable payments was
devised in 1975, when the Bechtel Foundation (whose contributions are tax write-offs) gave a $100,000 grant to the World
Wide Permina Fund. This contribution was the largest single
grant made in 1975, and it represents about 30 percent of
the Bechtel Foundation's total gifts for the year. According
to its articles of incorporation, World Wide Permina is chartered to "further the cultural ties between the U.S. and the
Republic of Indonesia."

At present, however, the extent of World Wide Permina's
activities is providing a scholarship for *one* Indonesian student
in the United States. The only imaginable reason why Bechtel
has neglected to expose this obvious rip-off is that World Wide
Permina has an interlocking board of directors with Pertamina
Corporation, the scandal-ridden Indonesian oil and gas monopoly with which Bechtel has millions of dollars of construction
contracts. In fact, until he was fired and placed under house
arrest for corruption, Pertamina's president, Indonesian General Ibnu Sutowo, also chaired the World Wide Permina Foundation Board. It was under Sutowo that Pertamina negotiated
most of its major contracts with Bechtel to build a multi-
billion-dollar complex of gas pipelines, liquefaction plants and
liquefied-natural-gas ports throughout Indonesia. Since corporate donations to World Wide Permina are co-mingled in the
foundation's Bank of America custody account, there is no
way of knowing whether Bechtel's $100,000 ever lined the

pockets of General Sutowo. But it certainly hasn't been spent on cultural exchange with Indonesia, and Bechtel knows it.

Although an occasional "grant" can help grease the way to a minor contract or favor, in Bechtel's league, bribes are a relatively ineffective way of doing business. The company's oil-rich Middle East customers care more about whether or not Bechtel builds in Israel, which it does not, or whether it continues to abide by the Arab boycott of Israel, which, in effect, it does, and for which the Justice Department sued Bechtel in 1975.

Most of the people Bechtel deals with on a decisive basis don't need cash. They need billion-dollar Eximbank financing and friendly U.S. foreign policy. So when George Shultz tells the president of Tai Power Corporation of Taiwan that he can arrange a $100-million loan guarantee from the Eximbank to finance new nuclear generators, or promises to do what he can to delay the diplomatic recognition of the People's Republic of China for a couple of years, he is offering something that money can't buy and something Taiwan knows he can deliver. So to Bechtel, which could easily dish out Shultz's salary in bribes every year, it made business sense to hire Shultz instead.

A Woman's Place at Bechtel

The Bechtel bureaucrats dislike no one so much as the federal government's Equal Employment Opportunity Commission. "They have a reputation for being by far the most militant and aggressive," states one interoffice memo to Employee Relations Manager W. E. Squires. "Their joy in life seems to be pursuing the cause of some downtrodden minority and getting a big fat check from some big fat corporation. Friends who have been close to these agencies say they actually run up and down the hall waving the checks when they get them. I don't think they are as interested in justice as they are in the checks."

The memo never clarifies whether the writer means bribes or fines, but the tone suggests that it doesn't really matter. One way or another, compliance with affirmative-action laws is expensive. The memo, summarizing one case of "a paranoiac nut" who complained to the EEOC about Bechtel, reads, "It cost Bechtel a lot of money with the supervisory and employee man-hours spent with the investigators."

Bechtel's strategy is to wait until it is told to clean up its act before complying. "If we anticipate what they want and automatically implement, then they won't have anything else for us to do and they will really have to think something up," the memo continues. The last sentence is prophetic. "We've gotten by so far, but those days are over."

Since the memo was written, five class-action suits have been filed against Bechtel for discrimination against women. But the suit Bechtel is fighting the hardest was brought by Linda Martinez before the memo was written, in August of 1972.

Martinez, a Philippine woman, claims that she was denied equal pay and promotional opportunities because she is a woman. She complained about it and, her suit charges, she was forced to resign under pressure. In 1975 the Federal District Court in Northern California ruled that her case could proceed as a class action. This means her suit is now filed on behalf of thousands of women workers, and Bechtel stands to pay out millions in back pay to women who were "denied hire, transfer or promotion because of their sex, denied equal compensation for performance of similar work because of their sex or experienced retaliation because of complaints of sex discrimination."

Bechtel won't say how many women in the class have stepped forward to complain. "It's not exactly a popular move." "And," one class member told me, "what hurts most is the number of women who won't talk to me." *Martinez v. Bechtel* is being followed closely by nervous corporate attorneys across the nation.

Although women's lot has reportedly improved at Bechtel since Linda Martinez filed her suit, one still has to look about a yard and a half down from the top of the organization chart before finding a woman's name. As of 1976, there were no women paid more than $30,000. (There still may not be, but since *Newsweek* magazine published Steve Bechtel, Jr.'s, salary last year, Bechtel payroll records have been placed in the same vault as nuclear secrets.)

The most important women to Bechtel are not employees but the wives of men who work there. In a way curiously reminiscent of military bases, each Bechtel office has a chapter of "Bechtel Wives," a club whose members are treated to occasional guided tours of faraway projects and frequent luncheon speeches by company executives like George Shultz.

Buried in Sand

Bechtel's phenomenal metamorphosis from muleskinner to sovereign state is not entirely surprising in a country whose economy has become dominated by a handful of multinational corporations. A corporation whose annual sales are often greater than the GNP of the country it is developing is bound at times to seem indistinguishable from a country itself. Dealings at every level take on an ambassadorial tone: contracts sound like treaties, salesmen act like diplomats and meetings between Steve Bechtel, Jr., and the Chief of State resemble summit conferences.

And like any nation, Bechtel mythologizes its work. With boundless energy, the lovable and imperious Steve Sr. has created an almost evangelistic mystique. His medium is *Bechtel Briefs,* a slick four-color monthly magazine in which T-shirts have been airbrushed on photos of workers and smoke has been removed from photos of exhaust pipes and chimneys. The purity of a fairy-tale workplace is matched by the righteousness of endless morale-building editorials addressed to Bechtel customers, workers and friends around the world. These editorials invariably repeat the Bechtel line: mass technology is salvation for a backward world.

The Bechtels know as well as any multinational executive that their brand of development has failed to meet human needs, that unemployment and poverty have frequently increased in Third World nations invaded by Western technology and that all too often the elite decides to protect its new industries from restive workers and peasants with U.S.-armed military dictatorships.

The villain is not development itself, or technology itself. Rather, it is mass centralized technology that is shaped and installed to meet the needs of Bechtel profits and local elites, rather than that of the population as a whole. Does India, for example, need a nuclear power plant, or solar-heat collectors in thousands of villages? Does Saudi Arabia need Jubail, or better protection for the way of life of its desert nomads? All too often, the expansion of centralized high technology merely gives added power to a tiny, repressive ruling group.

Since 1950, when Bechtel finished the infrastructure of the giant Arabian-American Oil Company, small revolutionary wars have raged throughout the Arabian peninsula—wars deliberately hidden from American view behind a media-manufactured preoccupation with energy. The CIA-supported coup in Iran installed one of the most brutal autocracies on earth, and Bechtel's 12-volume industrial-development plan for the country has strengthened, not loosened, the Shah's grip. U.S. aid to Saudi Arabia is partly used to support a crack "White Army" trained for internal repression. And the rivers of Indonesia have more than once been swollen with the corpses of slaughtered peasant rebels who lost their land to "development." And through it all, Bechtel builds and builds and builds.

Christopher Rand, an international-oil-industry consultant, worked for Bechtel for two years as an administrative specialist in the company's international petroleum division. He left Bechtel in 1971 and in 1975 published a book called *Making Democracy Safe for Oil,* an exposé of the oil industry's impact on resource nations. As far back as 1973 Rand was able to see projects like Jubail coming:

"It was a natural culmination of everything Bechtel and Saudi Arabia were doing. Billions of U.S. dollars were piling up in the Saudi treasury. Something had to be done to get that money back into the U.S. The easiest was to convince the Saudis that they could become an important industrial nation and build an infrastructure for them. Well, it's a ridiculous notion. The Saudis do have a tremendous energy base, but that's about the only advantage. There is no economic justification for a petrochemical complex there—particularly one that will generate 6,000 tons of sulphur a day, that in today's market can only be dumped in the desert. There's probably a market for aluminum, but Jubail is not well situated on the world's bauxite shipping routes; and steel? Steel is a farce. There is no rational justification for a steel mill in the Saudi peninsula.

"Jubail is a massive WPA project. Instead of employing idle workers, it's employing idle dollars. There's no question that dollarwise it's the biggest industrial boondoggle in history."

The desert has a way of protecting itself. Sands shift mysteriously from place to place and over the years have buried settlements throughout Saudi Arabia. The sands of the Dahana Desert will shift, Rand predicts, and cover Jubail before the end of the century.

Behind the Story

Early in 1976 a group of Bay Area journalists started meeting
informally on a weekly basis to discuss a common frustration. They
all wanted to write an investigative article about the Bechtel
Corporation, headquartered in downtown San Francisco, but none
of them had the time or the resources to do it. The reporters included
Henry Weinstein of the *San Francisco Examiner,* Mark Dowie of
Mother Jones, David Weir and Lowell Bergman of *Rolling Stone,*
as well as freelancers Nora Gallagher and Paul Grabowicz. They
all considered the story a supreme challenge. The company was
huge, secretive, and owned by a politically well-connected family
that tightly guarded its privacy. Bechtel was among the largest
construction companies in the world; it was still privately held and
therefore largely unaccountable to the public; its executives were
hired right out of the presidential Cabinet, and it was a key developer
of exotic technologies like uranium enrichment and coal slurry
pipelines. There was perhaps no other private group with as large
a stake in the Middle East. Yet Bechtel was virtually unknown to
the American public.

The reporters met for a time in the home of political activist
Alvin Duskin, who was sympathetic to their project. Everyone
agreed that a story had to be done, but no one could propose a
means to do it. Eventually the group disbanded, but not before
some valuable files had been pooled.

Less than two years later, Mark Dowie decided to revive the
Bechtel project. He was the publisher of *Mother Jones* magazine,
but still found time to pursue editorial projects and wanted to pick
up where the reporters' group had left off.

Investigative reporting often is the province of young writers,
at least in the magazine world. It is a common pattern for magazine
writers to move away from investigative articles into books or
columns or analytical writing when they can. The time, expense,
and toil of investigative work eventually encourage them to pursue
more profitable and less frustrating reporting.

Not so Mark Dowie. He didn't even try journalism until he was in his late thirties, and then it was on his own time, after hours at *Mother Jones.* Dowie's background was business and finance. He'd worked at the Bank of America and had been an economic consultant to some Bechtel-owned companies. To avoid a conflict of interest, he carefully excluded all information, contacts, and records from his former business connection with the Bechtels for this story.

Dowie quickly established a reputation as one of the best investigative reporters writing about corporations. In 1976 he co-authored with Tracy Johnston an exposé of the Dalkon Shield intrauterine device, which was a National Magazine Award finalist. Then he won a National Magazine Award in 1978 for his article about how Ford Motor Company knew that the gasoline tanks on its Pinto automobiles could explode when hit from the rear.

In suit and tie, Dowie, with his neatly clipped hair, can easily pass for the executive he once was. He knows the language and customs of the corporate world from the inside. He doesn't have to fake it. In researching the Bechtel story, however, Dowie's ability to go undercover was worthless. This corporate empire is as closed to outsiders as is the CIA.

To start with, Dowie pulled together the files from the disbanded reporters' group and met with Weir and Bergman to get a commitment from the Center for Investigative Reporting for help on the project. The story would require considerable documentation. Bechtel history had to be compiled from old books, *Who's Who,* legislative hearings, and obscure articles. Cynthia Kasabian and Scott Zonder, college interns at the Center, were enlisted as research assistants.

Dowie hoped that Bechtel would cooperate, or at least grant him an interview. After all, Dowie's purpose was to expose not so much corporate *mis*behavior by Bechtel as its corporate behavior, period. He wanted to write a story about how the system works, not how it breaks down. And the Bechtel story included success on every level. Telling the untold stories of how the system works, as well as how it doesn't work, is a recurring theme in the Center's brand of investigative journalism.

While the rest of the research team launched an elaborate library and public records search for material about Bechtel, Dowie called corporate headquarters to try to arrange an interview with a top company official.

Tom Flynn, a friendly ex-reporter who had gone to work for Bechtel's public relations division, came over to the Center's office and met with Dowie and Weir. Flynn did most of the questioning: "Who are you guys? What do you want? What have you heard about us? What will you do with any information you find?" Dowie was noncommittal about where he intended to publish the story. The reporters feared that the giant corporation would be very suspicious of the muckraking journal *Mother Jones*. Their suspicion that the article would be critical of Bechtel later proved justified.

For a few weeks after the meeting, Dowie thought he might get his official interview. Flynn said he was trying to get approval. But, as Dowie describes in his preface to the magazine story, he eventually realized that Bechtel had no intention of cooperating. Flynn apparently was just leading him on.

Dowie kept up the pressure, however. "I waited for Flynn to come out of his office at night or for lunch and I'd walk down the street with him. I kept bugging him to get me some interviews with officials, to get some cooperation, some background material on the history of the company, anything."

Dowie's reason for writing the article under the auspices of the Center, as opposed to being candid about his *Mother Jones* connection, stemmed from an earlier story printed in the magazine. One of the magazine's founders, premier investigative reporter Paul Jacobs, had written a startling exposé of the Bechtel-built Tarapur nuclear power plant in India in 1976. Jacobs's article was based on secret documents leaked by someone inside the company.

Jacobs had recently died from cancer which he believed was caused by radiation exposure during his coverage of nuclear weapons tests in Nevada in the 1950s. Before his death he told Dowie that he had never found out who his source was. He also gave his Tarapur files to Dowie.

By carefully rechecking the routing slips on the Tarapur documents, Dowie thought he was able to figure out who had been Jacobs's source at Bechtel. Dowie asked to meet with this official, but he refused and denied ever knowing Jacobs.

Lowell Bergman, another Center staff member, helped Dowie quietly approach other Bechtel officials in the hope of finding a friendly source. Somebody had given them a copy of Bechtel's telephone directory, which listed the employees' home numbers. The pair painstakingly checked out dozens of possible sources when they were away from their offices—the one time they might possibly agree to cooperate. Many were friendly at first, but most cut the reporters off whenever the first controversial question was asked. Soon Dowie found out why. Bechtel employees were given oaths of secrecy to sign when they joined the company, and again when they left. This was an organization obsessed with secrecy.

Dowie also tried another classic reportorial technique—hanging around the cafés and bars where Bechtel employees went for lunch and after-work drinks. "In a company like Bechtel," observes Dowie, "the engineers hang out in one place, the 'corporados' in another. After a while you know where to go and strike up conversations. You can learn a lot that way."

One employee Dowie met was a Bechtel photographer, who said that the company required that photographs in the company newsletter, *Bechtel Briefs,* be airbrushed. All the smokestacks came out smokeless, and half-dressed workers all ended up in T-shirts.

One of Dowie's *Mother Jones* associates, Steve Parker, met a Bechtel company lawyer in a bar. He warned Parker that if the upcoming piece "mentions the word *bribe,* we'll sue."

By this time Flynn had a final answer for Dowie on his request for an interview. "Flynn called and said, 'This time it's for good. We've decided we're absolutely not going to cooperate, and the decision comes from the top.'"

"I said, 'Steve, Jr.?'"

"He said, 'Yes.'"

Dowie asked for an explanation and Flynn said, "Because you stole documents from us for the Tarapur story."

Dowie was incredulous. "You mean that Steve Bechtel believes we broke into your most sensitive nuclear files in a tightly guarded corporate building and stole documents?"

"Mark, he has to believe that," Flynn replied.

Dowie then realized that for security-conscious Bechtel, believing the alternative (and true) explanation for the Tarapur story was worse. "Steve simply could not afford to believe that one of his vice-presidents had broken the corporate oath of secrecy. But I love the image of Jacobs and I—these two reporters—breaking into his building, cracking a safe, and taking that stuff. To this day, I bet he believes we broke in."

Dowie continued his search for knowledgeable sources outside the Bechtel empire. He found a man who had worked for Bechtel soon after World War II and who now worked for the CIA. He had a remarkable memory for details of Bechtel's activities.

And the extensive public records search, organized partly by the Center staff and interns, also uncovered some useful tidbits. In John McCone's confirmation hearings as under secretary of defense in 1950, Dowie found valuable statistics on Bechtel's large war profits, as mentioned in the story. The confirmation hearings were obtained from the government documents room at the University of California library.

A large file on Bechtel was also available from the Data Center, a nonprofit library in Oakland that specializes in corporate profiles. Dowie and other team members copied all the material they could find about the secretive company, including a massive Freedom of Information Act file on Bechtel's numerous government contracts.

"By putting it all together I started getting a pretty good picture of Bechtel," Dowie says. "But not before I had spent an awful lot of time reading." Once he had absorbed as much as he could, Dowie started to write. He discovered that analyzing all his information was just as necessary as the research. Investigative stories like this need a theme to pull the information together; in this case, it was that large-scale centralized technology helps to increase the power of small, powerful, centralized ruling elites. This overview comes only after extensive interviews and reading, and it distinguishes investigative journalists who understand how the forest develops from those who see only the trees.

When his first draft was ready, Dowie passed it around to his colleagues at the Center and the magazine for comments. Meanwhile, the *Mother Jones* staff hatched a brilliant plan for ensuring that this story would have impact—at least inside Bechtel itself.

Early on the morning the issue was to be released, a collection of *Mother Jones* staff and their friends quietly surrounded the Bechtel headquarters in downtown San Francisco. Just before 8, as Bechtel employees arrived for work, each was offered a free copy of the magazine "with an interesting story about your company in there."

Most took the free copy. Conspicuous in their refusal were a few high-level executives who bustled by without acknowledging the leafleteers. Minutes later, however, a number of secretaries were sent downstairs to pick up copies for those officials who had chosen not to grab one themselves.

The article was also well read outside the company. In the days immediately following its release, Dowie learned that Bechtel was about to hire yet another well-known government official—Richard Helms, former head of the CIA. Since it was too late to use this information in his story, Dowie leaked it to *San Francisco Chronicle* reporter Mike Taylor. Taylor had covered Bechtel and helped Dowie with some files during his investigation.

Bechtel, meanwhile, was readying its official response to Dowie's story. This rebuttal was released in the *Contra Costa Times,* a suburban newspaper near San Francisco that had earlier printed a short version of Dowie's article distributed by Pacific News Service. As part of its account, the company flatly denied any connection with the CIA. The following day, the *Chronicle* broke the Helms story on the front page.

In the months that followed, many other reporters started examining Bechtel. One of the best, and longest, pieces to appear was a front-page article in the *Wall Street Journal.* The article relied heavily on Dowie's reporting and had the added strength of an official corporate interview—the kind Dowie tried so hard to obtain but was denied.

Dowie's article, a ground-breaking exercise in corporate reporting, was named a finalist in the public service category for a National Magazine Award in 1979.

In the years since "The Bechtel File" appeared, Bechtel's public profile has risen considerably. Ronald Reagan's election in 1980 brought Bechtel executives Caspar Weinberger, George Shultz, and W. Kenneth Davis into powerful positions in the new administration. Stephen Bechtel, Jr., was selected as the first chairman of the National Academy of Engineering, a government advisory group. When it was revealed in 1982 that U.S. Middle East negotiator Philip Habib was also a Bechtel consultant, the corporation's influence on government policy briefly became a national story.

The increased public scrutiny has spurred Bechtel to gear up its public relations efforts. Soon after Mark Dowie's article was published, for instance, Bechtel ran a series of full-page ads in major national magazines entitled "We're Bechtel." When a reporter at a Billings, Montana, newspaper prepared critical stories about Bechtel construction there, the company PR representative, Tom Flynn, reportedly flew to Montana to squelch them. According to the *Billings* (Montana) *Gazette,* Flynn met with others and discussed whether the reporter "smoked pot, chased women, or gambled a lot." Flynn told the same paper that Dowie's article was "a hatchet job from the beginning" and that the later *Wall Street Journal* story "was just a lazy rewrite of the *Mother Jones* article."

Mark Dowie continues his investigative reporting at *Mother Jones* and has won several more national journalism awards. Center for Investigative Reporting interns Scott Zonder and Cynthia Kasabian have gone on to staff reporting jobs at the *Riverside* (California) *Press-Enterprise* and the *San Francisco Examiner* respectively.

Bechtel continues to build and reap profit. The coal slurry pipeline remains a political battle in Congress. A House committee approved a bill in 1982 to make the pipeline easier to build. Opponents, like the head of the National Coal Association, say they "are fighting the forces of evil" to stop the pipeline. The sex discrimination suit against Bechtel was settled out of court. The plaintiffs were awarded $1.375 million and attorney costs, and Bechtel was required to perform job audits for women employees who felt that their jobs were misclassified.

In 1978, then Bechtel executive Caspar Weinberger told Bechtel employees: "The future of Bechtel has to be very optimistic. But our future is necessarily very closely intertwined with the economy of the future. As we get larger, we cannot consider our own future independent of the economy, or of governmental economic policy. Bechtel is sufficiently big so that it cannot divorce itself from governmental policy or from the economy."

NewTimes

JULY 10, 1978 $1.00
THE FEATURE NEWS MAGAZINE

"**B**lack Panthers have committed a series of violent crimes over the last several years. Now, disaffected Panther Party intimates and others have told *New Times* about the scope and nature of this violence — about arson, extortion, beatings, even murder. There appears to be no political explanation for it; the Party is no longer under siege by the police, and this is not self-defense. It seems to be nothing but sense- less crim- inality, di- rected in most cases at other blacks. There is even a secret wing of the Panthers, known within the Party as 'the Squad,' to administer the brutality. And at the center of it all is Panther founder Huey P. Newton."

THE PARTY'S OVER

by Kate Coleman with Paul Avery

7

The Party's Over

by Kate Coleman with Paul Avery

Several weeks ago, a 30-year-old black woman went to police in Oakland, California, to report she had been kidnapped and sexually assaulted. She said the incident had occurred two days earlier, in the afternoon. The woman gave this account:

While waiting for a bus in crowded downtown Oakland, she had stepped into a phone booth to make two quick calls. She spoke first with her fiancé, and was about to call her mother when a gold Cadillac pulled up nearby and a huge man got out. The woman later guessed he stood 6 feet 7 inches and weighed about 400 pounds.

"Mr. Newton would like to see you," the man said, gesturing toward the late-model Cadillac.

"I don't know any Newton," the woman replied.

A light-skinned black man with a large Afro got out of the Cadillac and beckoned to her. Then the big man, indicating a gun in his pocket, said, "You'd better come with me." He pressed up against her and she could feel the barrel. He warned that if she yelled for help, "I'll blow your brains out all over the phone booth."

Both men then shoved her into the back of the car, and the big man took the wheel, leaving the other man in back with the woman. "You know where to go," he told the driver, and the car sped off toward the industrialized section of West Oakland, where it pulled in behind a building and stopped. The man in back snorted some white powder and began bragging to the woman about his sexual prowess, about what a "superior" man and lover he was. He started to unbutton her blouse, then tried to lift up her T-shirt underneath. She shoved him away. "No bitch pushes me around," he yelled, smacking her across the face. He went for her shirt again, pulled it up and began fondling and kissing her breasts. When she resisted, he burned her left wrist with a cigarette and called her a "street whore."

The driver turned around in his seat. "Huey, can't you see she isn't a street woman?" he said. He urged that they let her go, but the man in back told the driver that he should just follow orders. At that, the driver pulled out a pistol and directed the woman to do what she was told. She stopped all resistance then. And when the man in the back seat ordered her to fondle his penis through his pants, she obeyed, but he was dissatisfied with her efforts. He ordered her to excite him, yet despite her attempts, he failed to get an erection. Finally he pulled the woman's slacks down to her knees and ordered that she spread her legs while he performed cunnilingus on her. It lasted about five minutes.

Afterward, he went through the woman's purse and took out $46 in cash. He carefully examined her wallet and warned her, "Now I know who you are and where you live. If I hear anything about this, you'll be taken care of." Seeing pictures of her three children, he threatened them, too.

The big man headed the Cadillac for North Oakland, where the woman was released. Later, she estimated the ordeal had lasted about two and a half hours. The man in back handed her five dollars—"to catch a cab," he said—and threatened to kill her if she took action.

Badly shaken, the woman went to her mother's house. Her brother and her fiancé arrived soon after. She had been so affected by the experience that she fainted several times that evening, until finally her family brought her to the emergency room at Doctors' Hospital in Oakland, where she told the examining physician the whole story. The doctor urged her to call the police, but the woman was too frightened. It was two days before she reported the incident, and then only at the urging of her fiancé.

The woman told Oakland police her assailant was Huey Newton—founder and leader of the Black Panther Party. She said she had recognized him "from seeing him on TV and in the papers," but she identified him again from police photos. And from the sheaf of photos she unhesitatingly identified the big man as Robert Heard, Newton's 6-foot-8-inch bodyguard, who has been variously described as weighing between 380 and 470 pounds.

Police began the paperwork on her complaint, anticipating the arrest of Newton and Heard on charges of kidnapping and sexual assault. But the woman refused to press charges. She remembered the threats and was terrified.

After various parts of the woman's story surfaced locally, Newton and his lawyer, Sheldon Otis, insisted that Newton had nothing to do with the attack—"assuming it even took place," Otis said. They said he had been exonerated by a privately commissioned lie detector test. But a source close to the district attorney's office says the test was poorly conducted—that only four questions were asked, and that the two dealing with sexual assault were unspecific enough that Newton might have been able to pass a test he would otherwise have failed.

Nevertheless, Newton's defense team made copies of the lie detector test available to reporters as a way of refuting the woman's story. But a refutation was unnecessary. Even with prodding from the police and assurances of protection, the woman still refused to press charges, fearing Panther retribution.

The woman had good reason to be afraid. Over the last few years, Newton and other Panthers have moved like a street gang through the Oakland area. They have, say reliable sources, committed a series of violent crimes—including arson, extortion, beatings, even murder. Unlike the skirmishes that marked the Party's infancy in the late sixties, the recent incidents appear to have no political explanation. The Panthers are no longer under siege by the police, and this is not self-defense. It seems to be nothing but senseless criminality, directed in most cases against other blacks—sometimes Panthers themselves.

Most of these crimes remain open on police ledgers. The victims are too frightened, or the evidence too circumstantial, to bring Newton or his Panther subordinates to trial. Only a few of the incidents, in fact, have been covered in the Oakland and San Francisco press; some have never been reported to the police.

Now, after six months of interviews with disaffected Party intimates, the police and others, it is possible to learn the scope of recent Panther violence. It is possible, too, to see how the wave of brutality has affected the Black Panther Party—and the effect has been great. Already, the Party's support in the community has diminished, its grant money has dried up, and valuable workers and supporters have left. The Panther day care center/grade school is still operating, as is the free health clinic, but these institutions exist side by side with another Newton creation of an entirely different sort.

New Times has learned that there exists a secret wing of the Party, assembled originally by Newton as his own palace guard, loyal to him against any contender. Within the Party, the group is known as "the Squad." By all appearances, the Squad is simply a team of Newton's bodyguards—but they often operate like underworld hit men.

An uncanny duality has grown up around the Panthers— a myth and a reality, difficult to penetrate and sort out. Over the years, many supporters have regarded Panther militance as a legitimate response to police brutality and the country's long history of racism. Now, confronted by Panther behavior that seems to defy explanation, some Bay Area blacks and leftists nevertheless continue to protect and defend the Party. There has been a fear that any exposé of the Panthers would play into the hands of reactionary forces and hurt the entire black community. Party support has dwindled, but to many people, still, the Panthers—and above all Huey Newton—are liberators of oppressed blacks, heroes standing up to malignant police forces, great teachers in the vein of Mao Tse-tung and Ché Guevara. Also, illegal government actions, aimed with particular zeal at the Panthers by the FBI and other agencies (as revealed two years ago by the Senate Intelligence Committee and subsequent Freedom of Information Act lawsuits), created a well of sympathy for the Party—and suspicion of efforts to expose it.

But, there is a growing sense among many sympathizers and ex-Panthers that it is Huey Newton himself who has discredited the Party—and, by seemingly gratuitous violence, betrayed the principles on which it was founded.

It was in the fall of 1966 that Huey Newton, the son of a Baptist minister, founded the Black Panther Party, along with his friends Bobby Seale and David Hilliard. The Oakland-based Panthers marked a departure from the trend of black cultural nationalism then on the rise in the ghetto, a nationalism that declared all whites the enemy. The Party argued that black liberation could not be won without the support of white revolutionaries and radicals, and it welcomed them in the fight against a common ruling-class enemy. The Panthers' "Ten Point Program" went further than any nationalist group's demands by calling for "all power to the people" and the armed self-defense of blacks.

In Oakland, particularly, blacks had little power. That predominantly black city was run until very recently by a white Republican administration and a police department described by a local black politician as "no different from the most rabid, cracker police force in a small Mississippi town."

To keep an eye on the police, Newton and his fellow Panthers began patrolling Oakland ghetto streets on weekend nights, defiantly toting shotguns, pistols and a copy of the California Penal Code. The Panthers, though, were careful to remain within the law. They advised Oakland residents of their legal rights and acted as an armed presence to prevent police brutality. The effect on the left was electrifying. The outcry on the right prompted state legislators to draft a bill that made it illegal to bear unconcealed arms. In May 1967, a delegation of Panthers went to the California State Capitol carrying their weapons. They were lobbying against the bill, but the furor unleashed by their disciplined military presence assured its passage.

The trip to the Capitol was well publicized, but the incident that would catapult Newton to national prominence came later, on October 28, 1967. Newton's car was stopped by Oakland police that night, leading to an exchange that ended with Newton shot in the stomach, one policeman wounded, and Newton charged with murdering the other officer, John Frey. Newton pleaded innocent. His story was that Frey had called him "nigger" and probed his genitals while searching him. He said that he had been shot point-blank in the stomach and had not shot back. But in 1968, a jury convicted Newton of voluntary manslaughter and he went to prison.

While in prison, Newton became a political martyr. "Free Huey" buttons cropped up everywhere—and the West Coast–based Peace and Freedom Party, dedicating itself to support the Panthers in a black-white coalition, adopted "Free Huey" as one of its slogans. (The Peace and Freedom Party also made Eldridge Cleaver its candidate for president of the U.S. in 1968. Cleaver, the celebrated *Soul On Ice* author, helped run the Panthers when Newton went to prison.)

During this period, white leftists and liberals flocked excitedly to the Black Panther Party because they saw it as a nonracist revolutionary vanguard. The Party was self-consciously modeled after the Algerian FLN, with its urban guerrilla warfare tactic of deliberate skirmishes with police. Leftists saw Newton as the only black leader dedicated to Marxism but also capable of transforming ghetto blacks into a disciplined revolutionary army. (Newton affected a swagger stick to go along with the Party's militarism, and went by a variety of lofty titles over the years, including Minister of Defense, the Supreme Commander, the Supreme Servant, the Servant and, most recently, President.)

In predominantly black Oakland, only 2 percent of the police force was then made up of minorities. Panther claims that the police were an occupying army, and that law enforcement agencies were out to crush the Party, were concepts embraced immediately by white leftists. When, in 1968 and 1969, these law enforcement agencies raided Panther offices across the country, resulting in hundreds of arrests and a long list of dead and wounded blacks, Panthers and many white leftists alike viewed armed struggle as imminent.

The money began to flow into Panther coffers as never before, and prominent white liberals and leftists, including such people as then–Yale University president Kingman Brewster and author Jessica Mitford, raised money or spoke publicly in support of the Party. It was the era of Radical Chic, of Leonard Bernstein's swank New York cocktail party for the Panthers. And everywhere, liberals and leftists were demanding that Huey be freed.

In the summer of 1970 he was freed—his conviction reversed because the judge had erred in his instructions to the jury. Newton faced two more trials on the charge, both ending in jury deadlocks. Finally the district attorney declared that any further attempt to prosecute Newton would be futile, and the case was dismissed.

When he came out of prison in 1970, Newton brought with him plans for major changes in the Black Panther Party. He reversed the stand on armed insurrection, saying there was little support for it in the black community, and that the cost to the Party in lives and resources had been staggering. Instead, Newton called for "survival programs pending the revolution," and began putting Party resources into projects such as the Black Panther school, the free health clinic, food giveaways and sickle cell anemia testing.

In style as well as content, Newton backed away from the militant posturing of Eldridge Cleaver. Cleaver used to visit local black churches (accompanied by his leather-jacketed Panther bodyguards) and stand in the pulpit addressing the congregation as "motherfuckers," demanding support for the Party. As with the Panthers' "off the pig" rhetoric, the obscenity was part of a "revolutionary" style. But when Newton was released, he ordered Panthers to clean up their language and attend church regularly, a move to win over mainstream blacks. (Cleaver, meanwhile, had fled the country well before Newton's release to avoid trial on charges stemming from a 1968 shoot-out with Oakland police. From Algeria he ran the international wing of the Panthers.)

But as the Panthers assumed a nonviolent stance, there flared within the Party an intense power struggle between two factions—and it threatened to destroy the Panthers. Ideologically, the split came over Newton's orders to back away from "military" skirmishes with the police.

The underground, military wing of the Party was committed to immediate armed struggle, viewing Panther "survival programs" as symbolic alternatives to existing institutions, useful primarily as propaganda to build support for the Party. But Newton pushed through his changes despite the underground's objections. And to solidify his position, he expelled the Party's militants, who formed the only organized group within the Panthers tough enough to challenge him. One of the first to go was leading Los Angeles Panther Elmer "Geronimo" Pratt. In his wake went the entire New York chapter. Cleaver protested strenuously from Algeria, but Newton's break with Cleaver went beyond ideological matters. It was a public battle between two titanic egos, exacerbated by Newton's fears, after nearly three years in prison, that the Party had slipped beyond his control. He worried that even in Algeria, Cleaver posed a threat to his leadership. (The FBI, it was later learned, exploited this fear by forging defamatory letters from Newton and Cleaver as a way to play on their mutual paranoia.)

To ensure his authority, Newton closed most of the 30 Panther chapters nationwide, calling loyal members to Oakland. But warring between the factions continued, and people on both sides were murdered. Newton loyalist Sam Napier, for example, the national distributor of the Panther newspaper, was cut down by bullets in New York. The atmosphere became so volatile that when Geronimo Pratt's pregnant wife was stabbed repeatedly and killed in 1971, many attributed the murder to the ongoing internecine warfare.

Ultimately, Newton prevailed, beefing up his one-man rule of the Party. But he remained plagued by insecurities for years, sometimes doubting his oldest and closest lieutenants. In early 1974, in a move that puzzled and upset supporters, he expelled co-founder David Hilliard from the Party. So great was Newton's displeasure that he went into the Panther school and personally pulled out all four of Hilliard's children.

Hilliard, Newton's friend since childhood, was in prison at the time for his role in the 1968 shoot-out with Oakland police, the same incident that forced Eldridge Cleaver to flee the country. According to Panther insiders, Newton told Party members that Hilliard had orchestrated a coup against him, and Newton charged Hilliard's wife, Pat, a tireless Party worker, with misusing Panther funds.

David Hilliard's expulsion sent out severe shock waves. He was widely loved, and regarded as the heart of the Party. Hilliard was the organization man who ran the Panthers when both Newton and Bobby Seale were in prison and Cleaver was out of the country. He had worked unflaggingly for Newton's release. To those who knew Hilliard, the "coup" story put out by Newton seemed preposterous. And to this day, even to close friends outside the Party, Hilliard professes bewilderment about the real reasons for his expulsion.

It was against this backdrop of insecurity, and to guarantee his dominance over the Party, that Newton created "the Squad." (But the Squad was also an outgrowth of a much earlier fascination Newton had with small-time gangsterism— pimping, running card games and burglarizing houses in the Berkeley hills, activities he has acknowledged in his autobiography, *Revolutionary Suicide*.) Newton selected Squad members himself. A source familiar with the initiation rites describes the process:

"There would be some guy who had come into the Party off the streets. He'd work his ass off doing the hard, day-to-day stuff that keeps the Party going—you know, standing on the corner with the sickle cell anemia cans or hawking the paper. After a while he'd get the summons to go up to [Newton's] penthouse—that alone would be very flattering, because those people lived in dire poverty. But then he'd be up there with Huey and they'd snort cocaine together, and then he'd be told he had been selected for the Squad. For somebody low down in the Party, the whole thing would wow them— the coke, the good liquor and just being able to hang out with Huey." Party members have also related stories about

the Squad sharing women with Newton. The carousing together, with the accouterment of good cocaine, was a major
reward of Squad service.

The Squad itself has always been small, reportedly made
up of two "fire teams," usually with five or six men each.
The duties of Squad members varied, but frequently they accompanied Newton when he ventured out into Oakland's tough
night life, into the bars and after-hours joints. It was during
such forays, say the police and other sources, that Newton
and the Squad began the practice of extorting money from
bars, pimps and dope dealers.

The practice appears to have had its roots in a legal fund-
raising effort begun by Newton in the summer of 1971. The
Panthers began a boycott of black-owned liquor stores when
recalcitrant owners refused to accede to Newton's demands
that they pay "reparations" to the black community by contributing money to Panther programs. Negotiations ended the
boycott in early 1972, and although no money ever changed
hands, in Newton's mind the principle was firmly established:
The Panthers were entitled to a piece of the action from businesses selling liquor to the black community.

Now, with the Squad, these payments from bars and clubs
began to look suspiciously like protection money. The amounts
paid by different owners varied, but some clubs were said to
be shelling out as much as $500 a week. Yet none of the
owners was willing to come forth and testify against Newton or
Squad members. It has been a nettling problem over the years
for law enforcement officials. They know what is going on,
the black community knows what is going on, but no one can
do anything about it because victims won't go to the police.

One club owner did have his nephew contact the office of
Representative Ron Dellums (D-Ca.). "The man's uncle had
just opened a bar," says Dellums aide Don Hopkins, "and
he said that it appeared the bar was not going to be successful
because of the extortion demands of the Black Panther Party.
I raised the possibility of going to police, but he discounted
that as a choice."

Newton enjoyed the tough night life in Oakland and Berkeley. He bragged once of being a "two-fisted drinker"—and

he was a two-fisted fighter as well. A lawyer who has worked for the Party says fighting "is one of Newton's forms of recreation—like the fastest gun in the West." His rap sheet bears this out, beginning with his arrest at 16 for beating a schoolmate with a hammer. Newton has subsequently said he used poor judgment ("I was immature then"), but there were other scrapes in the years that followed. (At 22, for example, he stabbed an unarmed youth in the head with a steak knife.) Newton could be particularly violent when crossed, or when he felt himself to be.

This streak of vengefulness would become characteristic of the Squad, too, as those who didn't comply with the extortion demands would learn. There were the fires at the Fox-Oakland Theater in 1973. The first blaze occurred on August 10, the second on December 5. Both were arson, in the opinion of investigators. The estimated property damage came to $89,000.

The fires were set within two days of scheduled rock concerts, promoted by Oakland businessman Ed Bercovich. He had leased the theater from its absentee owners and finally secured an Oakland City Council special permit to put on live entertainment. The city council gave its approval in part because Bercovich had worked out a deal with a local youth group to hire unemployed teenagers in Oakland—a large majority of them black—to clean up the theater, sell tickets and usher.

Newton resented it. The Black Panther Party had once had a subletting arrangement at the Fox-Oakland to show movies. Newton had dreams of taking over the theater and turning it into a cultural center, with the kind of live entertainment that Bercovich had succeeded in lining up. But the theater's owners weren't interested in Newton's plans.

Shortly after one of the Fox fires, Newton intimated to a penthouse visitor that the blaze had been set by the Panthers as retaliation. But he left out another part of the story: Bercovich had refused to pay extortion money to the Party.

Months before the first show was even scheduled, Bercovich says, he was approached by a Panther go-between, the owner of a bar frequented by Newton and his friends. The go-between urged Bercovich to come to some kind of agreement with the Panthers. He offered to set up the meeting, telling Bercovich the Panthers wanted "a piece of the action." And he warned that if a deal wasn't made, not one show would go on—"they would burn the place down," as Bercovich remembers it.

"Everything he said would come true, came true," Bercovich says, shaking his head sadly. "And I had all those kids working for me."

Even as he and the squad acted like thugs, Newton continually tried to conceal his "bad-ass nigger" side from his educated friends, just as he submerged his intellectuality beneath a macho exterior when he sortied out with Squad members to the bars of Oakland. One former intimate characterizes Newton as "schizoid," chiding himself for having taken so long to realize it. "He had different faces for different people," he says. "I never saw him crazy, never saw him brutalize people. I only saw him in his intellectual mode. He'd talk about Zen Buddhism or dialectics. It was always intellectual questions. It's interesting, because I have a non-intellectual friend, and when Huey ran into *him* at a party, the only thing Huey'd talk about was dope, street stuff and fights—like bragging about the last fight he was in. Huey would never talk politics to this guy—ever! With *me,* he never talked about anything else."

Newton managed his image most of all with wealthy or intellectual supporters; and while such people sometimes caught glimpses of the high-handedness with which the Party was run, they told themselves that Newton stood outside such practices. But most of these sympathizers were not around when Newton beat Party members, sometimes ordering Squad members to hold their guns on them when he did. (An eyewitness says that when Newton beat Seale bodyguard Carl Colar, he even ordered Len Colar, Carl's brother, to train his gun on the victim. Newton then pummeled Carl—with fists and a lead pipe.) And most sympathizers did not see the harsh disciplinary actions of the Squad, which over the years included, according to a number of sources, beatings, bull whipping and "mud-holing." (The mud hole, a deep pit dug on the site of the Party's first school in Oakland, was filled with cold water before the Panther being punished was thrown in. When he or she tried to climb out, the others would beat the Panther back down.)

One former Party member traces the severe discipline to the Panthers' sense of themselves as an army at war. In that context, infractions real or imagined had to be dealt with swiftly. But long after the Party abandoned urban guerrilla warfare, the corporal punishment remained.

Few sympathizers saw the cramped dormitories where the Party rank and file lived; they saw only the inside of Newton's apartment, or took tours of the school. There always seemed to be cadres willing to do the work of the Party, but supporters may not have known that many Panthers left over the years, slipping away from Oakland in secrecy, lest they be caught and beaten.

Panther sympathizers may have seen little of this, but to others Newton's erratic side was more visible, and experiencing it tested their activism sorely. Such was the case when Newton single-handedly destroyed a potential chapter of the Party in Texas in early 1974, according to a Bay Area activist who traveled there a year after the incident.

The group in Texas, People's Party II, was a grass-roots organization that operated several enterprises—including a store and a nightclub—to raise money for service projects in the black community. The group was considering becoming a chapter of the Black Panther Party, and Newton, in turn, wanted to bring the Texas business operation under the Panther aegis. So far along was the proposed merger that Newton and a small entourage flew to Texas to inspect the local setup. One of the former leaders of People's Party II told the visiting Bay Area activist that from the start of Newton's visit, the Texas people found his behavior disturbing. It seemed to his hosts that Newton was on drugs.

On Newton's last night in Texas, he met with the group in its nightclub. Decked out in a cape, he strutted around the room screaming, "I am the Supreme Servant!" He made a play for the woman leader of People's Party II, asking her to dance. She told him she was there with someone else. An argument ensued. In the course of the altercation, Newton hit the woman, delivered a severe beating to her escort, and threatened to kill another person who tried to intervene.

The incident ended as quickly as it had begun. Newton

left the bar and headed back to Oakland in the morning. But the woman told the Bay Area activist that the man Newton had beaten flipped out shortly afterward and was still institutionalized—a year later. The woman herself admitted to being so devastated that she had not done anything political since the incident. Moreover, she said, the local party was demoralized and weakened by the startling affair.

This behavior was in sharp contrast to Newton as genial host to scores of luminaries who answered his summons to share fine cognac and long, rambling conversation. Visitors would arrive at Newton's penthouse apartment in Oakland and find themselves ushered into a modern, expensively furnished living room of brown leather couches and stark walls. They would breathe in the heavy scent of gardenias floating in a brandy snifter. And Newton would flatter his guests with attentiveness. "When I was up there," says Alameda County Supervisor John George, a black lawyer boosted into office with Panther support, "*he* would serve me. He'd bring me a drink or a sandwich—and he would fix it himself. He didn't ask Gwen [his secretary] to do it. He would sit sipping Remy Martin and we would talk. He always seemed so happy to have someone to talk with."

Because of Newton's charm, guests such as John George willfully ignored the dark rumors they heard about him. "I like him," George says, shaking his head in a troubled manner. "That is why I may continue to excuse and excuse." Among some of Newton's former intimates, too, there is a tendency to excuse his violence—or even to deny it. Take the case of Bobby Seale, who founded the Party with Newton and Hilliard.

In 1974, Seale, who was then the Party's chairman, reportedly was beaten and had to be treated by a doctor for his injuries. By several accounts, Newton ordered his bodyguards to train their guns on Seale to ensure he didn't fight back while Newton administered the beating. After the attack, Seale left the Party and disappeared from public view, emerging only within the last year to publish a book.

Reached by phone in Philadelphia, where he now lives, Seale denies he was beaten. "It's not true," he says. "The police put out a lot of crap initially. *I've* even heard that off and on, but I don't pay any attention to it. Whoever said that is lying." But it was said by many who were not police, who were in a position to know—including someone who treated his injuries.

"What injuries?" Seale screams into the phone. "I had no injuries whatsoever! I don't give a damn who said it. Tell them I said they're a flat black-ass, motherfucking liar, or a white-assed liar—whoever the hell they are."

Seale's departure came in July 1974, just as Newton, according to the Alameda County district attorney's office, police and various witnesses, was embarking on a bizarre rampage of intermittent violence that would stretch over 18 days. It began on July 30 with a run-in he had with two plainclothes cops in the Fox Lounge in Oakland. Newton accused them of following him simply to harass him. He turned belligerent, the police said, and pointing a finger gun-like at one of the officers, screamed for bodyguard Robert Heard to "shoot him, shoot the pig-ass motherfucker—shoot him!" When Heard slipped his hand into the briefcase he carried, the policemen drew their weapons. Inside the briefcase was a loaded .38 caliber revolver and $1,000 in cash. Heard was busted. Later that night, with other officers for reinforcement, Newton was also arrested, along with Panther heavies Larry Henson and Flores "Fly" Forbes.

It was just the kind of event to jack Newton up. It heightened his paranoia, "made him crazy," as one of his friends says. Six days later Kathleen Smith, a 17-year-old prostitute, and her friend Crystal Gray were standing on an Oakland street corner hustling Johns. There were other prostitutes in the vicinity as well. It was a slow evening, a Monday before midnight. Crystal and Kathleen—or Kathy, as she was called by the other women—smoked a joint together. They were both feeling "mellow," as Crystal later testified at a preliminary hearing, when a big, fancy metallic-colored car cruised by their corner. Crystal hailed the occupants with a "Hey, baby!" The car kept going and stopped at the light. Both women noted with some appreciation that the car was a Mark IV Continental. Ten or fifteen minutes later, Crystal noticed the same car again, parked at the corner on a side street. She saw one of the occupants—"the light-skinned one"—get out.

"Which one of you ladies called me," Crystal later quoted him as saying.

The two women exchanged glances—those "what's-his-trip" expressions—and stepped back, sensing trouble. The man stared hard at them. Suddenly, Crystal said, he lunged forward and struck Kathy. "Her eyes got big," Crystal later recalled, and Kathy stumbled backward. Crystal was angry and said to the man, "Say brother, why did you hit my girl friend? She didn't do nothing to you."

The man's chilling response, she said, was to draw a small silvery gun from his breast pocket. Crystal yelled to Kathy to run, and she herself made for the nearby Ebony Plaza Hotel. Hearing her cries, the other prostitutes, too, ran inside the hotel. All except for Kathy. Crystal went back outside to see what had happened to her friend. As she did, a shot rang out. Rushing to the sidewalk, Crystal saw the same man standing over Kathy's slumping body. The Mark IV slid out of its berth and swung over toward the tableau of a wounded Kathy, held in Crystal's arms. The light-skinned man jumped in the car and it sped off.

Kathy had been shot in the jaw and was unconscious. The trauma from the wound damaged her spinal column and put her in an immediate coma; it was a half-death that lingered for 96 days. When hospital authorities finally decided to move Kathy's inert body to a nursing home to continue life-sustaining treatment, the shock of the move was too great for the small spark of life still left in her. She died.

Three prostitutes identified Huey Newton as the man who pulled the gun on Kathy. One of them was Crystal Gray, and her testimony, authorities believed, would be the most convincing to a jury.

Eleven days after the shooting of Kathleen Smith, two young women stopped in at the Lamp Post, an Oakland bar nominally owned by Newton's cousin Jimmy Ward but run by the Panthers. They ordered hamburgers and then, according to the police statement of one of the women, Helen Robinson, Robert Heard came to the table and began to "get smart" with her friend, Diane Washington. Washington sassed back and it turned mean. Heard whispered something to a "little guy," and the next thing they knew, the "little one" came over and grabbed the other woman, Helen Robinson, by the jacket. He yanked her off her chair, and then he and Heard began pushing her back and forth. They each socked her whenever she came within their grasp. The "little guy" was Huey Newton, the two women said.

According to Robinson's statement, the two men then knocked her to the floor. Eventually someone in the bar—Robinson is not sure who—grabbed her by the collar and threw her into the street. Several times she tried to return to get Washington out, but each time she was rebuffed.

It was seven or eight minutes before Washington managed to escape from the bar. Robinson noted that Washington's lip was "big and bleeding, her jaw was swollen and her eye was kind of black." Robinson said that Washington had actually made her way out of the bar at one point, but that Huey Newton came out after her and "dragged her right back in." The women called police that night, and six days later made a complete report and identified Newton and Heard from a series of 12 photos marked with numbers—no names.

The Lamp Post bar incident had occurred in the early morning, about four A.M. Later that day, in the afternoon, there was more bloodshed, this time in Newton's apartment. The victim was Preston Callins, a handsome, middle-aged, middle-class black tailor. His account of the incident, two days after it happened, was tape recorded by police.

Callins said that three weeks earlier he had been introduced to Newton at the Lamp Post by a mutual friend. The two had met before but didn't really know each other. Callins did know, however, that Newton ordered his clothes from a men's store in San Francisco, and that the store, in turn, farmed its orders out to Callins. Callins told this to Newton in the Lamp Post and suggested they eliminate the middle man—that Callins make Newton's clothes for him directly. Newton agreed, gave Callins his phone number and suggested he give him a call. After trying for several days, Callins finally reached Newton and was invited to come over and measure him for a suit.

The tailor arrived with his materials packed in a sample case. Newton greeted him and began showing him around the penthouse apartment. "He did everything but get down to business," Callins later told police. "He was drinkin' some cognac. I think he paid $19 a bottle for this cognac . . . and he was drinkin' the whole time . . . and drunk as a skunk. Very potent stuff. I asked him to pour me just a little taste. I wanted to see how it tastes, you know." In a show of hospitality, Newton told Callins he would order a bottle of the same cognac for him to take home, and he did so by speaking into an intercom to a woman in another room.

Seated comfortably now in the presence of another man whom Callins said was Newton's brother-in-law or possibly his uncle, the two began to talk. "He says, 'I'll tell you what. Everybody's been rippin' me off, Preston, on getting clothes made,'" Callins recalled. " 'Now, if you give me a full price on a suit, one price,' he said, 'I'll have all of my clothes made from you.' I said, 'I can make you a suit for $180 with my material.' "

But Callins said he never got around to showing Newton the materials in his sample case. "I had a suit that I had on that he kept telling me he didn't like . . . and I said, 'Well, I didn't bring this suit over here for you to like . . . I'll show you some samples.' But he wouldn't let me show him any . . . So he said somethin' like, he said, 'Oh, god-dammit. I've been ripped off! Blah, blah, blah, blah.'

"I said, 'Oh, baby, don't feel that way,' and when I said 'baby,' that's what started the whole thing, because I have a habit of callin' my friends . . . 'baby,' you know—my wife, my brothers, my other friends, I call 'baby,' and he didn't like that.

"He jumps up and he goes buggy. 'Nobody calls me no damn baby.' " Then, Callins said, Newton marched from the dining area where they had been sitting and returned with a .357 revolver. "I'm sitting talking to his brother-in-law across the table," Callins said, "and he [Newton] whacked me . . . I mean a hard blow right across the back of my head while I was sitting at the table. Blood shot everywhere. Then he turned around and whacked me on the other side . . . Then he said, 'I'm gonna shoot you!' And I said, 'Aw, man, you gonna invite me to your home to start some stuff for nothing. What's wrong with you?'

"So he says, 'Uh, man, you called me a baby and I don't like you no way. You're a little bit yellower than I am. I don't like you.' "I said, 'Aw, man, get off of this shit!' So then he hit me again, and he hit me and knocked me on the floor . . . he kicked me in the mouth, and by that time I was tired of being hit. I jumped up and hit him in the mouth . . . knocked him upside the wall . . . by that time I was bleedin'. I was bleedin' a lot . . . I had lost, I bet you, three or four . . . pints of blood. I couldn't be no match for that little youngster there."

Callins managed to make it to the apartment door, unlock it and stumble out into the hallway, but Newton followed. Now he had a different gun. The first was of no use to him any more: The grips, Callins told police, had broken on his head. Callins tried to hide in a small recess of the hallway.

"He says, 'I'm gonna kill you!' He came and he followed me . . . and he made me go back, and by that time I was just bleeding everywhere. By the time I got to his door I just fell on the floor. Blood all down the hall, and all in his apartment. I saw his brother-in-law. I told him, I says, 'You, you must be out of your mind . . . Can't you stop this maniac from doing what he's doin'?' "

The other man tried to calm Newton down. In the meantime, Callins said, Newton had called in two of his bodyguards.

Newton beat him again, according to Callins' statement, and then brought out a tape recorder and tried to pressure Callins into making statements that would exonerate him. "He asked . . . questions like, 'Did you come in my house and molest me?' I said, 'No.' . . . And each time he hit me. Each time he slapped me . . . Boom! . . . He said, 'Didn't you do me wrong in my house?' I says, 'No, I didn't do wrong, I came here in peace. I came to make your clothes . . . you offered me a drink, I took a little shot, and you got drunk, and then you started hittin' me upside the head with your pistol and I couldn't stand it. That's why I hit you back!' "

Callins said the two bodyguards then brought a car around

from the garage. Callins was ordered out of the building. He asked for his sample case, and the "big fellow" (whom he later identified as Robert Heard) retrieved it for him. Oddly, Callins said Newton ordered Heard to get the gift bottle of cognac for Callins to take home. The two bodyguards then ushered Callins downstairs, placed newspaper on the floor of the car (so Callins wouldn't bleed on the carpet) and drove him home. They ordered him out and chucked his sample case onto the sidewalk beside him. As Callins fumbled with his garage door lock, he fainted. His wife called the police and an ambulance.

Callins was taken to Kaiser Hospital in Redwood City, where his four depressed skull fractures required neurosurgery. When police visited him in intensive care to take his statement, Callins told them, "Every time he hit me with that pistol you could hear the bones crash."

In a preliminary hearing last fall, three years later, Alameda County Deputy District Attorney Tom Orloff called Callins to the stand to give testimony against Newton on the pistol-whipping charges. The tailor shocked the courtroom when he said that while he remembered the beating, he could no longer recall the perpetrator. He said his memory loss was a result of the injuries he suffered. Despite the playing in court of his tape-recorded statement to police shortly after the beating, in which he clearly described Newton as the sole assailant, Callins could not be shaken from his testimony. What Callins failed to tell the court, *New Times* has learned, was that he had recently received $6,000 from the Newton side.

Callins refuses to comment on his testimony. When asked about the money, his lawyer, Howard Moore, denies Callins was paid off for his silence. "Anybody has the right to sue anybody in civil court," he fumes, implying that the $6,000 represented settlement of claims Callins had against Newton. Alameda County records, though, show that Callins never filed suit. Sheldon Otis, Newton's lawyer, says that Callins passed along "verbal demands for civil damages for injuries to his person." Beyond that, Otis refuses to comment on the matter. (He was not involved in arranging for the payment.) Howard Moore puts it this way: "Mr. Callins had a claim against Mr.

Newton for personal injuries and that claim has been resolved."

By the end of August 1974, police had filed a variety of felony counts against Newton. There was the assault charge stemming from the Fox Lounge altercation with the plainclothes cops, which was later amended to include charges relating to the shooting of Kathleen Smith, the beating of Preston Callins and the incident with the two young women at the Lamp Post. When Kathleen Smith died nearly three months later, the charges were amended again—to include a murder count.

But Newton was long gone by then. Sources say he had fled to Mexico, and from there, by boat, to Cuba. The Cubans granted him sanctuary on the condition that he keep his nose clean, live modestly and work. Newton agreed.

When Newton failed to show up for a preliminary hearing in late August, Panther lawyer Charles Garry met with reporters to announce that Newton had jumped bail and fled because pimps in Oakland had put out a contract on his life. To prove it, Garry played a tape-recorded phone conversation he had had with then–police chief Charles Gain. Gain had called Garry to say that an underworld source had tipped off police to the contract. But Gain's phone call had actually taken place almost a year before Newton left the country.

As Newton fled to Cuba, it seemed to many in Oakland that the Party was breathing its last gasps. But that judgment was premature. There were to be three years of impressive and previously unimaginable Panther inroads into the Oakland political establishment. This would all occur under Elaine Brown, Newton's successor.

The glamorous, 34-year-old Brown had come to Oakland four years earlier from Los Angeles, where she had interrupted a singing career to work for the Panthers. She was smart, articulate and completely loyal to Newton—qualities that helped her rise quickly through the ranks. With Newton's blessings as he left the country, Brown became chairperson of the Party. Even from Havana he remained Number One, conferring regularly with Brown by telephone—monitored by the CIA—and more private messages delivered by trusted couriers.

But it was Elaine Brown who engineered the Party's sudden acquisition of respectability.

Brown buzzed about Oakland in a red Mercedes and always dressed with the panache of a young woman executive. She had a flair for public relations, using the Panther school, begun under Newton, to gain favorable publicity for the Party and to impress state and county officials. And from Alameda County, the cities of Oakland and Berkeley, the state of California, as well as private donors, she landed a series of service and educational grants for the Party that came to over $300,000. (Part of the grant money funneled into the Party came from the Law Enforcement Assistance Administration [LEAA], and was earmarked for a Panther program to help juvenile delinquents. Bay Area leftists noted with amusement that the LEAA, formed in the days of "law and order" to aid local criminal justice systems, was a favorite agency of the Nixon Administration.)

During Elaine Brown's tenure, Oakland's first black mayor, Lionel Wilson, and Alameda County's first black supervisor, John George, were both helped into office by the crucial campaign support of the Panthers. One year before his election, John George had been Brown's campaign chairman when she herself ran for a seat on the city council in 1975. (She waged an impressive campaign and finished second.) "She got *all* the Democratic groups' endorsements," George says. "They recognized that the Panthers were moving into the legitimate political arena and that it was better to work with them than against them." In previous Panther attempts at public office, most Democratic politicians had been skittish about forming alliances with a Party that had Newton at the helm. In Newton's absence, the way was open for cooperation and trade-offs.

Elaine Brown's rapport with politicians didn't stop at the Alameda County line. In 1976 she went to the Democratic National Convention as a Jerry Brown delegate, and the governor couldn't have failed to notice that when nearly all of his other California delegates had switched their votes to Jimmy Carter (in a show of unity once his nomination was assured), Elaine Brown remained steadfast in voting for him. Perhaps that is why the governor agreed to see her when she came to Sacramento to lobby for completion of the Grove Shafter Freeway in Oakland, a project stalled by his freeze on highway construction funds. Speaking on behalf of an ad hoc organization formed largely by Republican businessmen in Oakland, Elaine Brown argued that without the Grove Shafter Freeway, a huge downtown development planned for Oakland would not be built. Thousands of jobs were at stake, she said, and she had won a guarantee from the development's backers that a percentage of the jobs would go to hard-pressed minorities.

"She said she didn't give a damn about the freeways, all she wanted was the jobs," says J. Anthony Kline, legal affairs secretary to the governor, who attended the meeting. "She was very convincing. We did what she wanted done. We agreed to complete the freeway."

But despite the high regard in which she was held by officials in Oakland and Sacramento, there were others who quietly referred to Elaine Brown as the "Dragon Lady." Sources say she had a pronounced vengeful streak. A local television reporter, for example, says Brown (who was then press spokeswoman for the Party) called him after he had broken the story of Bobby Seale's disappearance and "resignation." The reporter says Brown told him, "We know who you are, and if you come to Oakland, you're in trouble." After that, he says, he stopped pursuing the Seale story and has not wanted to cover the Panthers since.

Elaine Brown's precise relationship to the Squad is not clear. It is known, though, that the group continued its criminal activities during her administration. And there are no reports that she moved against it. Some Squad members served as her bodyguards; but unlike Newton, Brown did not tour the streets and bars with the Squad on shake-down runs.

During Newton's three-year absence, there were a series of robberies, shootings and murders that police regard as the work of the Squad. Other sources close to the Panthers share that belief. Witnesses in most of these cases refused to make formal identifications; in others, identifications were impossible because the assailants wore ski masks.

All of the cases are unsolved, save one murder for which

a Panther, George Robinson, was convicted. (The conviction was later reversed because of an illegal police search.) But Oakland and Berkeley police, who are careful not to simply list any unsolved crime as Panther-related, see Squad involvement in the following cases:

- Tommy Jackson was a doorman at The Brass Rail, a Berkeley after-hours bar operating as a "private social club" and regarded in the surrounding community as a headquarters at the time for cocaine dealers. At 6 A.M. on August 27, 1974, the 19-year-old Jackson was admitting a customer when a car pulled to the curb and several black men inside opened fire with shotguns. Jackson was killed and several customers in the bar were wounded. Club owner Wilbert La Tour had reportedly balked at Squad demands for money, although he denied it to the police. Case still unsolved.

  The Brass Rail was the scene of two other murders. Willie Ralph Duke, 24, was a heroin dealer who, police informants said, was making payoffs to the Squad. He had reportedly missed a payment because he had lost the money gambling. While Duke was drinking at The Brass Rail on January 25, 1975, with three Panthers and club owner La Tour, Billy Carr approached Duke and suggested they step outside. Police have theorized that the 21-year-old Carr was attempting to warn Duke that he was going to be killed. As both men began to walk away from the bar, say witnesses, the three Panthers suddenly pulled guns. Two of them opened fire and shot Duke. Carr tried to stop them and was also shot. Both men died. Neither La Tour, who saw the shooting, nor the other witnesses would name the three gunmen. Case unsolved.

  La Tour himself was found murdered four months later. Oakland police, acting on a tip that he was dead, went to La Tour's apartment and found his car gone. A week later another tip was received that La Tour's car could be found in the San Francisco International Airport garage with his dead body inside. It was. Long dead. The body had been stuffed head-first into a sleeping bag and jammed into the trunk of the car. Case unsolved.

- On April 26, 1975, Vernon McInnis, a dope dealer known on the streets as "Preacher Man," was gunned down by two shotgun blasts and five .45 caliber shots. Several days before his murder, McInnis had been approached in the Lamp Post to buy a copy of the Panther newspaper. He refused, reportedly saying that the Panthers "rip people off." The remark led to an argument with Panthers Robert Heard and George Robinson, both Squad members. McInnis was bounced from the bar and killed several days later. George Robinson was convicted of the murder, but the conviction was reversed because police had improperly conducted their search of his car when he was arrested. (The district attorney's office is appealing the reversal.) Although the motive established at the trial was the Lamp Post altercation, several sources familiar with the case believe the killing had much more to do with drug-related payoffs to Panthers.
- Two other shootings involving shotguns were thought to be the work of Panthers because the spent shells found at the scenes had markings almost identical to those in the McInnis case. Police could not act on the evidence, though, because there were no eyewitnesses (as there were in the McInnis case) and because shotgun casing marks are not as specific as those from hand guns. One case involved Philip Cole, an owner of the Black Knight bar. Cole was reported to have been the victim of Panther extortion, although he angrily denies it. On September 12, 1974, he was shot at on the street. (The bullets missed.) Cole could not identify his assailants. In the other case, a week before the Vernon McInnis murder, two men were shot soon after leaving the Lamp Post. Willie White lost both an arm and a leg in the shotgun blast, and James Harris died from the wounds he received in the back of the head. Both men had been in an argument with a Lamp Post cocktail waitress that had widened to include others. Case unsolved.
- In February 1975, one dope dealer was robbed at his home by two armed blacks in ski masks, and another dealer was kidnapped by three black men and killed. Police suspect the Panthers because of reports that both men were being shaken down by the Squad.

Finally, there is the still unexplained murder of Betty Van Patter, the Party's attractive, 45-year-old white bookkeeper. She was a Berkeley liberal who dabbled in the more faddish aspects of the occult, but was nevertheless described by a former associate as "a first-rate bookkeeper, very responsible."

Van Patter landed her job in the summer of 1974. She was hired originally to keep books for the Panther school, but her duties expanded soon after to include bookkeeping for the Party itself and for the Lamp Post bar. Although pleased to be working for the Panthers, Van Patter told some friends that the Lamp Post was not paying its taxes, and that money was taken directly out of the cash register and passed along to Party members. Van Patter was known to be fastidious about her work, and she didn't like going along with accounting procedures she considered shaky.

Betty Van Patter disappeared on Friday, December 13, 1974, after having stopped in at one of her favorite Berkeley bars. She had entered alone, say acquaintances, and was unusually quiet. Several people who were in the bar recall that a black man came in, handed her a note and then left. Van Patter left the bar, alone, at about 9:30 P.M. and was never seen alive again. Her corpse was found 35 days later, floating in San Francisco Bay. Probable cause of death, said the coroner's report, was "a powerful blow to the skull." Death had been immediate.

It is not known whether the Panthers had anything to do with Van Patter's murder. But there are indications that Elaine Brown had grown irritated with the Party's bookkeeper. Asked about Van Patter after her disappearance, Brown angrily described her to a Panther colleague as an "idiot" and "stupid," charging that Van Patter wouldn't come to work if the "moon was out of phase." But her biggest complaint about Van Patter was that she was inquisitive, and vocal in her complaints about irregularities in the Party ledgers. "Betty wanted to know too much of everything," Elaine Brown confided. "And she was getting into the Lamp Post." In response, Brown told the colleague, she fired Van Patter. "I was scared of her getting into my [city council] campaign books and all the other stuff," Brown said. "She started asking about where money was going.

She started telling me about why Jimmy's taxes need to be paid." (Jimmy Ward, Huey Newton's cousin, is the owner of the Lamp Post.)

Van Patter's murder could not have come at a worse time for Elaine Brown, who was then running for the Oakland City Council. Four days after the body was found, police questioned Brown in the office of Panther lawyer Charles Garry. She insisted she had terminated Betty Van Patter's employment on December 6—a full week before Van Patter's disappearance. Brown produced "copies" of Van Patter's severance check, work record and notice of termination to support her claims.

But Fred Hiestand, a lawyer who has done work for the Party, told police he had seen Van Patter on Tuesday, December 10—on Panther business. The day after he saw Van Patter, Hiestand saw Elaine Brown. He told police Brown announced to him at that time her *intention* of firing Van Patter at the next opportunity.

If the discrepancies in Brown's statements had become public knowledge, her campaign could have collapsed. But none of it leaked. And the case is still unsolved.

As Elaine Brown ran the Party in Oakland (with the Panthers' new-found respectability untarnished by the violence police link to the squad), Huey Newton cooled his heels in Cuba. He had no particular desire to assimilate into the socialist society around him, Cuban sources say. Newton held no regular job; he hung out. And he closely watched developments in the United States (a Democrat in the White House, disclosures of FBI illegalities involving Panthers) and, of course, developments in Oakland. He picked his time—last summer— and returned to stand trial for the murder of Kathleen Smith and the beating of Preston Callins.

Newton must have been heartened by the favorable publicity that greeted his return. The press played up to him, dutifully recording his praise of the Cubans and his charges of police and FBI harassment of the Party. But while he may have been winning a public relations battle, his trial loomed ahead as a much tougher fight. Crystal Gray, the eyewitness to the Kathleen Smith shooting, was still firm in her identification

of Newton as the killer, despite her admission that she suffered
from night blindness and was high on marijuana at the time
of the shooting.

Then came "Richmond"—the shorthand way that people
in the Bay Area now refer to the frightening incident of October
23, 1977. After Richmond, the Party would begin quickly to
crumble.

On that night last October, Mary Matthews, a 56-year-old
black woman, was having trouble sleeping. Lying awake in
bed, she heard someone tampering with the front door of her
home in Richmond, California, 15 miles north of Oakland.
It was about five A.M.

"Who is it?" she yelled.

No response. She thought whoever it was had gone away.

But a short time later she heard someone pulling on the
screen door in the rear of her house. Mary Matthews called,
"Who is it? What do you want?" There was no answer. The
noises continued.

Quickly then, she leaped out of bed—although usually she
is slow and considered in her movements. She retrieved her
.38 revolver and, without wasting a gesture, dialed Richmond
police. While holding the phone she heard the sudden sound
of ripping metal and realized the screen door had been torn
completely off its hinges.

Someone was out to kill her. It had to be that, she thought,
because there was so little in the house that anyone would
want to steal.

As she recited her address to the police the first shot was
fired outside. The lock, she thought, he's shooting off the lock.
She dropped the telephone receiver on the floor, pointed the
gun at the back door and fired. The very act of firing the
gun she had kept for so long, but never used, panicked her
further—that, and a fusillade of return fire, the muzzle flashes
coming through the doorway and lighting up her kitchen. She
ran to a small room in the rear of her house to hide, locking
the door behind her. Cowering in there behind the furniture,
it seemed forever before she heard the crackling of police radios
that indicated she might finally be safe.

Outside Mary Matthews' door was a pool of blood and a

12-gauge shotgun. On the sidewalk lay the dead body of a black man. From the trail of smeared blood, police could tell the man had been dragged and then dropped; and the blood went beyond the dead body, indicating another assailant had been wounded. In searching the area along the Richmond ghetto street, a block of corrugated metal warehouses interspersed with a few houses and vacant lots, police found a second shotgun, an automatic rifle and ammunition. They also found discarded clothing similar to that worn by the dead man. From these items, police surmised there were at least three assailants, and that the discarded blue overalls and watch caps were probably donned to be shed after the killing in order to make eyewitness identification difficult. It was a cold, planned murder attempt.

But why Mary Matthews? It didn't make sense. What would anyone have against this middle-aged mother and grandmother who worked as a bookkeeper out of her own modest home?

The answer came from the pink clapboard house directly behind Mary Matthews'. She owns that house as well, renting its two apartments to single mothers with children. One of the women was dark-skinned and pretty, barely five feet tall. She approached the police and said she was the one the gunmen had come to kill, not Mary Matthews. She identified herself as Raphaelle Gary—known on the streets as Crystal Gray.

Newton was due in court the very next day, October 24, for a preliminary hearing in the Kathleen Smith murder case. Crystal Gray was also scheduled to be there to testify against him. (The charges involving the altercation with plainclothes cops at the Fox Lounge and the beating of the two young women at the Lamp Post were eventually reduced to misdemeanors and severed from the Smith and Preston Callins cases. All charges are still pending. The Smith-Callins trial will probably begin in August or September.)

It was hours before Richmond police verified the fingerprints of the body in blue overalls outside Mary Matthews' house. The dead man was Louis T. Johnson, a 27-year-old Black Panther who lived in Berkeley in a house with other Party members. In a preliminary autopsy performed later that day, a bullet was removed from the back of Johnson's skull. Mary

Matthews was blameless—it was not her gun that had shot him. Johnson had been hit accidentally by one of his fellow assailants.

It was a botch. They had attacked the wrong house—and they failed to kill anyone but one of their own. Moreover, another of the assailants had been wounded in the hand, judging by one of the gloves police found on the scene: It was ripped and bloodied.

What had happened in Richmond was not publicly revealed until the following morning, when Deputy District Attorney Tom Orloff broke the bizarre news in Oakland's Municipal Court. In an outraged voice, Orloff called the incident in Richmond a "planned assassination" attempt of the "most important witness" in his case against Newton. Orloff linked the dead assailant to Newton, saying among other things that Johnson had recently visited Newton when he was briefly jailed after returning from Cuba. But outside the courtroom—free on $80,000 cash bail—Newton denied any involvement in, or knowledge of, the Richmond affair, hinting at nefarious doings by the police. "At this point I wouldn't be surprised if the police set anything up," he said. He claimed not to know Louis Johnson. (Crystal Gray was given police protection and began her testimony later that week.)

Newton's suggestions of a police setup looked unlikely when, four days later, it was revealed that Flores Forbes—a Squad member arrested with Newton at the Fox Lounge—had sought emergency treatment at an Oakland hospital for a gunshot wound in the hand consistent with the torn, bloody glove found in Richmond.

Forbes arrived at the hospital with his hand bandaged, using an old music book as a crude splint. Unwrapping the bandages, the attending physician saw that the whole back of Forbes' hand had been torn away. Forbes told the doctor he had been injured in an industrial accident with a rivet gun. The man who accompanied Forbes, Panther Nelson Malloy, backed his story, but the doctor knew a bullet wound when he saw one, and said he would have to report it to the police. At that, the two men fled the hospital.

Publicity about Richmond was potentially so damaging to

Newton's case, and the Party itself, that Newton finally agreed to meet with two reporters. Looking thinner than before he left for Cuba, Newton was attractively decked out in a pin-striped three-piece suit donned for a courtroom appearance earlier that day. He tried to convince the reporters that Panther Flores Forbes was only peripherally connected to the Party, but local newspapers had already revealed that Forbes was on the payroll of a Panther youth service program and was intimately involved in some of the Party's violent activities.

Sipping cognac, Newton conceded that the gunmen may have been "overzealous and figured that they would hunt down a witness." But he nevertheless denied that he or the Party were involved. He insisted that both Johnson and Forbes had quit the Party "a few weeks before the trial started. I don't remember exactly what date." But in any event, Newton said, they were no longer Panthers at the time of the Richmond attack.

A few days after that interview, several tourists in the Nevada desert about 40 miles from Las Vegas heard a moaning sound a few yards off the road. Then they noticed a man's feet sticking out from under a pile of rocks. The tourists snapped a Polaroid picture of the shallow grave and brought it to local rangers, who rushed to the site and unearthed a seriously wounded black man, buried alive and left for dead. He had been shot twice and was paralyzed from the neck down.

When Las Vegas police questioned him in the hospital, the man gave a fake name and said he had been robbed and shot while hitchhiking; eventually, though, he admitted to police that he was Nelson Malloy, the man who had accompanied Flores Forbes to the Oakland hospital the day after the Richmond assault. The story Malloy finally told sounded like something out of the annals of the Mafia—loyal soldiers turning on other loyalists when ordered from above.

Forbes, Malloy said, had come to his house after the attempt on Mary Matthews' life. Malloy had only recently arrived in Oakland, summoned by Newton bodyguard Robert Heard. Before that, Malloy had worked in the Panthers' small Winston-Salem, North Carolina, chapter to set up a free ambulance service for poor blacks in the community. He was dedicated, a believer. After moving west, Malloy went to work at the Party's free health clinic in Berkeley, impressing clinic personnel with his diligence and aptitude.

Perhaps Forbes went to Malloy for help because of his paramedic skills. Malloy bandaged Forbes's shattered hand and wrapped it in the music book splint, but his medical experience was insufficient and he knew it. He told Forbes that surgery was necessary, and that he could not perform it.

It was then that the two men went to the hospital in Oakland, only to flee in fear that the doctor would turn them in. According to Malloy's account to police, they remained in hiding until Oakland Panther Rollin Reid drove them to the airport the next day. Forbes and Malloy took a Western Airlines flight to Las Vegas. There they were met by Panther Allen Lewis, who drove Forbes to a Las Vegas hospital where he was treated under a phony name. Malloy told police that both Reid and Lewis arrived several days later at his hotel room with "orders" to drive him to Houston because Las Vegas was getting "too hot." Malloy dutifully climbed in the back of a rented van and the three left Las Vegas.

About 45 minutes later, Malloy said, Reid and Lewis stopped the van for a "rest break." Malloy said he was standing beside the van when the two men pulled pistols and shot him in the back and left arm. He dropped to the ground but remained conscious while they dragged him off the roadway and piled rocks on top of him.

Malloy believes—and police in the Bay Area agree—that Flores Forbes was executed by Lewis and Reid. Police describe the shooting of Malloy and the probable murder of Forbes as a "house-cleaning" effort to prevent any possible implication of Panther higher-ups who may have ordered the Richmond assassination attempt. Lewis and Reid, being sought for the shooting of Malloy, have disappeared.

Much of the support for Huey Newton prior to Richmond began to seriously erode when the dead gunman outside Mary Matthews' home proved to be Panther Louis Johnson. The chilling account told by the permanently paralyzed Nelson Malloy about Forbes, Lewis and Reid seemed to confirm the Party's involvement in Richmond. And when the Bay Area press heavily covered Malloy's release from the Las Vegas hospital, in a wheelchair, and his return home to a Winston-Salem hospital ward aboard a plane chartered by his aggrieved family and old friends, the Panthers had never looked worse. Alameda County Supervisor John George, for example, a long-time Newton supporter, was deeply troubled by the direction the Party had taken.

But suddenly there was another blow, and it had the potential to harm Newton and the Party in the local political arena as much as the Richmond and Malloy incidents: Party chairperson Elaine Brown had disappeared.

The disappearance triggered rumors that Brown might be dead. She wasn't, but there were other accounts that she had been physically beaten in a climactic power struggle with Newton after his return. So persistent were these reports that in Los Angeles (where Brown had reportedly fled after a speedy exodus from her Oakland apartment in the middle of the night), police circulated to local hospitals a description of her alleged injuries—severe swelling of one eye and a broken nose.

Nearly a month after her disappearance, Brown's letter of resignation from the Party was finally made public in the Bay Area press. Saying her decision to quit was "made with Huey's understanding," she wrote of "unhappiness in personal matters . . . My mental and physical strength, after 10 years, were waning, in fact nearly collapsing." A doctor who has treated Party members says, however, that colleagues in Los Angeles told him that Brown did receive the injuries described in police circulars, and that she was treated for them. (Repeated attempts to reach Elaine Brown were unsuccessful. She did not respond to messages left for her at an office in Los Angeles where she is reportedly editing film scripts and writing songs.)

The theories surrounding Brown's sudden departure have run the gamut from unrequited love for Newton (who married his long-time secretary, Gwen Fontaine, in Cuba) to opposition to the Richmond assassination attempt, to the reassertion of male dominance of the Party now that Newton had returned. But whatever the reason, her resignation, along with Newton's return and the Richmond attack, began to signal the end of

the Party's era of legitimacy. Richmond, especially, was a jolt
to many sympathizers, who now found it impossible to over-
look reports of Panther brutality.

The Party's problems were soon compounded by disclosures
that Panthers had mismanaged investments and government
grants. The grants had been administered by an offshoot of
the nonprofit Educational Opportunities Corporation (EOC).
This offshoot, the EOC Service Corporation, was created under
Elaine Brown's leadership to run the Party's school. One man
formerly close to the Panthers says that funds channeled
through the EOC Service Corporation were used to "keep
the Squad sweet," meaning to establish steady income and
fringe benefits for the heavies. This was confirmed in part by
a newspaper account that grant dollars approved for Panther
programs paid the rent for Robert Heard and Squad member
Larry Henson in an expensive apartment on Oakland's Lake
Shore Avenue. Oakland *Tribune* reporters Pearl Stewart and
Lance Williams broke that story and also reported that Heard
and Henson, as well as Flores Forbes and another Panther
facing serious charges, were all on the payrolls of the Party's
grant-funded projects.

When he learned of the Panthers' financial irregularities last
fall, Oakland Mayor Lionel Wilson resigned from the board
of the Party's school, where he had served even before his
election. A city audit of publicly funded Panther programs,
meanwhile, showed a wide pattern of irregularities. (For example, investigators could find no evidence that Panthers on the
programs' payrolls were even "physically in attendance," although their paychecks were cashed, bearing signatures that
looked like possible forgeries to city auditors.) These irregularities might have been overlooked, or allowed to be rectified
by the Party, were it not for the controversy surrounding Newton and the Richmond affair. Eventually, when the city council
voted to cancel Oakland's contracts with the Panthers, the
move was uncontested. (Mayor Wilson abstained because of
his former board position.) Some in Oakland think the city
council action still might not have been so drastic if the Panthers had not, on one particular application for school grants,
listed Newton as the head of the EOC. "It was just plain

stupid of the Party," one observer says. "They should have kept Huey completely out of it."

Mismanagement and misappropriation are old charges against the Panthers when it comes to money. One doctor who formerly worked at the Party's free health clinic says bitterly that "the clinic always came last." Funds awarded to the health facility by the City of Berkeley "were frequently siphoned off and used for other projects, like Bobby Seale's campaign for mayor [of Oakland in 1973]," the doctor says.

Amazingly, the Party has maintained a steady flow of money over the years, despite grumblings from some supporters that money went only to the highest echelon of the Party, and that Newton let other members rot in jail while he and ranking Panthers always made bail.

Considering all the money donated to the Panthers, the Party by now could have been financially solid if there had been careful investment and moderate spending. But there wasn't. "They could have been big, real big, as rich as the Muslims," one former supporter says. "But they blew it. They were always fucking up with money." Several weeks ago, the IRS put a $200,000 lien against the now-defunct Stronghold Consolidated Productions, Inc., the New York–based Panther corporation set up to handle the flow of money from Newton's books. The corporation, which also purchased real estate for the Party, was accused by the IRS of not paying its corporate taxes from 1971 to 1973. There is even some indication that the IRS might hold Newton personally accountable for the money. If he or the Party as a whole must pay the lien, it could well bankrupt both.

Now there is no one left in the Party with any power to challenge Newton's supremacy. The identification of the Panthers with Newton and Newton alone is complete. "I am we," he has sometimes said, and one suspects he sees himself as inseparable from the Party. What he does, Newton has written, he does in the name of all black people.

But what he has done, in fact, is to destroy the Party he created. The grants are gone now. The clinic and school still have their doors open, but the Panther newspaper has published only intermittently in recent months. Each week brings more defections from the already decimated Party. They often take place unnoticed, but the impact is great—as when newspaper editor Michael Fultz quietly slipped out of town in May. It was people like Fultz who did the back-breaking legitimate work of the Party. Now, what remains is an isolated Huey Newton, surrounded by his muscle and his lawyers.

New Times recently asked Newton for an interview but he declined. He would grant one, he said, if this story concerned the Panther school—and only the school.

Even as Newton awaits trial on the Smith-Callins charges, violence continues to swirl around him and the Party. At 4 A.M. on a Sunday in late March—two days after an Alameda County board recommended to the Oakland City Council that grant money for the Panthers be cut off—a $5,000 Datsun 260 Z belonging to Oakland *Tribune* reporter Pearl Stewart was fire-bombed. Two hours earlier, a separate fire had been set in a boxcar next to a *Tribune* warehouse. The door of the boxcar had been pried open and the newsprint stored inside torched.

Stewart had been writing articles critical of the Panthers for months. Coincidentally, she lived in the apartment building where Panthers Henson and Heard had lived until it was revealed (in one of her stories) that their apartment was paid for with EOC grant money. Stewart says the locks on the security garage, where her car was parked, had not been changed since Heard and Henson moved out. (Although she points out that the garage could be entered without a resident key if someone were intent upon doing so.) The fire-bombing incident was a chilling reminder of Richmond, and it was not lost on the Oakland City Council, which acted the following day to halt *all* funds for the Panthers.

Newton spends much of his time these days in Santa Cruz, where he is working toward a doctorate at the University of California. He is in a program called "History of Consciousness." Enrolling at Santa Cruz shortly after returning from Cuba helped bolster his public image; and Newton also scored points by landing an appointment in February as a student teacher at Merritt College, a nonpaying job that will count toward his Ph.D. (Newton's brother Melvin runs the school's liberal arts department.) It didn't matter that Newton showed up late for his first class, looking and sounding as if he had a hangover (he had been celebrating his 36th birthday the night before). It mattered only that the job carried respectability.

But even as he pursues his Ph.D. there are reports that Newton has returned to his old routines. Once again he is said to be frequenting the bars in Oakland and Berkeley, accompanied by Squad members. And once again stories of extortion demands are making the rounds. "He's back to his same old stuff," one source says, "hitting up the clubs, the pimps and the dope dealers." Not all of the barroom sorties involve extortion. On May 11, in the small town of Seacliff, 20 miles south of Santa Cruz, Newton and Robert Heard got into a barroom fight with a 26-year-old white, Kenny Hall. The sheriffs' office has been unable to reconstruct the events precisely but has determined that during the fight at least one handgun was drawn and at least two shots were fired. Heard and Newton were both seen with a gun, according to the sheriffs' office. Hall was unarmed. Afterward, Newton and Heard fled the bar but were arrested later that night. Kenny Hall was treated for a minor head injury, suffered when he was knocked into a glass divider.

Police in the Bay Area find the situation frustrating. Their hands are tied because victims and witnesses will rarely step forward to testify against Newton or his friends. Police cite the recent incident at the Cafe D'Elegance, an after-hours club in Berkeley. Newton was there, making his rounds, when a pimp reportedly accosted him and complained about the shake-downs of his women. Newton, said one witness, ordered his bodyguards to draw their guns. No one was permitted to leave while Newton ranted and lectured his captive audience on political theory for about a half-hour. But nobody in the club that night ever pressed charges.

Undoubtedly, much of the reluctance to testify against Newton stems from fear. But there is also a lingering feeling among some blacks and white radicals that Newton was once an important leader in the fight for equality, and that sending him to prison would serve the interests of racists.

The Seacliff brawl made local headlines and prompted Deputy District Attorney Tom Orloff back in Oakland to ask that Newton's bail in the Smith-Callins case be raised from $80,000 (which Newton had posted in cash) to $200,000. (Panther watchers were already amazed at the speed with which Newton had raised the $50,000 cash bail for the Seacliff incident.) After several days, the judge in the Smith-Callins case set an additional cash bail for Newton at $75,000. Newton showed up in court on May 19, the day the bail decision was to be handed down, with a slew of supporters from the Party, including Panther school children, to face the crowd of reporters. At his side was his wealthy, long-time supporter, Hollywood producer Bert Schneider. Newton was placed in custody for a scant 15 minutes before the extra $75,000 surety bond came through. When it did, he was released. (On June 15, news broke that Newton's lawyer, Sheldon Otis, had bowed out of the case and been replaced by Michael Kennedy, a close friend of Schneider's.)

Now it appears to be a waiting game all around. The police, stymied by reluctant witnesses, won't move against Newton without solid evidence, for there is sensitivity about Panther cries of police harassment. Besides, law enforcement officials believe they have a solid case against Newton on the current charges, and that he will be put away. Victims of continuing Panther extortion are also waiting. Their attitude is, Why bother doing something about it now? Why risk trouble when it will be resolved in the courts? Huey will be convicted, and the rest of them will be too weak to continue.

But some believe that Newton will do anything to avoid prison, despite his boast years ago that he could do hard time because there was a side of him that liked solitude. These observers believe Newton will jump bail and leave the country once again—although it is not certain whether Cuba would receive him so readily this time.

And there are others who think Newton is intent on self-destruction, on going down in a blaze of glory. Look at the titles of his books, they say—*To Die for the People* and *Revolutionary Suicide.*

Behind the Story

By the mid-1970s, there were dozens of journalists in the San Francisco Bay Area who knew enough details about the Black Panther party's seamy underside to write a story. But no one wanted to. A sort of conspiracy of silence had grown up around the Panthers. Some of the reporters who covered their activities were so impressed by their achievements that they felt justified in ignoring their problems. Others worried that any attempt to look into the rumors of murders, drug deals, and other crimes committed by certain Panthers would be labeled a police-inspired hatchet job. Beyond this was an even greater fear—that if the rumors proved true, reporters might be placing their lives on the line to do the story.

Under the circumstances it was going to take an extraordinary journalist to do the Panther story—somebody not only exceptionally brave but also thick-skinned enough to endure the criticism from friends and colleagues that would inevitably follow. Somebody like Kate Coleman.

By her own admission, Coleman loves to create a scene—a sort of one-person political street theater. At a radical-chic reception for Jane Fonda, for instance, Coleman showed up wearing a construction helmet and jumpsuit. While a reporter at *Newsweek* in 1968, she refused to shake hands with presidential candidate Hubert Humphrey when he visited the magazine, calling him a "war criminal."

When it comes to her journalism, freelancer Coleman is equally brash. For a piece on hookers, she went out and tried hooking. To write a psychological portrait of a beauty contest winner, Coleman took Miss America out to dinner and found out that she didn't like men. During an interview with Eldridge Cleaver, she asked him the question, "Do you beat your wife?" and somehow got him to answer "Yes." More important, she also got him to admit that he and Bobby Hutton had ambushed the Oakland police in their famous 1968 shoot-out. Whatever it takes to do a story the way she thinks it has to be done, Coleman does it. And in every story, along with the flair, is considerable substance.

In the fall of 1977, *Politicks* magazine, a soon-to-be-defunct

publication based in New York, asked Coleman to write a profile
of Panther leader Elaine Brown. Attractive, powerful, radical, black,
and a woman—Brown had all the attributes for what Coleman
calls a "fluff piece."

But Coleman rebelled. "I told them [the editors] I wouldn't do
it because I'd heard some awful things about the Panthers—things
that nobody wanted to publicize."

To her surprise, *Politicks* responded with a challenge: "Why don't
you do *that* piece?" The magazine was calling her bluff.

Hesitantly, with atypical caution, Coleman began asking around.
In a Berkeley café she chanced upon someone whom, through
mutual friends, she knew she could trust. This person had had
years of direct contact with Panther leaders and had recently become
disillusioned over their use of violence.

"It was the bitterness and cynicism that I heard from this and
other sources that intrigued me," Coleman explains. "They were
hinting that there were all kinds of terrible things—murders and
so on. They were terrified to give me specific information, yet they
desperately wanted the story to come out. I think that when anybody
involved in news catches that tone from a source, it's just
irresistible."

Coleman realized the story would require time and money beyond
what *Politicks* could offer, so she decided to try to sell the piece
to a better-financed magazine. But first she had to overcome another
barrier.

"I didn't want to do this story alone. I felt the insecurity of
being a white person leveling a finger at black people." So she
began to look for a black partner.

An old friend, Carolyn Craven, a black reporter then working
for the local public television station, agreed to help. And a black
reporter for a small left-wing journal said he also would join the
team.

Coleman's partners both understood the political sensitivities of
doing the Panther story. Many former and current party supporters
would denounce their effort as a return to the racism that has so
often characterized reporting on black activists in the past. Like
Coleman, both partners had been activists themselves.

For her part, Coleman's political activism had always combined the serious with the humorously dramatic. She had been a leader of the Free Speech Movement while a student at the University of California in Berkeley in the early 1960s and had also been deeply involved in the antiwar and civil rights movements. Later, while living in New York, she had been a Yippie—one of the political pranksters led by Abbie Hoffman and Jerry Rubin.

But Coleman always had a serious side as well, and this helped her land the job at *Newsweek* in 1965. Throughout twenty years of journalism and activism, Coleman says she has held to one strong belief—that "racism is the ugliest thing about America." It was the unique combination of iconoclastic courage and sensitivity to both the good and the bad sides of the Panthers that made Coleman the perfect person to do the story she now felt had to be done.

She had written about the group before. In 1974 she sold a profile of Huey Newton to the *New York Times Magazine.* It was a "glowing" feature, but it was never published. The *Times* held the piece for eight months and then killed it. Soon afterward, Newton's legal troubles started compounding—the murder charge following the death of seventeen-year-old prostitute Kathleen Smith, the beating of tailor Preston Callins, the fights in bars with undercover narcs and various women. Nevertheless, Newton remained a hero to most of the Left. Panther sympathizers reacted knee-jerk style to each new charge against Newton, labeling it a police setup.

Coleman, however, believed that "you can't cover up forever; you can't perpetuate a myth based on lies. Somebody simply had to do this story." She was motivated by more than the crimes. She had heard reports that Newton was mistreating his "young, idealistic followers." Coleman felt such treatment was a "murder of the spirit."

Coleman and Craven approached the Center for Investigative Reporting for help. "We wanted 'how-to' help and psychological support," Coleman says. "I'd never done anything of this sort before."

The Center's role in the investigation quickly expanded. Within weeks, Coleman's partners had drifted away. As the mother of young children, Craven felt especially vulnerable to any possible violent reprisals. Her early research on the Panthers convinced her that some members of the group were easily capable of assaults on people they didn't like.

During this time Coleman's house was burglarized twice. The first time her television was taken. The second time her entire house was ransacked, and the door to a file cabinet containing all her notes for the story was left open. Although she felt certain that the burglaries were not Panther-related, Coleman also knew that Newton knew she was working on her story. The break-ins, therefore, made her acutely aware of how vulnerable she would be to a Richmond-style assault on her home.* Meanwhile, her male colleague also left the reporting team, and Coleman was once again alone.

Center staff members had heard the rumors about Panther crimes and decided that the Panther story needed telling. Staff writer Paul Avery, a veteran investigative reporter, agreed to join Coleman in her investigation.

Avery was a brand-new kind of partner for Coleman: soft-spoken, in his mid-forties, and the divorced father of two teenaged daughters. Avery lived alone on his houseboat in Sausalito across the bay from San Francisco. He had covered the police beat for the *San Francisco Chronicle* for three years. There he developed excellent sources that he maintained for years after. Before joining the Center staff in October 1977, he co-authored *The Voices of Guns,* a book about the Symbionese Liberation Army and Patricia Hearst.

In contrast to Coleman, Avery had not been a sympathizer of the Panthers, though he did not oppose them either. He hadn't been politically active. But he brought a nuts-and-bolts knowledge about working with official sources to get documentation of criminal activities, and this was a skill that was needed to make the Panther story a success. Twenty-two years of newspaper reporting had given Avery the contacts and instincts necessary to judge whether he was getting "good information" or some kind of police "plant." There were few reporters with his kind of savvy around; fewer still willing to tackle the Panther project.

For any reporter there are special risks in working with law enforcement sources. They have custody of exclusive, derogatory

---

* This incident, as described in the story, had only recently occurred.

information about people, and some police officials are tempted to abuse their power by using reporters to help convict criminals or damage enemies. Avery, however, knew how to sift out the bad police information from the solid.

For Coleman, acquiring a police source was a new experience. The former Yippie started by calling the Oakland police department and asking for a meeting. When she arrived at the department's downtown headquarters, she found three men waiting for her: "a guy from vice, a captain, and an undercover cop." The three told her that the department would not cooperate in any way with her inquiry. Instead they grilled her, suspicious of her intentions and her activist past.

By the time the session ended, Coleman was convinced that she was not going to have a police source after all. But a few days later, a man from a Bay Area law enforcement agency contacted her as a result of the meeting with the Oakland police. He explained that he was an intelligence officer with access to his agency's entire file on the Panthers.

The ground rules for their relationship were quickly established. Her source might decide to let Coleman copy notes from his agency's files, but she could not make copies. For her part, Coleman insisted on obtaining a file number for any piece of information the intelligence officer supplied her—this would protect her against being fed bogus data. She agreed she would not refer to the intelligence officer in her story other than as a "police source."*

Paul Avery, meanwhile, obtained a similar source in the nearby Berkeley police department.

To ensure accuracy and avoid the pitfalls of reporting information slanted by the law enforcement viewpoint, Coleman spent all the rest of her time tracking down former Panthers, sympathizers, and others who knew what was going on inside the party. Some of her sources were black, some white.

At the Center, staff members located an editor who was excited about the story: Jonathan Larsen, editor of *New Times* magazine in New York. Larsen agreed to pay the reporters a monthly fee over the several months of investigation, as opposed to the usual

---

* Coleman's source was recontacted during research for this book and refused to be identified more specifically.

lump sum payment upon delivery of a manuscript. Though the overall story fee was extraordinarily large for a magazine story, it still did not adequately compensate the work of two skilled reporters over the six months of the project.

With the *New Times* contract in hand, Coleman and Avery had the luxury every good investigative piece requires—time. They met with potential sources repeatedly in order to develop their trust. Coleman noticed that her meetings with former Panthers and Panther sympathizers followed a pattern. At first they were reluctant to cooperate; then they gradually agreed that the story needed to be done; and finally, many of them agreed to tell what they knew. Some became enthusiastic enough about the project to convince knowledgeable friends to cooperate. Eventually Coleman had dozens of leftist sources to complement her one police source. About six of these sources proved vital to the story; all requested anonymity.

Anonymity is a tricky issue for reporters. It weakens a story in the eyes of readers who wonder about the reliability of the unnamed sources, and it makes the story's validity vulnerable to critics who charge that anonymity is a license to lie. As long as a source remains unidentified, the reader is unable to make an independent judgment about his or her credibility. The reporter, on the other hand, must often give a source anonymity in order to obtain the kind of explosive information contained in "The Party's Over."

In addition to their sources on the left and in law enforcement, the reporters met with colleagues at the *Oakland Tribune,* Pearl Stewart and Lance Williams. Both reporters had recently started to produce excellent daily coverage of Newton and the party's affairs, including its financial dealings.

Until this point, Coleman had been careful not to share any of the information she was uncovering with the people she was interviewing. But there usually comes a point in most investigations where in order to get more information you have to give some in return. In this case, Coleman started turning over material that would be useful to the *Tribune* reporters in return for copies of documents they were locating. This was a time-saving move to avoid duplication of effort.

In addition, by a stroke of good fortune, Coleman was able to engage in what is usually a more dangerous kind of trading—with her intelligence source.

Throughout the investigation, Coleman was particularly wary of letting the officer know any of the details she was finding, for fear of unwittingly becoming an accomplice in any law enforcement effort to "get" Newton or other Panthers. The Panthers and the various police agencies shared an intense mutual hatred; Coleman did not want to get caught in the middle. Now, however, she happened upon a completely unrelated piece of information of value to the law enforcement people which she had no reservations about turning over.

A sensational murder case had recently occurred in Oakland, and the police were unable to discover suspects or a motive for the crime. Through a contact, Coleman found out that a kilogram of ET—the base for LSD—had been stolen from the house. This knowledge was evidence that the crime had been drug-related. She decided to tip her intelligence source to this information, in the hope that he would be more cooperative with her Panther investigation.

From the first time they met privately, the intelligence officer had pressed Coleman for some sort of exclusive information that would demonstrate her reliability. Knowing that she was an ex-Yippie, he initially tried to find out where Abbie Hoffman, then a fugitive, was living. Coleman laughingly dismissed these inquiries, but his persistence worried her. Was it necessary to become some sort of "snitch" to get legitimate help from law enforcement? The drug murder tip proved the perfect solution to the problem. After that, her source stopped bothering Coleman for information and simply helped when he could.

Coleman also realized that not all officials involved in law enforcement activities share the same viewpoint about groups like the Panthers. She and Avery did not even approach the FBI for help, since neither of them trusted the Bureau's information, given its history of illegal spying and disrupting Panther activities.

Avery continued reporting on the story, and comparing the information pouring into the reporters' offices from their various sources almost on a daily basis, Coleman and Avery began to develop their research into an article. Coleman was responsible for the writing. She started churning out a draft that eventually ran to nearly a hundred pages, while Avery drafted specific sections and edited the whole. The pair had become an effective team. "Paul's contribution was incalculable," Coleman remembers. "He was willing to listen to me at two in the morning. Now, that's a good partner!"

Both were obsessed by the effort to piece together an enormous puzzle. They had, by Coleman's estimate, ten pieces of information for every one they could fit in the story. They decided to use only that information that was "multisourced" and consistent with the best-documented cases. Rumors, unsubstantiated charges, or pieces of information supplied only by law enforcement officials were dropped.

By the time she'd finished the first draft, Coleman felt she had become "semi-hysterical. Both Paul and I were punch-drunk. . . . We were both single; we had no sex lives left, no boyfriends, no girlfriends, no nothing. All we had was each other, the piece, and the Center."

They also had paranoia. Always a companion during this kind of investigation, in this case it became extreme. *Tribune* reporter Pearl Stewart's car was firebombed after her critical stories about the Panthers started appearing. And the bodies of Panthers involved in the Richmond incident were discovered. Threats, direct and indirect, from people still active with the Panthers were received by Coleman, Avery, and Center staff members. As a result of these threats, the Center decided to relocate its office temporarily once the story appeared.

Coleman turned to political friends for protection. These activists—some of whom were black—supported her right to finish her story and offered armed bodyguards at her house to help her do it.

The finished draft was "restrained" in tone, according to Coleman, and a departure from the flamboyant style she usually favored. She included much of the Panthers' history in order to record accurately the political context within which their decline was occurring.

The editors at *New Times* were dissatisfied. They felt the draft was too long and cumbersome and would not hold their readers' interest. Editor Larsen decided to fly Coleman to New York for the final rewrite and editing process. When negotiating the deal with *New Times,* the Center's staff had insisted that the authors and the Center retain final editorial review of the manuscript in order to preserve the confidentiality of sources, to protect against libel, and to preserve some of the political analysis that all agreed was necessary. The editors at *New Times,* for their part, prided themselves on their sensitivity to the political implications of the piece. "The political context was essential to us," editor Scott Kaufer remembers. "Without it the article would not have interested us at all."

The process of achieving a final manuscript took three weeks. Coleman stayed at a hotel in midtown Manhattan in a room she remembers as "dark and dingy, with a bed too soft, terrible lighting, and no room service after ten P.M."

Larsen had assigned Kaufer to the piece because he considered him his best editor. When Coleman went to her hotel lobby to meet Kaufer for the first time, she saw two men waiting—a distinguished gray-haired man reading a newspaper and a "kid over in the corner." To her surprise, the "kid" was Kaufer. Coleman surmised that Kaufer was just out of college and in his first magazine job. In fact, he was an experienced editor who had worked at *Boston Magazine, World Magazine,* and *I. F. Stone's Weekly.*

The editor-writer relationship was far from smooth. Almost instantly, according to Coleman, "war broke out." "We were at each other's throats," Kaufer remembers. Kaufer told her to cut the article significantly, including some of the history, the political analysis of the Panthers, and a long section on Elaine Brown. The magazine, Coleman says, wanted the story "jazzed up, sensationalized, and focused more on Newton." Kaufer has a different recollection: "The piece was boring. We wanted it to read better."

Coleman fought back, determined to preserve the story as she felt it should be. "It was the first time I had ever fought for something other than myself, and it gave me great tenacity. Always before I felt that fighting [with editors over a story] was a sign of being a prima donna. But now I realized that I *was* a prima donna, my stories are prima donnas, and they deserve the effort. After all, I felt I'd risked my life with this story. So I learned how to fight. I also learned how to compromise."

Kaufer had redrafted the piece, but Coleman angrily denounced it and telephoned the Center office to announce that she was withdrawing the piece from *New Times* to sell it elsewhere. At parties in New York she had already sounded out several editors who were interested in seeing the manuscript.

But then she reconsidered. "I decided to try to work out my differences with *New Times*. After all, it's the magazine that pays you in the beginning that is truly the most committed to a story like this. I may have found the same problems or worse if I had gone to another publication."

Kaufer and Coleman grudgingly "went back to the drawing boards" and surprised each other by finding a way to work together. "I realized I could slick it up a bit without compromising integrity," Coleman says. She also started to recognize that the young editor had considerable talent.

Once a final draft was agreed upon, another hurdle remained. Coleman had to sit through the fact-checking and libel-reading processes with the magazine's lawyer. After conferring with her colleagues, Coleman overcame some doubts and turned over the names of some of her confidential sources. "I believe that you have to tell your top editor and top lawyer who your important sources are because they're going down the line with you. But I made it clear to them I was never going to reveal those names in a court of law. I had told my sources I would go to jail before revealing them and I meant to keep my word."

Once certain changes had been made out of libel considerations, the manuscript concentrated more on Newton. In addition, for purposes of attribution the final version used the phrase "according to police sources," when in most cases the authors had corroboration from confidential sources as well. "It turned out to be easier to write it that way than to go through the elaborate contortions to describe people I had to protect and whose identities I couldn't give away," Coleman explains. Later, however, when Newton attacked the piece for relying so heavily on the police, Coleman regretted her decision. It was essentially an editing judgment not to mention the confidential sources, who were actually her most important suppliers of information. "I got in trouble in that case for the sake of grace in writing."

Coleman had one further regret. Just as the piece was nearing publication, the sexual assault on the Oakland woman occurred. This incident seemed to make a strong lead, since it was timely and an exclusive newsbreak. Although the story came from nonpolice sources, and Coleman still believes it was solid, she now feels it was a mistake to start the article with it. In the rush to make deadlines, reporters and editors often select something that seems "hot," but in this case Coleman feels the choice undercut her deliberate, nonsensational writing style in the rest of the piece.

Newton's response to the story was swift. At a press conference in Oakland he denounced it as filled with "lies" and accused Avery of "possibly" being a "paid agent of the police" and Coleman of being "Avery's dupe." Newton also announced that he would file a $6¼-million libel suit against *New Times,* Avery, and Coleman. This legal action never materialized.

The article proved to be something of a dirge for Newton and the Panthers. The Panther Free Medical Clinic closed in early 1980, as did the Panther newspaper later that year. In 1982 the Supreme Court threw out a $100-million lawsuit filed by the Panthers against the Justice Department, FBI, and CIA. And in September 1982 the California attorney general's office opened an investigation into charges that the Panther school had diverted $285,000 in state and federal funds to personal accounts. This followed closely on charges by the FBI that Newton and other associates were improperly benefiting from the school.

Newton eventually was acquitted of killing Kathleen Smith when a key prosecution witness told a startled jury that she had lied in identifying Newton as the killer. Newton's other legal problems have included arrests on suspicion of drunken driving while he was free on bail for an illegal weapons charge.

Elaine Brown has left the music business and is now reportedly a law student in Los Angeles. Preston Callins, who changed his story about being beaten by Newton after receiving a payment from one of Newton's lawyers, died of a brain tumor.

Kate Coleman continues to live in the Bay Area and write

controversial stories. The Panther article sparked disagreement among local political activists, some of whom felt that it never should have been written. Others, however, told Coleman that they now think she was correct in writing it.

Paul Avery became a reporter for the *Sacramento Bee*. He continues to do investigative stories and often writes about the criminal justice system.

New Times magazine, a valuable outlet for muckraking since its beginning in 1973, was acquired by a large entertainment corporation soon after the "Panther" article appeared. It closed for economic reasons at the end of 1978.

In the late 1960s the Black Panthers were among the most powerful and influential black groups in the country. Former FBI director J. Edgar Hoover, who waged a secret, illegal war against them, once called the Panthers the most dangerous group in America. Recently, however, Huey Newton, who earned a doctorate in the history of consciousness in 1980, was quoted as saying that the party is now only a "state of mind."

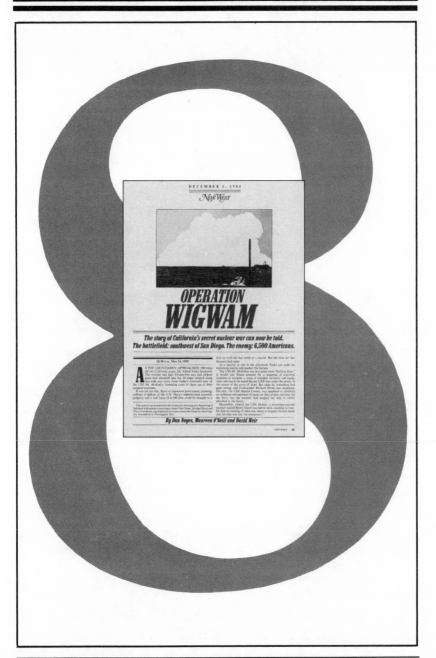

DECEMBER 1, 1980

New West

OPERATION
WIGWAM

**The story of California's secret nuclear war can now be told.
The battlefield: southwest of San Diego. The enemy: 6,500 Americans.**

12:30 P.M., May 14, 1955

A S THE COUNTDOWN APPROACHED, 200 miles off the California coast, Dr. Alfred Focke hesitated. The weather was bad. Fifteen-foot seas and 24-knot gusts had smashed into the 30 ships arrayed along two wide arcs away from Focke's command post on the USS *Mt. McKinley*, knocking some of them out of their assigned positions.

It was not too late. Years of top-secret government planning, millions of dollars of the U.S. Navy's sophisticated scientific gadgetry and a task force of 6,500 men could be brought to a

This article was prepared at the Center for Investigative Reporting in Oakland with research assistance from Clare Peine. Michael Kepp and Tracy Freedman and financial assistance from the Fund for Investigative Journalism in Washington, D.C.

boil up until she had tenth of a second. But the time for that decision had come.

At a quarter to one in the afternoon, Focke put aside his remaining doubts and pushed the button.

The USS *Mt. McKinley* was five miles from "Surface Zero." It would take fifteen minutes for a sequence of electrical impulses to activate a series of complex circuitry and equipment and reach the bomb buried 2,000 feet under the ocean, in the center of the array of ships. But close by, something had gone wrong, and Commander Richard Purdy was desperate. His ship, the USS *Mission County*, was supposed to maintain an elaborate arrangement of buoys in their proper positions for the blast, but the weather had tangled the ship in cables attached to the buoys.

Meanwhile, aboard the USS *Molala*, a seventeen-year-old seaman named Barry Nicoll was below deck cleaning latrines. He had no warning of what was about to happen; he only knew that his ship was on "on maneuvers."

By Dan Noyes, Maureen O'Neill and David Weir

NEW WEST

CHAPTER

8

Operation Wigwam

by Dan Noyes, Maureen O'Neill, and David Weir

12:30 P.M., May 14, 1955

As the countdown approached, 500 miles off the California coast, Dr. Alfred Focke hesitated. The weather was bad. Fifteen-foot seas and 24-knot gusts had smashed into the 30 ships arrayed along two wide arcs away from Focke's command post on the USS *Mt. McKinley,* knocking some of them out of their assigned positions.

It was not too late. Years of top-secret government planning, millions of dollars of the U.S. Navy's sophisticated scientific gadgetry and a task force of 6,500 men could be brought to a halt up until the last tenth of a second. But the time for a decision had come.

At a quarter to one in the afternoon, Focke put aside his remaining doubts and pushed the button.

The USS *Mt. McKinley* was five miles from "Surface Zero." It would take fifteen minutes for a sequence of electrical impulses to navigate a mass of complex circuitry and equipment surrounding the bomb buried 2,000 feet under the ocean, in the center of the array of ships. But close by, something had gone wrong, and Commander Richard Purdy was desperate. His ship, the USS *Marion County,* was supposed to maintain an elaborate arrangement of buoys in their proper positions for the blast, but the weather had tangled the ship in cables attached to the buoys.

Meanwhile, aboard the USS *Molala,* a seventeen-year-old seaman named Barry Nicoll was below deck cleaning latrines. He had no warning of what was about to happen; he only knew that his ship was out "on maneuvers."

At a tenth of a second before 1 P.M., an awesome rumble came from far beneath the turbulent Pacific. History's first deep underwater nuclear blast sent a force two and a half times as powerful as that released at Hiroshima hurtling toward the surface, and Operation Wigwam was officially under way.

This is the story of that operation, a one-bomb atomic battle off the coast of California. It is an eyewitness account, based on the memories of the men who planned and executed the explosion as well as those who were its victims. Because many of the official records and movies have recently been declassified, it is probably the most detailed inside story of atomic sea war ever made public. It is a story that changed the lives of Focke, Purdy and Nicoll forever.

Nineteen fifty-five, the year Albert Einstein signed the Pugwash Manifesto renouncing war, was a time when Americans were learning the fears of the nuclear age—fear of the Russians, of spies both inside and outside our borders and of the terrible dangers of radioactive fallout. There was a rush to build bomb shelters, and school children were drilled to crouch under their desks when mock air raid sirens sounded.

As part of an intensive effort to find out what our enemies could do to us before they did it, the U.S. government detonated fifteen nuclear bombs during 1955. There were no enemies at these explosions, only thousands of American servicemen.

Wigwam, an operation so secret even its code name was a classified term, was one of the fifteen. Planning for it began at least two years before H hour. In complete secrecy, Focke, at that time a navy explosives expert, started working as scientific director of the project. He was quietly transferred from the Naval Electronics Laboratory at Point Loma up the coast to the University of California's Scripps Institution of Oceanography at La Jolla. There, working ostensibly as a marine physicist, Focke started devising the scientific components of the test.

The peaceful Scripps campus, high on a scenic cliff above a wide Pacific beach, looked like a relaxed academic outpost devoted to understanding the ocean at its doorstep, but the task force of Scripps scientists quietly working within held the highest government security clearances. They knew that what they were readying was an experiment—no one had ever shot off an atomic bomb deep below the sea before—and an experiment involving human life. But the navy officers and the scientists assigned to the project felt that they had good reasons for that experiment.

In the aftermath of World War II, antisubmarine warfare was one of the U.S. Navy's major preoccupations (it remains so to this day). According to an "operation plan" developed by the Armed Forces Special Weapons Program in 1954, "the chief objective of Operation Wigwam is to determine with satisfactory accuracy at what ranges, under various conditions, a submarine or surface vessel will be destroyed by a deep underwater atomic explosion. The second objective is to determine the hazards to the delivery vehicle and its supporting forces." In other words, the naval personnel being assembled for the blast were unwittingly participating in a nuclear "war games" experiment.

This work was complicated, as another navy report later observed, "by the inability of anyone to predict to any satisfactory degree the extent and type of surface and subsurface phenomena." No one knew, for instance, whether the ocean would be able to contain the shot or whether the radioactive blast would explode out into the air and contaminate the surface. Unknown, too, was how powerful a shock wave would be created by the explosion—and what that would do to the ships near the blast site.

The uncertainty surrounding the test was not surprising given the overall lack of scientific knowledge about the oceans at the time. "Oceanography," a Scripps public information officer recently confided, "only really came of age after World

War II, when the military became interested in the oceans."
The navy, for example, underwrote almost the entire Scripps
budget during the fifties, and the institute's director was Roger
Revelle, a former navy expert in the oceanographic aspects
of atomic testing.

The Wigwam task force of Scripps scientists, including Focke
and Revelle, was given the task of locating a suitable area
between 200 and 600 miles off the California coast for the
blast. They chose a spot at 28° 44' north latitude and 126°
16' west longitude, 450 nautical miles southwest of San Diego,
and declared the area a "biological desert."

By mid-April 1955, a month before D day, the Wigwam
planners were caught up in a whirlwind of secret sessions,
classified memos, top-level security clearances and emergency
conferences.

On the morning of April 12, six key officials plotting the
test gathered at Point Loma for an urgent meeting. They had
three big worries: the press, the public and the tuna. Present
at the meeting were Focke; Rear Admiral John Sylvester, commander of the navy's Wigwam task force; Focke's military
assistant, Captain Jack Lofland; two marine biologists from
Scripps; and Dr. W. R. Boss, an Atomic Energy Commission
(AEC) official. The AEC was worried about the public. "It
must be acknowledged," noted an internal AEC memorandum,
"that in the event of an unanticipated accident involving radioactive contamination, public opinion might exert sufficient
pressure to cause delay or cancellation of future testing."

In addition, the AEC's Division of Biology and Medicine
had protested the idea of an atomic blast so close to the West
Coast for fear it might disrupt the ailing tuna industry.

A year earlier, during a series of nuclear detonations code-
named "Castle," at Bikini atoll, Japanese tuna boats had reported landing 480 metric tons of radioactive fish, and panic
had swept American supermarkets.

The U.S. tuna industry was already in dire straits, thanks
to the intense competition from Japan. Canning executive
G. C. Van Camp Sr. had told the AEC that another scare would
"wreck the industry," throw thousands of people out of work
and focus public anger on the entire nuclear testing program.

Now, at their Point Loma meeting, Focke, Sylvester and Lofland were told by the AEC's Dr. Boss that the Food and Drug Administration (FDA), which normally monitored tuna for radioactivity, didn't want any part in checking tuna after the Wigwam blast. This news greatly upset the military planners.

Boss then explained that the FDA could still be convinced to take part if the navy would provide the expert personnel. But Sylvester said that all the navy's radiation safety experts would be needed at the test site in case the "shot vents and some of the water or mist hits ships of the task force."

The planners' major concerns were for the scientific and military results of the test; concern for the possible hazards facing the thousands of men stationed at the blast site appears to have been secondary. In fact, the navy originally wanted to stage a much larger operation, but the event had to be scaled down because of a "reduced budget." Radiation standards set for the operation allowed exposure to ten times the amount of radiation considered safe for the public in 1955.

On the afternoon of April 12, after the morning meeting at Point Loma, the AEC's Boss toured one of the tuna canning plants, posing as a Scripps scientist in the company of bona fide Scripps scientists, in order to plan a monitoring program. The AEC scrupulously avoided letting anyone know that it was involved monitoring tuna for radioactivity—the agency even discussed using UCLA as a front to reimburse fishermen for any "hot" fish that might have to be discarded.

The Wigwam architects would have preferred to keep the test secret, as some of the other nuclear blasts had been. But the large scope of this test, involving 6,500 men on 30 ships, as well as what they termed their "public relations" tuna-monitoring effort, made a news leak inevitable. Furthermore, there was the "serious international problem" that Mexico and South American nations were major consumers of Pacific fish. The AEC worried that President Eisenhower's Atoms for Peace program might be undermined as a result.

So, during the weeks leading up to the blast, AEC officials fabricated their strategy: "If the test operation is conducted as planned, without any untoward incident, it is felt that by development of a proper public information plan, adverse public reaction can be held to a minimum." A draft press release written two weeks before the blast set down the official line: "No radioactivity at all has been found in commercial fish arriving from the area."

Despite the best efforts of Scripps and the AEC, however, when a carefully worded press release was finally issued several days before the detonation, it aroused anger in the West Coast fishing industry and in some state officials as well. Seth Gordon, director of the California Department of Fish and Game, sent a letter to the AEC contesting the "biological desert" label Scripps had pinned on the blast site: "We know there are no deserts in the ocean. Fish in greater or lesser abundance are found everywhere."

The protest died quickly, however, when the AEC quietly pointed out to industry officials that "the less said about the affair to the press the better."

As part of its "public information plan," the Pentagon also lied about the size of the bomb. The *San Diego Tribune* was leaked the story that the blast's yield was "thought to have had an energy equivalent of 1 to 5 kilotons, certainly smaller than 20 kt. . . ." The bomb was actually 30 kilotons. As for press coverage of the blast itself, an internal AEC memo bluntly stated, "There will be no access by correspondents."

As the countdown to H hour began, Focke and his small circle of atomic warriors reviewed every detail of their heavily classified operation. Each stage of the test was code-named according to a common theme, dating from earlier military glories. The tuna-monitoring effort was labeled "Pow-Wow." Pretest sub models were "Papooses." And the simulated submarine hulls that were to be used as targets of the blast (to determine the "incipient lethality" of underwater nuclear bombs) were called "Squaws"—because, according to Focke, "that is what gets squeezed inside the Wigwam."

With the press, the public and the tuna industry all under control, the only variable the navy had not prepared for was the weather. For Commander Richard Purdy and his crew, the weather made all the difference.

1:00 P.M., May 14, 1955: H-Hour

Fifteen minutes after Focke pressed the button on the *Mt. McKinley,* the bomb exploded, propelling three giant radioactive gas bubbles toward the surface 333 fathoms above. The water rifled skyward at a speed of 200 miles per hour, breaking into the atmosphere with poetic symmetry. Surface Zero became a boiling white circle two miles in diameter. Domes, then plumes, of churning water rose up, each higher than the last, until a column of water higher than the World Trade Center towered above the midday sea.

Shock waves from the blast thundered through the ocean, slamming into the circle of barges, tugs, LSTs, destroyers and an aircraft carrier. Among the shock waves was one that had rebounded off the hard rock bottom 16,000 feet below.

Some of the ships were tossed up like bathtub toys. A barge at Surface Zero disintegrated; another nearby roller-coastered 40 feet up and down in the roaring white foam.

Lying flat on the deck of the command ship, *Mt. McKinley,* not far from scientific director Focke, a chief petty officer looked up to see the king post superstructure "vibrating like tuning forks." A military report later said two of "the ships appeared to flex as the shock wave traveled from bow to stern."

Aboard the USS *Fort Marion,* boatswain's mate Walter Johnson felt a fine mist rain down on him.

On the *Molala,* seventeen-year-old Barry Nicoll was ordered up on deck from his job cleaning the latrines. Halfway up the ladder he felt the blast. Like many around him, he had no idea what was happening. He looked toward the white mountain exploding out of the Pacific and gasped.

A 28-square-mile area of ocean churned like a giant caldron. The displaced water crashed noisily down again, this time pushing a new wall of boiling water out from Surface Zero—toward the ships. Suddenly, a gargantuan white wave over 600 feet high threatened the ships. It surged for more than a mile and then died down, shooting out breaker after breaker in concentric circles away from Surface Zero.

Downwind from the blast, beneath the 330-billion-cubic-foot

radioactive plume drifting southward, Captain Ross Pennington readied his ship, the USS *George Eastman,* to sail near
Surface Zero. The ship's power had been knocked out by the
initial force of the blast, and Pennington and several of his
crew members had to leave their shielded control area to get
it going again. A secret report later noted that the men were
working under "extremely hazardous respiratory conditions."
Once the *Eastman* got moving, it looked from the other ships
as if it were sailing into a mountain of radioactive water.

Upwind of Surface Zero the *Marion County* was still trying
to get out of the blast area. Commander Richard Purdy was
trying to calm his men, who were screaming and running
around uncontrollably in the face of an advancing 1,900-foot
wall of water. Purdy kept his senses, stabilized the ship, and
put the engines into reverse. The *Marion County* started to
back away from the blast area—it could no longer go forward
because its bow door had been damaged in the rough seas.

The research ship, the *Horizon,* that carried most of the
Scripps scientists, also was incapacitated by the blast. The scientists panicked as the ship drifted helplessly into the circle
of radioactive water downwind. "Inside the bomb area it was
so hot you'd be killed," remembers Dr. Theodore Folsom, a
Scripps oceanographer. "When we drifted into the hot water,
the needles on the radiation range finder went way off. I yelled,
'Get the hell out of here.' " Folsom took advantage of the
situation, however, by dropping measurement devices overboard. The ship finally got going and moved quickly out of
the danger area.

Within ten minutes of the blast, the land masses ringing
the Pacific echoed the sound of the explosion. At that time,
the Coast and Geodetic Survey reported the rumble as an
earthquake. Instruments at Cal Tech measured it at the equivalent of 4.1 on the Richter scale. The shock wave reached a
Greek freighter more than 600 miles away from the blast site,
steaming off the Golden Gate. The ship radioed the Coast
Guard, "Has San Francisco just been hit by a severe earthquake? We have been badly shaken but are all right and will
return to render assistance if needed."

Thirty-two minutes after H hour, the sound of the explosion

reached Hawaii. Echoes from each of the islands in the Hawaiian chain reverberated back to Point Sur. Later the sound-bounce from each of the Aleutians off Alaska came in, followed by an echo from Japan.

Not long after the volcanos of water subsided, sharp bursts of automatic gunfire erupted from ships deployed around Surface Zero. It was cleanup time, and some of the radioactive debris was being sunk by gunfire. Barrels scattered over a three-mile radius were sunk to 16,000 feet below, where they joined one of the three sub hulls and a barge that had already sunk.

Other waste-disposal activities were more complicated. The simulated submarine hulls designed and built especially for Wigwam, surface barges, instrument platforms, buoys, pontoons and cables used in the test were now the record of history's first deep underwater nuclear explosion. The buoys and pontoons were retrieved by designated ships and placed on deck for the return voyage home. The barges and two surviving sub targets were rigged up for the 500-mile tow back to the mainland.

Then there was the 3.1-square-mile circle of foam that defined the perimeter of the most highly contaminated water from the blast. Scripps scientists followed this "hot" water for 40 days before losing its track 120 miles west of Surface Zero. Any migrating fish that came in contact with what the scientists labeled the "undulating sheets" of radioactive water would have absorbed it and possibly have become dangerous to eat. (As anticipated, the one-month tuna-monitoring effort after the test did not find any radioactive fish from the Wigwam site, although it did detect a few "hot" specimens from the 1954 Castle area.)

The process of retrieving radioactive debris naturally exposed the ships (and their crews) to high levels of contamination. According to one report, "the main deck and topside spaces [of the USS *Chanticleer*] were contaminated from 2,500 to 25,000 counts per minute as a result of the ship's work in a contaminated water area." Eugene Gordon, a seaman on the *Chanticleer*, remembers that "men went around the deck with Geiger counters. The ship was hot. We had to deep-six a lot of the stuff on deck, including a vat of potatoes."

According to the report quoted above, "personal clothing contamination up to 50,000 counts per minute was experienced. [However the Geiger counters were calibrated, 50,000 counts would have been highly radioactive.] Attempts to launder contaminated clothing in shipboard facilities were not successful in a reduction to permissible levels. Holding for decay, in addition to laundering, appeared to be necessary." The report went on to state that "highly contaminated sinkable objects, not essential to the mission, were discarded overboard."

Among the largest pieces of radioactive waste were the two surviving submarine hull targets. Each was 132 feet long. In order to raise one of the subs to facilitate towing, groups of divers had to enter the radioactive water and readjust the cables and weights holding the subs down. The navy placed a high priority on salvaging these target hulls because expensive, delicate instrumentation had been placed on board in order to measure the effects of the blast.

Once the sub hulls were ready, two ships began the arduous job of towing them toward San Diego. Halfway back, however, the main cable holding one of the sub hulls broke, and it sank to the ocean floor thousands of feet below.

The next day the cable towing the third sub hull started tearing apart. The radioactive hull was carefully maneuvered to about 100 feet of water somewhere off either Santa Catalina or San Clemente island (there are conflicting reports on exactly where). There it was sunk in waters that are used by abalone divers, fishermen and recreational boaters. As late as five years later, in 1960, a diver who had been involved in Operation Wigwam reported seeing the sub hull still in place. (Checks of navigational charts of the region have failed to locate the sub hull in 1980, however.)

The possibility that low-level radioactivity might have been released into these recreational waters off the California coast cannot be discounted, though it is not addressed by any of the declassified reports released by the navy to date.

While the radioactive sub hulls were being towed back to land, the ships carrying "hot" buoys, pontoons, cables and boxes of contaminated water docked in San Diego. Large cranes lifted this radioactive debris from the test onto the docks. Its ultimate resting place is unknown, but according to Dr. John Gofman, a nuclear critic trained in both nuclear physics and medicine, it was "very irresponsible" to bring the test waste back to land.

Finally, two ships involved in Operation Wigwam—the USS *George Eastman* and the USS *Granville S. Hall*—were purposely exposed to radiation. The *George Eastman* was equipped with a special "wash-down" system, which essentially consisted of garden spray-type hoses. This system was only 14 percent successful, however, according to a recently declassified military report. Radiation levels on the *Eastman,* for example, reached 500 milliroentgens per hour one day after the blast. This level, though undoubtedly short-lived, indicates that the ship became "hot" enough to constitute an extremely hazardous environment for its crew—especially since it went on to its next assignment at Operation Redwing, farther out in the Pacific.

Fourteen months later, in August 1956, Captain Ross Pennington and his crew stood on deck as the *Eastman* approached the Golden Gate.

Suddenly the tug sent to meet the ship appeared. To Pennington and his crew the tug was a ghostly sight, completely draped in canvas, with crew members wearing what Pennington's wife, Mary, waiting for him at berth at Hunter's Point, recalls as "white, spacelike suits."

As the ship docked at Hunter's Point, a radiation detector was placed at the bottom of the ladder. Mary Pennington watched as her husband descended the ladder. Her heart dropped when he was turned back. He and the crew had to change their shoes, which were "hot" from walking around on the deck of the radioactive ship, before they were allowed back on land.

After this chilling start to their reunion, Pennington explained to his wife what had happened at Wigwam and Redwing—that the *"Eastman's* purpose was to be exposed to as much radiation as possible."

Richard Purdy's Nightmare

After the blast, Richard Purdy had to back his damaged ship, the *Marion County,* 500 miles to San Diego. Then he went home to the cottage in Encinitas where he lived with his wife, Ruth. Purdy seemed all right for a couple of days. He took Ruth to a party for all the commanders involved in the operation, although as usual he did not tell her what had happened at sea. At the party several officers mentioned to Ruth that her husband deserved a medal for the way he had calmed his crew and navigated the damaged ship back to port.

Richard Purdy had participated in many of the hottest firefights in the Pacific during World War II, including Okinawa and Midway. Purdy said that after one battle he was responsible for towing two boatloads full of dead friends and companions, whose bodies were decomposed beyond recognition, out to sea and then sinking them. After completing this mission, Purdy said he was given two bottles of bourbon and told to "go to the officer's club and drink it off." He was not the type who could forget, however—time and again the standard commendation forms filed in his naval record indicated the deep and unusual compassion he felt for the men serving under his command.

Purdy had enlisted in the navy, refusing an appointment to the Naval Academy arranged by a congressional contact of his father's. He had quickly risen through the ranks and was pinstriped captain of his first ship at the age of 28, just as World War II was breaking out.

Although he felt he had seen the worst of war's horrors, Commander Purdy had not been prepared for his first glimpse of nuclear devastation. That came in 1954, when he was ordered to tow a nuclear bomb-blasted ship back to the mainland from the South Pacific. Purdy's ship, the *Marion County,* towed it all the way back to San Diego. A newspaper report called it the longest ship tow in naval history.

Ruth Purdy says her husband could not get the image of that ship out of his mind. Nothing he had seen in the war had prepared him for the advent of weapons that made commanders and seamen and human judgment itself irrelevant.

Steaming backward into San Diego after Wigwam, Purdy said later, was like reliving the towing of the disabled ship from the South Pacific the year before. At home with his wife, Ruth, in Encinitas in late May 1955, Purdy was even quieter than usual and had trouble sleeping. Within days, after viewing an executive showing of the film clips of Wigwam with the assembled naval brass, Richard Purdy suffered a complete nervous breakdown. He was transported off to the psychiatric ward of a nearby veterans' hospital, where he was kept for six months. He refused the navy's offer of a 100 percent psychiatric disability and demanded to return to sea. Because of his record, the navy complied. He was given charge of the rescue effort to pick up anyone who went down at sea in airplane crashes off San Diego. There wasn't much to do, and a few months later, at the age of 44, he retired, his brilliant naval career a shambles.

Not long after the blast, while Richard Purdy was slowly backing the *Marion County* toward San Diego, seventeen-year-old Barry Nicoll, aboard the *Molala,* started vomiting. As soon as the ship reached San Diego, Nicoll was transferred to a nearby VA hospital, where other symptoms started appearing in rapid succession.

Nicoll was told he had been hit by 390 roentgens of radiation from the blast (a dose of 300 is considered potentially lethal by some experts). The admitting physician noted in his official health record that Nicoll had suffered chills, general malaise, loss of appetite and headaches after "exposure to radiation on maneuvers consisting of atomic warfare."

Nicoll's hair stopped growing—he didn't need a haircut for the next six months—and the hair on his chest fell out completely. (These symptoms were omitted from his official health records.) He developed severe thyroid trouble. Part of his thyroid was removed, but other symptoms kept appearing. His spleen hurt; his lymph nodes were swollen. The hair loss and gastrointestinal problems were classic indicators of radiation exposure.

During his six-month stay at the hospital, Nicoll continued

to have the terrible headaches and other symptoms. All this time he was afflicted by a mysterious quenchless thirst.

Nicoll was told he was suffering from mononucleosis, but he felt the doctors were hiding something from him. "Every day, groups of doctors would come in to look at me—five or six of them at a time. Some were foreign—they couldn't speak English. It made me feel important to have so many interesting people coming in to see me—I was only seventeen. But it also got me worried."

Nicoll says he was visited at the hospital by a navy captain who said, "Under no circumstances are you to mention what you've seen or where you've been. If you do, I'll take care of you." (Recent attempts to locate the officer have failed.) Nicoll says he obeyed the command for the next 25 years.

D Day Plus 25 Years

For almost a quarter of a century silence surrounded Operation Wigwam. For the men who had devised and executed the maneuver, these were years of success and achievement. The scientists at Scripps rose to the top of their fields. Their names achieved prestige in the marine labs that ring the coasts of the world's great oceans. Many of them directly benefited from their involvement at Wigwam, publishing papers on the tendency of radioactive pools of water to resist diffusion by the ocean or the relative lack of biological productivity in the eastern tropical Pacific.

Members of Scripps's Wigwam task force publicly downplayed the threat of radioactivity to fish on several occasions. In 1957 testimony before a congressional subcommittee probing fish contamination from the Castle nuclear blasts, Scripps director Revelle suggested that just because fish were "hot" didn't mean they were inedible. He stressed that only "one-half of 1 percent" of the catch in question, which was landed by Japanese fishing fleets, was radioactive. This, however, did amount to 480 metric tons.

While they were publicly minimizing the threat of radioactivity in the oceans, Scripps scientists were also publishing research papers in journals such as *Limnology and Oceanography* that indicated that marine organisms exposed to radioactivity concentrated many dangerous isotopes (including strontium 90) to levels thousands of times that found in the seawater itself. This "biomagnification" represents a serious health threat to people (such as the entire population of Japan) who rely on fish for a large part of their diet.

Scripps also was involved in the navy's controversial ocean-dumping practices, monitoring sites like the Farallon Islands area off San Francisco, where nuclear waste was dumped for twenty years. In 1957 Scripps reported no "easily detectable amounts of radioactivity" at the Farallones. But recently, evidence has surfaced that leaking drums have released radioactivity thousands of times higher than the background levels.

Furthermore, Scripps performed atmospheric research for the CIA, which critics charge is investigating weather modification schemes; developed technology for the CIA's mysterious *Glomar Explorer* mission; constructed a prototype of a "floating island" that could serve as a mid-ocean airfield; and conducted undersea research for the navy. Press speculation on the latter has centered around the potential use of low-frequency sonar in submarine warfare or the firing of benthic nuclear missiles. The institute's current director, William Nierenberg, who is an expert in antisubmarine warfare, consulted on Project Agile, a Department of Defense-funded counterinsurgency operation. Scripps has carried out extensive nondefense research as well, including deep-sea drilling and manganese nodule mining work, useful to industry.

The technical evaluations Scripps scientists prepared of the Wigwam blast have now been released, along with other military and AEC reports, under the Freedom of Information Act. They reveal that:

- Largely because of the adverse weather conditions, 70 percent of the experiments planned for Wigwam were failures.
- "The Wigwam detonation produced sufficient airborne activity to have given radiation doses many times tolerance to exposed personnel located approximately five miles down-

wind." (At least two ships—the *Eastman* and the *Granville Hall*—were about five miles downwind at H hour.)

- Air monitors stationed at San Diego measured a higher level of radioactivity over that city within four days of the blast. The radioactivity skyrocketed from ten to twenty times normal background levels over the next nine days.
- The frightening "base surge" created by the blast was characterized as an "insidious hazard" that turned into an "invisible radioactive aerosol."

Johnny Atomseed Comes to San Diego

In September 1979 one man finally broke the 25-year public silence about Wigwam. In Honolulu, Elroy Runnels, 46-year-old father of four, announced to a room packed full of television lights, cameras and reporters that he was suing the government for exposing him to lethal radiation at Operation Wigwam. Two days later Runnels was dead of leukemia.

At this point, a determined activist named Tony Hodges entered the scene. Hodges, an old friend of Runnels's attorney, was outraged by the government's refusal to pay Runnels's disability claim. He managed to obtain the navy's declassified film and official written report of Operation Wigwam and scraped together enough money for an early December budget-fare flight from Honolulu to San Diego. His mission was to force the Wigwam story into the public arena.

Hodges's effort was only a partial success, but the publicity he engineered did indirectly help unravel the conspiracy of silence about the blast. A graph of high levels of radioactivity over San Diego, after Wigwam, was shown on local TV and alarmed residents concerned about fallout and cancer.

Mayor Pete Wilson directed his Quality of Life Board, headed by sociologist Joseph R. Gusfield of the University of California at San Diego, to investigate the possibility that the city's air had been contaminated by Wigwam. "We were very skeptical of the military people the Pentagon sent out to talk to us," Gusfield said in a recent interview. "We knew they were just PR people." Nevertheless, when the commission issued its report last April, it concluded that there was no evidence to dispute the official version of events at Wigwam— and that the air over San Diego had not been dangerously radioactive. The report suggested that another atomic bomb set off at the Nevada Test Site around the same time may have been responsible for the measured increase.

Officials of the Department of Energy (DOE), which has taken over some AEC functions, flatly deny that the Nevada test could have been the culprit. "All of our fallout was blown due east on those particular days," stated information officer David Jackson in Las Vegas. "The sharp increase in radioactive half-lives over San Diego was probably due to Wigwam," said DOE physicist David Wheeler.

Amid the finger-pointing back and forth, neither side was disputing the main issue: that radioactive fallout had been injected into the atmosphere. Although it may not have created an immediate health threat to San Diegans, this burst of fallout contributed to the globe-circling belt of man-made radioactivity that endures to this day. At its peak, in 1962, the weapons testing was cumulatively responsible for approximately 13 percent of the background radiation hitting people in the Northern Hemisphere.

One of those watching the Wigwam controversy on San Diego TV last winter was Richard Purdy. By December 1979 Purdy knew he was dying of lung cancer. His nervous breakdown had led to a drinking problem during the years of quiet retirement in Encinitas.

Once he realized that Operation Wigwam was declassified, Purdy ended his long silence about the test. Ruth was shocked: Her husband had never mentioned the test except once, nine years after the explosion, when he had developed painful cataracts in both eyes. That condition had caused an experienced Navy physician to ask him whether he had ever witnessed an atomic explosion because, according to the doctor, "it's the kind of condition many atomic veterans suffer."

Now Richard Purdy started reliving his personal nightmare once again. He told Ruth about the wall of water charging his ship, the *Marion County* seeming to bounce eighteen inches off the ocean, the men screaming, the damaged bow door, his crippled ship drifting toward Surface Zero—all as part of a "peacetime maneuver" staged against his own men. For the first time in 25 years, Ruth Purdy began to understand why her husband had gone crazy.

On his deathbed, Purdy called in a young neighbor, Ron Josephson, and spoke haltingly into a tape recorder, detailing everything he could remember about the blast. The sick man's voice explained why he was finally setting down his record of Wigwam. "It's too late for me, son, [but] I feel they were all left holding the bag—all those crews. Not just on my ship— hell, no—but all those crews."

Three weeks later Ruth Purdy watched her husband bleed to death in the final stage of his cancer. A special bed, ordered weeks earlier from the VA so Purdy wouldn't have to leave home at the end, arrived too late to be of any use. Ruth Purdy was now a widow of the nuclear age.

While San Diego was still in tumult over whether Wigwam had doused it with "hot" air, Tony Hodges, whom the mayor's PR man had dubbed "Johnny Atomseed," was telephoning Sacramento, trying to interest aides to Governor Jerry Brown in the test. A few days later, Brown held a midnight screening of the declassified Wigwam film, to which he invited dozens of antinuclear activists who were staging a five-week sit-in at his office.

After viewing the blast movie, Brown issued an immediate call for the federal government to publicly release the names of all servicemen involved in Wigwam so they could receive suitable medical treatment.

The following day, at his home in West Covina, Barry Nicoll noticed a small news account of Brown's statement. Despite the catalog of repercussions he had suffered after Wigwam, Nicoll had eventually recovered enough to finish his navy duty. He married, started raising a family and found a job. In spite of recurring illnesses—including a second operation in 1959 to remove the rest of his thyroid—Nicoll became a successful teamster, made good money and acquired a nice house with a swimming pool. But in 1979 Nicoll fell out of a truck-trailer while unloading it.

That accident seemed to unleash his post-Wigwam symptoms in exaggerated form. "The doctors told me I was like a loaded gun. What happened to me in '55 put me in a condition where the trauma of my accident triggered my diabetes, my headaches, my thirst—everything."

Now, Brown's call for the identity of Wigwam victims raised Nicoll's hopes for government compensation. "All these years I kept quiet about it," he explains. "It was under a cell in my mind that was not to be opened. I never even told my family. But once I started talking it spilled out like water over the falls."

Nicoll wrote Brown a letter, explaining how he had been exposed at Wigwam. But the governor never answered, apparently because of a staff oversight. "That hurt me more than anything else," he says. "When I saw that notice in the paper I felt a togetherness with Governor Brown. But now I wish I had never seen it. It's too painful. I'd like to come face to face with Governor Brown and ask, 'Why'd you call for our names?' "

Rocking in his chair, gulping gallon after gallon of fluids, Nicoll says he today suffers severe headaches "two-thirds of the time." He has to go to bed by 9 P.M. every night because he feels exhausted, even though he cannot work. If he wears his glasses longer than twenty minutes at a time, his vision blurs.

Two radiation-illness experts consulted for the preparation of this article stated that no definitive diagnosis could be made of Nicoll's multiple health problems. His exposure at Wigwam has been complicated by years of intervening events, particularly his accident in 1979, and the possibility that he may have suffered from unknown inherited conditions. Both doctors, however, felt his problems may have been exacerbated by exposure at Wigwam. "Nobody has done a study to see if there is a connection to radiation of any of these diseases," points out Dr. Gofman. "Virtually nothing has been done to find the effects of low-level ionizing radiation on these diseases or other health problems. Although good evidence exists that cancer and leukemia are induced by low-level radiation, other medical disorders simply have not been studied."

Today Barry Nicoll is trying to decide how to meet his

growing medical bills. He says he is a loyal citizen—both of his oldest sons are in the air force with his blessing, and he still raises and lowers his American flag every day. "But what burns my butt is how they went about covering this all up— all these years." He has retained a lawyer to look into suing the government.

"It's a disgrace that the government is not at least studying these men," observes Gofman. "The reason they aren't is that they would frighten the public and the military planners. But the government has an obligation to find out what happened to them. The servicemen weren't even like guinea pigs—you study those at least. These men were like sheep."

During a six-month investigation for *New West* and ABC News's *20/20,* the Center for Investigative Reporting found 36 men who participated in Operation Wigwam. Fourteen of them had suffered from diseases that could be traced to radiation exposure at Wigwam:

- Charles Fleming, a civilian technician for Scripps, was in a small airplane that flew directly into the radioactive plume above Surface Zero to measure radioactivity after the shot. He developed a mysterious condition that caused his bones to crumble and died last summer of a heart attack.
- Walter Johnson, the boatswain's mate who felt a fine mist filter down on him after the explosion, developed a severe skin rash within a year and a half of the test. The VA says it has lost his medical records from that period. Today, 25 years after Wigwam, he still has to keep a sign above his bed: DON'T SCRATCH!
- James Heiner, a third-class petty officer on the USS *Curtiss,* also developed a painful skin disorder, resulting in welts, discoloration and severe itching. The condition has come and gone since the test and does not respond to any medication.
- Archie Gary, who was on the USS *Comstock,* suffers from a similar skin condition.
- John Stillwell was on a salvage tug that towed one of the contaminated submarine hulls back from the test. He devel-

oped cancer and had to have half of his jaw surgically removed.

- Earl Branham, a pipe welder temporarily on the USS *Comstock* during the test, has leukemia. He was told by the VA that his medical records are missing.
- Robert Wilhite, from the USS *Wright,* recalls being "appalled that the navy would allow its men outside during the blast without any protective clothing." Wilhite had his right lung removed due to cancer in 1971 and now has cancer in his left lung.
- Marche Rothlisberger, administrative officer to Task Force Commander Admiral Sylvester, developed tooth and gum problems as a result of a strange bone condition that appeared in 1966. His periodontist stated, "The underlying cause for his condition could have been radioactive exposure."
- John Brewer, who was on the USS *Fort Marion,* has skin cancer and cancer of the knee. He does not feel Wigwam was responsible for his diseases.
- Richard T. Fellis, who was on the USS *Chanticleer,* died in 1977 of cancer.
- Elroy Runnels is dead of leukemia.
- Richard Purdy is dead of cancer.
- Barry Nicoll suffers from undiagnosed disorders.
- Captain Ross Pennington, who sailed the USS *Eastman* toward Surface Zero, died last December of leukemia. He received a 100 percent disability evaluation from the government for his exposure to radiation in nuclear tests—apparently the only serviceman from Wigwam to be compensated so far.

Many of these men are hindered in their attempts to get compensation by the fact that they were not wearing radiation detection badges during the blast. Others have had their records lost or misplaced by the authorities. The government has not performed a comprehensive survey of the health effects of the Wigwam blast.

The Defense Nuclear Agency's (DNA) spokesperson, Lieutenant Colonel Bill McGee, stated pointedly, "We are not in the health defense business."

The DNA's official report on the Wigwam test, released last February, amounts to a whitewash of what actually happened at the blast. This 250-page version compiled by the Jaycor consulting firm of Alexandria, Virginia, suffers from the following major failures:

- Although a few high-level officials reviewed a draft, not one of the 6,500 participants in Wigwam was interviewed for the report.
- The report downplays the chance that Wigwam caused the radioactive "spike" over San Diego four days after the blast. An independent meteorologist and two radiation experts consulted by *New West* determined that radiation from Wigwam may indeed have been responsible.
- The report neglects to mention the substantial pretest concern that tuna or other commercial fish might be contaminated by the test. It also does not report that, despite AEC advisory committee recommendations that Mexico and other South American fishing nations be forewarned of the test, no international announcements were made.
- The report claims that all personnel were familiarized with the radiological hazards before the test, but few of the 36 participants interviewed for this article could recall any such briefing. Many, in fact, were not even told they would be witnessing an atomic explosion.
- The report claims that every participant was given a radiation detection film badge to wear during the test, but 14 of the 36 men interviewed for this article say they were given no badges.
- The report does not mention the full extent of damage sustained by ships involved in the test. No mention is made of the severe damage inflicted on the USS *Marion County,* described to *New West* by three eyewitnesses, or the *Eastman.*
- At one point the report claims that no servicemen received more than 0.425 roentgens of radiation from the blast, but elsewhere it says that the deck of the *Eastman* received 400 roentgens. According to John Gofman, "The ship would

have remained radioactive, at low levels, for months afterward, representing serious health consequences for the men on board in terms of eventual cancers."

It is apparent from this report and other similar documents that the U.S. government does not *want* to know whether its seventeen-year nuclear war had any victims. The official position is that the tests simply had to be done. Governor Brown is still the most prominent public official who has taken issue with the government over Operation Wigwam. Brown's aide Phillip Greenberg told *New West* that a detailed letter from the DNA earlier this year, which reiterated the conclusions of the official Jaycor report, answered all of Brown's questions about the blast at that time. Now, based on the new information in this article, it appears that he should reconsider calling for studies of the health effects of Wigwam, the government's obligations to California veterans and the hazards of materials dumped off the California coast.

Today the Scripps Institution of Oceanography is the largest center of its kind in the country. It no longer has to rely on the navy for most of its budget, and the days of coordinating nuclear blasts in the Pacific are a somewhat embarrassing memory.

The man who pushed the button at Wigwam, Dr. Alfred Focke, lives about ten miles from Barry Nicoll. He says that he would do it all over again today. But he also feels that "every prospective head of state should be required to stand within five miles to witness one of these small atomic bombs. The savings in eventual damage to humans could be incalculable."

Scripps officials were nervous during a recent round of interviews about their role in Wigwam. An internal memorandum, circulated by public affairs officer Chuck Colgan, advised that the staff hold a special meeting "to review the subject areas of Wigwam to be discussed with the reporters."

In addition, Nierenberg tried to deny that Focke was employed by Scripps while acting as Wigwam scientific director in 1955.

"No, we checked our records, and Focke was working for the Naval Electronics Lab at that time, not us."

Reminded that the institute's official history states that Focke was a Scripps employee at that time, Nierenberg then consulted with deputy director Jeffery Frautschy before returning to the phone: "Ah . . . yes, it seems Focke *was* with Scripps at that time, after all." His voice was unenthusiastic.

From his office overlooking the institute's picturesque loading pier for its fleet of research vessels, Frautschy recently reviewed Scripps' involvement in Operation Wigwam. Frautschy admitted that if the navy asked the institute to coordinate a similar test today, "We would have to take into account the shift in public opinion before agreeing to do it. We probably would say no."

Behind the Story

The large balding man with sunken eyes and colorless skin moved slowly to the podium. Orville Kelly looked like—and was—a dying man. Despite his painful lymphatic cancer and chemotherapy treatments, Kelly was maintaining an arduous speaking schedule in November 1979. This talk, before several hundred people at the University of San Francisco, was typical of the speeches he had been giving for days in various West Coast cities. Before he died, he said, he wanted to tell as many people as possible about the twenty-two atomic bomb tests he had witnessed as a serviceman in the Pacific twenty years earlier.

While slides of some of the nuclear explosions were projected onto a screen, Kelly spoke in a slow, deliberate manner about the physical and psychological problems he believed the tests had caused to the men stationed nearby. Dispassionately, he recounted the innocence and patriotism of the participants. His own cancer, he now felt, was a result of his radiation exposure during these tests. But the United States government denied his and others' claims for medical and financial assistance. He felt betrayed by the country he had served, and he had formed an organization, the National Association of Atomic Veterans (NAAV), to try to do something about it. Despite his declining health and his sense of betrayal, the tone of his speech was not bitter. Clearly he was still a patriot, a man happy to have served in the military. His straightforward manner moved many of those in the auditorium, and when he finished his speech, they rose spontaneously to applaud him.

One of those moved was Dan Noyes, the bearded, midwestern reporter from the Center for Investigative Reporting, who was investigating the atomic testing program. Noyes had first heard of Kelly and his organization a month earlier while researching Operation Wigwam. Now that he was seeing Kelly and his wife, Wanda, in person, his commitment to the story deepened. To Noyes, the Kellys represented the classic American story of decent people trying to correct what they feel to be an injustice. They were underdogs fighting a system that was rigged against them—a massive military bureaucracy that steadfastly refused to recognize the legitimacy of the veterans' claims.

It was the kind of story that had attracted Noyes to journalism in the first place, after several years' work in various nonprofit organizations. He saw investigative reporting as a chance to tell the underdog's side of a story.

The Kellys were two of many committed people that Dan Noyes, Maureen O'Neill, and David Weir got to know over the months they spent investigating Operation Wigwam. It was a wrenching experience to meet people, share their frustrations and fears, and then call back only to learn that they had died. Therefore, the reporters in the story were involved on a deeper emotional level than is normally the case. As O'Neill said later, "I found myself caring very much what happened to these people—once I knew them and their problems, in fact, I couldn't get them out of my mind."

The story began when an attorney in Hawaii named Cooper Brown telephoned the Center. One of Brown's clients, Elroy Runnels, had decided to sue the government because he was dying from leukemia that he felt had been caused by his exposure to radiation during Operation Wigwam. Brown was familiar with the Center's work on the health effects of pesticides, and he hoped to interest the staff in Runnels's plight.

Noyes answered Brown's call and was intrigued to learn that there had been an atomic test so close to the California coast— even if the story was twenty-five years old. During the conversation, Brown offered Noyes another bit of information that was even more interesting. Brown had talked to the widow of a navy officer who claimed that her husband had been involved in another underwater atomic incident near the California coast in 1964 or 1965. Noyes realized that, if true, this test would have been in violation of the limited nuclear test ban treaty that the United States had signed in 1963. Or, if it was a nuclear accident, it had never been reported. Either way, it was a story—*if* it was true. Noyes took the woman's name, Dawn Fellis, and her telephone number and immediately placed the first of many telephone calls to her in his attempt to assess her information.

Dawn Fellis had a vivid recollection of her husband returning, shaken, from a mission that he at first refused to describe. He was so upset, however, that he had quickly broken down and divulged what was apparently a top-secret matter. He told her only the barest details of what had happened, but his concern over his radiation exposure had lodged in her memory. Because she remembered that her husband had also been at Wigwam, the publicity generated by Runnels's lawsuit in Hawaii had led her to contact Brown about this other mysterious incident. Her husband had only recently died of cancer, and the Veterans Administration was not cooperating with her request for his medical records. She wanted to find out whether there was a connection between the tests and his illness. She told Noyes that another officer who had served on her husband's ship could verify her story, but that she had lost track of him since he retired and moved several years earlier.

Noyes contacted a producer at ABC-TV's *20/20* news program to suggest an investigation of Fellis's allegations. The Center and *20/20* had recently completed one investigative story together, and the producer readily agreed to help finance this new inquiry. With this financial commitment, Noyes and Maureen O'Neill began checking the Fellis story.

O'Neill took charge of the search for the retired officer, and she was well suited to this challenge. A determined, gregarious woman in her mid-thirties, O'Neill knew how to avoid taking "no" for an answer from just about anybody. This was her first investigative story, but she had years of experience as a legal researcher and office manager for a politically active San Francisco law firm. O'Neill loved to talk to people, and the challenge of persuading them to turn over information they weren't supposed to made the work fun. Her skill at getting people steeped in military secrecy to trust her with sensitive information was one of the keys to the ultimate success of the investigation.

Finding a missing person is a basic investigative task. In this case, finding the retired officer Fellis had told Noyes about would require two full weeks of O'Neill's time. Starting with only his name and an old address near San Diego, O'Neill first tried the Postal Service. It reported no forwarding address. Next, she called all the schools in the area where the man had lived in the hopes of tracing him through his children. Eventually she located the right school and obtained the children's names, but no new address. She checked through old telephone books and other public records that might give her a lead on his whereabouts, but again she came back empty-handed.

Next O'Neill checked back with Fellis to ask whether there was any military organization in the San Diego area that the man might have joined. She learned that an officers' service organization was a likely prospect, so she called it.

"I told the officer who answered that I was an old friend of the man's wife and used to live in San Diego and I was trying to contact them," O'Neill explains. "I said I wanted to reestablish a friendship. Over a two-day period of talking with this officer I finally convinced him to help me. He gave in and read me the man's Social Security number—which he was not supposed to do—and told me not to tell anyone where it came from."

O'Neill contacted a friend in a government agency who was able to plug the Social Security number into a military computer system in New Orleans in order to obtain the man's current address. By now it was the end of the second week of the search. She waited a day, and then she got what she wanted: the man's new home address, in Kansas.

Noyes, O'Neill, and Weir didn't want to use precious time waiting for a written response, so they tried to get the man's telephone number. He was not listed in local Information. Checks of "reverse directories" for the area also failed to uncover his number. Frustrated, once again they called Dawn Fellis and asked her to send a telegram requesting the man to call her. She did, and he called. Soon the reporters had what they wanted—a chance to talk to the retired officer directly.

Certainly they had bent the rules of journalism to find their man. Journalists often face the dilemma of whether to misrepresent themselves or their purposes in order to find a crucial piece of information. In this case, the reporters believed that the goal— finding out whether a violation of the test ban treaty or a major nuclear accident had occurred—justified the means they used to find this source. They agreed that O'Neill had to hide the fact that she was a reporter in order to locate the retired officer.

"Being a woman helped," O'Neill explains. "Speaking as a woman trying to find lost friends was what convinced the officer to be helpful. Military families often face this problem of finding each other after transfers, and so he sympathized with me. In a sense I was representing Dawn Fellis, who really did want to find these old friends, partly to tell them about her husband's death."

Reaching the lost man by phone in Kansas proved to be an anticlimax. He was unable or unwilling to recall anything about the Fellis story. A search that had taken ten days, cost hundreds of dollars in long-distance phone bills, and stretched journalistic ethics ended in disappointment.

The three Center reporters now had to discard the Fellis story (other attempts to verify it had also failed) and determine what else might be salvaged out of the material they had collected.

Fortunately, Cooper Brown had mentioned in his original conversation with Noyes that he thought the government had a film of Operation Wigwam. Noyes decided to send a Freedom of Information Act (FOIA) request to the Defense Nuclear Agency (DNA) for the Wigwam film. To his surprise, the film arrived within a matter of days, and he turned it over to *20/20* for copying. He also phoned Cooper Brown to thank him for the tip about the film. Brown asked if he could see it before it was sent back to the DNA, and Noyes agreed.

Sending the film to Brown triggered one of the most bizarre but significant chapters in the long Wigwam investigation. In Hawaii, Brown showed the film to sometime private investigator and full-time hell raiser Tony Hodges, who decided it would make dramatic television viewing for the citizens of San Diego. Thus the "Johnny Atomseed" incident, described in the *New West* story, was launched. Hodges's trip to San Diego catapulted Wigwam into a major story in that city. Soon a number of Wigwam participants were contacting the local media to talk about the health effects they believed they'd suffered from the test. By "networking" with San Diego reporters, the Center staff was able to obtain most of these names, some of whom eventually proved critical to the story.

Without Hodges's colorful antics and the resulting identification of new test participants, the Center might never have convinced *20/20* to pursue the Wigwam story after Dawn Fellis's allegations had to be discarded. A film on Wigwam that the government had produced to "deemphasize certain of the more dramatic aspects" of the test, according to FOIA documents, was ironically now being used by Hodges to stir up the entire city of San Diego.

At a press conference Hodges presented a graph from a military document that depicted radiation levels in San Diego rising dramatically in the days following the test. When the local media used Hodges's information and the film as their lead story, Mayor Wilson was forced to convene San Diego's Quality of Life Commission to investigate whether any public health problems had resulted.

There were further political repercussions from Hodges's whirlwind tour of the state. His repeated telephone calls to the governor's office attracted Governor Jerry Brown's interest in Operation Wigwam. Brown's staff called to say that Brown wanted to see the film. Hodges, however, had abruptly returned to Hawaii in order to take advantage of a low-priced air fare. Instead Noyes and O'Neill agreed to go to Sacramento to give the governor a special screening of the film.

Near midnight on a foggy December night, after the governor and his aides had attended a late-night staff Christmas party, the two reporters showed the fourteen-minute film to a group of bleary-eyed public officials, including Brown. His staff also invited dozens of antinuclear protestors to the screening. They had been staging a peaceful sit-in at the governor's outer offices for several weeks in order to draw attention to a nearby nuclear power plant.

Noyes and O'Neill returned to San Francisco in the early-morning hours, not sure what effect the film had had on Brown. They found out several days later when Brown issued a public protest of the navy's handling of the Wigwam test, giving the story another boost. At least one other Wigwam participant who would play a major part in the story—Barry Nicholl—came forward as a result of the publicity over the governor's concern.

Armed with the footage that had already created an uproar in San Diego (and appeared on the national ABC evening news telecast as well) and with the names of a number of men who had participated in the test, Noyes now asked the *20/20* producer whether he would commit to developing a story based on Wigwam alone. The producer said yes but added a proviso: the Center had to provide irrefutable medical evidence that the test had affected the men's health.

This turned out to be an impossible task, but not before Noyes, O'Neill, and others at the Center had made a major attempt to accomplish it. Compiling medical proof of the connection between the test and the men's illnesses was far beyond the Center's limited resources. The federal Centers for Disease Control was at that time studying the effects of one Nevada test on the servicemen who had witnessed it. That study took five and a half years and cost nearly $900,000, and according to the Pentagon it proved inconclusive.

At this point the reporters got another break. The DNA decided to prepare one of its first atomic test reports for the public on Wigwam. Substantial amounts of previously secret material would soon be "declassified." Partly because of the efforts of Orville Kelly and his colleagues, the plight of atomic veterans was becoming a political concern in Washington; the Senate had held hearings in mid-1979 on veterans' claims for radiation-related disability support. In addition, the Centers for Disease Control had identified a cluster of leukemia cases among veterans present at another nuclear test. The DNA now wanted to release information about Wigwam and other tests to demonstrate their cooperation in the investigation of possible health effects from nuclear tests. Because their records contained little evidence of radiation danger at Wigwam, the DNA considered it one of the military's "safest" tests and a good candidate for public scrutiny.

"We were overjoyed," Weir recalls. "We felt we could demonstrate that there had been adverse health effects for some of the servicemen, and possibly some environmental damage as well, from what the DNA considered one of the safest tests. We weren't concentrating on a 'bad' test where everything went wrong; it was one of the star tests. Problems at Wigwam, if we could document them, would obviously raise questions about the really dirty tests."

Weir and Center researcher Mike Kepp began to probe into the question of fish contamination near the test site. FOIA requests were rushed off to the Nuclear Regulatory Agency, the Department of Energy, and the Food and Drug Administration for studies carried out in 1955 to monitor radiation in the ocean and in fish caught near Wigwam's "Surface Zero."

Meanwhile, O'Neill was tracking down every Wigwam participant or widow she could find. She interviewed everyone extensively, usually over a period of weeks, to find out what they could remember about the test and how it had affected their health. She located some people by word of mouth, asking each participant to remember the names of others and then searching for them. She also gathered the names of people who had called the San Diego media or Governor Brown's office after Hodges's trip. And she placed notices in newsletters that atomic veterans might read, requesting that Wigwam participants contact her. Eventually O'Neill had located and interviewed three dozen men who had been at Wigwam.

"One of them was Charles Fleming," O'Neill remembers. "He was dying at that time, but he was an important source. He gave me the names of two or three other men and also tipped us to the fact that the radiated submarine hulls used in the test had been dumped somewhere off the coast—he thought near Catalina Island off southern California." Tracing what had happened to the three sub hulls at the test soon turned into another major investigation.

Others joined the search for sources. Noyes asked Chris Paine, a Center associate working in Washington, D.C., to check with veterans groups there to locate Wigwam participants. Paine found Ross Pennington, who was dying of leukemia in a Maryland hospital, and received an extremely important letter from him just before he died. Pennington had been the captain of one of the most heavily radiated ships at Wigwam, and he wrote Paine that he had been told his ship was measured for radioactivity and found "off-scale at over four hundred rems" right after the test. Pennington also felt that Elroy Runnels had good cause to believe his exposure to radiation at Wigwam had led to his leukemia.

Pennington died before O'Neill could speak with him, but she did reach his widow for a lengthy interview. "I always tried to get as much information as I could during that initial interview," O'Neill explains, "because often afterward people would be more hesitant. When I called out of the blue to talk about something that had happened twenty-five years ago, people would volunteer things like 'I remember that' or 'This is what happened.' Then,

later, they would realize that this was an investigation by the press
and they would become frightened. All those years in the military
had affected them and they worried that they might be doing
something against their country.

"Well, with Mrs. Pennington," O'Neill continues, "I caught her
off guard the first time we spoke. We talked for a good hour and
a half, and she gave me the whole story of how her husband's
ship had returned after Operation Wigwam to San Francisco Bay.
When I called her later, however, she refused to talk at all and
said she didn't want to do anything that might hurt the government."

During her interviews with atomic veterans and their families,
O'Neill was sympathetic, caring, and "a friend to some, a daughter
or sister to others." She feels that success in interviewing depends
both on caring about people and on putting them at ease. "If they
can look at you as a person, not just a reporter, they will relax
more and open up."

By this point in the investigation, in early 1980, the money from
20/20 had run out and there was still much work to do before
ABC could be convinced to broadcast a story. The three reporters
decided to risk pursuing the investigation on their own. They would
go back to *20/20* when they had more evidence of the adverse
health effects on the veterans. In the meantime, they decided to
try to sell an article about Wigwam to *New West* magazine. If
both assignments came through, they would be able to recoup the
cost of the full investigation.

For *20/20*, Noyes began preparing an extensive research packet
that included brief summaries of the health problems and
recollections of each of the men O'Neill had tracked down. Aided
by Center staff member Mark Schapiro, he also interviewed
numerous radiation and health experts to show that, although there
was no conclusive medical evidence connecting Wigwam to the
men's diseases, there was strong circumstantial evidence that a link
existed.

Even more useful in the effort to win ABC's approval for the
story was a meeting Noyes had with John Berger, a freelance
reporter who had written extensively on nuclear issues. Berger
showed Noyes a military catalogue that revealed that the
government had other film footage of Wigwam beyond the Public

Relations film the Center had already obtained. Through the FOIA, Noyes now secured copies of this material. For the first time the reporters could view the military's most revealing footage of the test. The scenes depicted the violence of the explosion in a far more dramatic way than the PR version—and ABC was pleased. Television is first and foremost a visual medium; good film footage is often a decisive factor for which investigative stories make it on the air.

By April, after reviewing the research packet from Noyes, ABC gave a tentative okay to proceed with the story. Most important, from the financially strapped Center's point of view, the network agreed to pay for the work done so far. Encouraged, the reporters convinced *New West* to assign a Wigwam article in conjunction with the *20/20* segment. Producing the stories simultaneously held certain risks—either outlet might feel slighted, for instance—but it also meant that both would benefit from a more thorough investigation. The Washington, D.C.–based Fund for Investigative Journalism also agreed to support some of the expenses of the *New West* story. Weir could now devote nearly full-time work to the final stage of the project. In the end, the Center was able to escape with only a small loss on an extensive investigation that stretched out over a year and involved seven researchers—the three main reporters plus Kepp, Paine, Schapiro, and Center staff writer Tracy Freedman. The final bill for the project topped $15,000.

For the *New West* article, the team concentrated on parts of the story that were peripheral to the *20/20* version: the involvement of Scripps Institute, the possible contamination of fish, the source of the elevated radiation levels over San Diego after Wigwam, the whereabouts of the radiated sub hulls and other detritus from the test, and the Atomic Energy Commission's planning process for Wigwam.

The team's extensive use of the FOIA finally began to pay off as packages of documents arrived from various federal agencies. Most of the material was relatively uncensored. "All kinds of documents were available which had been put together by the government at a time when there was no FOIA," says Weir. (The act was passed in 1966.) "Far more truthful information found its way into the files in those days, under the arrogant assumption that the public would never see it. Old information is generally better under FOIA. Few people in power are directly threatened by the release of very old data. So we got tons of twenty-five-year-old material, much of it very useful."

Sadly, as the investigation dragged on into summer, some of the sources for the story died from cancer. First, Chuck Fleming. Then, Orville Kelly. The timing of Kelly's death was particularly disheartening since network competition had prevented *20/20* from interviewing him for the Wigwam segment. A week before the ABC crew called to set a filming date, a rival crew from *60 Minutes* arrived to interview Kelly in his hospital bed for a story *they* were filming about the plight of atomic veterans. The *60 Minutes* producer told Kelly and his wife that he wanted an exclusive interview, and that if they allowed the *20/20* crew in it might torpedo the CBS show altogether. Rather than risk losing a story on the top-rated show in the country, the Kellys reluctantly declined the *20/20* request. A few weeks later, Kelly died. The *60 Minutes* program aired in the fall of 1980 and included the Kelly deathbed interview.

Another disappointment came when Weir finished analyzing the FOIA documents about fish contamination. Working with marine biologist and author John Culliney, Weir realized that although there was a reasonable chance that fish had been contaminated, nothing in the documents they possessed would allow them to print such a charge. The search for the exact site of the sunken submarine hulls also ended in failure, despite weeks of work.

By Labor Day the team had made extensive preparations for a final set of key interviews for both the *New West* and the *20/20* stories. Noyes, O'Neill, and Weir piled a large case of files into a rental car and headed south from San Francisco for Los Angeles and San Diego. After a day's drive, during which they reviewed their research, they stopped at a motel east of Los Angeles, where they were to meet a film crew and ABC producer Lowell Bergman the following day.

Early the next morning they located the house where Wigwam director Alfred Focke lived. While Focke reminisced about the test, his wife served the assembled crew of reporters and technicians cookies and lemonade. Focke was proud of Operation Wigwam. He saw it as one of his greatest moments in a long career of service to his country. Now retired and teaching at a small college near Los Angeles, he welcomed the chance to review his accomplishments and be in the spotlight once again.

Focke answered the reporters' critical questions with the civility of a college professor. Clearly, the view of the top-level decision makers at Wigwam was considerably different from that of the servicemen at sea level. His interview gave the team insight into the fascination the scientific-military planners had with nuclear explosions during that period.

Next the reporters traveled to La Jolla to interview Scripps officials. O'Neill had conducted a few preliminary interviews several weeks earlier and had found the scientists friendly and willing to discuss all aspects of the test. She had taped Ted Folsom when he said, "Oh, our instruments were so crude; the detectors were designed for medium- and high-range levels of radiation. We went to sea with no low-level gear; we drifted into the "hot" water areas and I yelled, 'Get the hell out of here!' "

Now, however, as O'Neill remembers, "We were back on campus with the *20/20* crew, and Folsom and the others clammed up. They talked only about what a safe test it had been. In fact Folsom spent most of his time on camera talking about how dangerous *other* tests had been. The Scripps people were so guarded, in fact, that nothing they said was used on the show."

The reporters were mystified at the about-face until a sympathetic Scripps employee surreptitiously handed them a memo revealing that before the *20/20* film crew arrived the Scripps Public Affairs Office had organized a special meeting of all the Scripps officials involved in Wigwam. Apparently the officials were cautioned to minimize the dangers of Wigwam while on camera.

The reporters also spent several days with former servicemen and their families, gathering valuable details about their participation in the test and their current medical problems. The start of a final interview with San Diego mayor Pete Wilson provided some much-needed comic relief. Because of the confusion over the simultaneous development of stories for both *20/20* and *New West,* the mayor had arrived for the Saturday afternoon interview expecting to be filmed for national television. But the *20/20* crew had decided not to include the mayor's involvement in their version and dropped out at the last minute. When the three reporters showed up in casual clothes, they found an obviously disappointed mayor in his suit and tie.

The last night in San Diego was spent over notepads and a bottle of good liquor as the reporters plotted out an organization of their massive files for *New West*. Weir was responsible for writing the bulk of the article, and the outline they developed that night held up well during the next several weeks of work. Noyes wrote the concluding section on the findings of the investigation, and O'Neill organized the files for an extensive fact-checking process. In order to write the lead to the story, Weir watched the Wigwam film clips and reviewed the transcript of the government films. For him, capturing the explosive power of the detonation was a technique for drawing readers into the story, and watching footage of the blast made the telling of the story much stronger.

One particularly sensitive decision during the writing stage was the reporters' inclusion of the information about Richard Purdy's alcoholism and psychological problems. "I talked with Mrs. Purdy a lot over the months," O'Neill remembers. "She freely told us about his drinking and mental problems, but then, near the end, she asked that we not use it. She didn't want his family to find out about it; she had hidden it from them for years.

"She was a wonderful person who had helped us and I felt bad about putting it in, but we believed it was part of the story. In the end she wrote us and agreed with our judgment, although she still wished we'd left it out. She was very pleased with the story overall, though."

The argument for using the material was simple. By the time the *New West* article appeared there had been numerous magazine and newspaper stories, even books, about health problems from nuclear weapons tests. By contrast, very little attention had been devoted to the psychological toll from the tests. In addition, the reporters felt that the very concept of nuclear warfare was insane, and that the reaction of Richard Purdy to Operation Wigwam was a natural human reaction.

The fact-checking process at *New West*, coordinated by magazine staff member Paul Cohen, took about two weeks. Editor B. K. Moran, who had met with Weir several times during the writing

of the story, edited the manuscript and skillfully moved the
Frautschy quote to the end of the piece, providing a summation
of the Wigwam story where it belonged.

Careful coordination with *20/20* set the end of November as
the time when both the magazine story and the television segment
would appear. Then, even though *TV Guide* announced the story
in its weekly edition, a last-moment scheduling shakeup pulled the
Wigwam story off the air. It was too late for *New West* to stop,
however, and the carefully constructed plan to coordinate the release
of the two versions collapsed.

The airing of the Wigwam story continued to be delayed at ABC
over the following months, raising concern that it might not appear
at all. The DNA's Colonel William McGee, in an attempt to affect
the *20/20* segment, sent a long letter to producer Lowell Bergman
denouncing the *New West* story as inaccurate. Noyes sent a detailed
memo to ABC refuting McGee's charges.

Finally, in March 1981, a year and a half after Noyes had received
the initial phone call from Cooper Brown, the story was aired with
ABC reporter David Marash as correspondent.

Since the two stories on Wigwam were released, there has been
little improvement for this country's atomic veterans. While
Congress has moved slowly on legislation to provide compensation
to atomic veterans, early in 1983 the Veterans Administration eased
slightly the guidelines for providing medical care to these men.

Orville Kelly's book on atomic testing, *Countdown Zero,* was
published posthumously in 1982. Cooper Brown left his law practice
to become general counsel of the National Association of Atomic
Veterans. Wanda Kelly became executive director of NAAV upon
her husband's death. Elroy Runnels's lawsuit lingered in the courts
after Scripps Institute settled its part in the suit in an out-of-court
payment. Colonel McGee did not answer a letter from Noyes
responding to McGee's criticisms of the *New West* article. Governor
Brown never mentioned Wigwam publicly again.

Former Scripps director Roger Revelle, however, did respond
to the *New West* story in a 1982 magazine article: "I don't have
any opinion or any knowledge of [the Wigwam health effects], but
I wouldn't be surprised. The AEC mission was really very high-
handed about radioactivity. It used to drive me up a wall the way

they'd lie and conceal and in general behave very badly. You just couldn't trust them. We [Scripps] stopped being involved [with atomic testing] after Wigwam."

Revelle went on to say, "These bomb tests made an anti-weapons man out of me. I feel very strongly about it. I don't think anybody should be developing nuclear weapons. Believe me, no one who's seen one of those things go off ever wants to see another one."

Investigative Techniques

Finding a good investigative story can be as simple as receiving a phone call about Operation Wigwam or as complex as figuring out why a package of Kool-Aid is in Afghanistan. In all good investigative stories, the reporter must recognize the potential of the information and be tenacious in tracking down the story. This awareness comes with experience, education, and alertness. It's what Doug Foster used when he saw someone out of place at the Teamsters convention, and why Suzanne Gordon became curious when she saw a newspaper clip about the Hunger Project. Tenacity, on the other hand, is mostly in the blood.

The First Lead

Stories begin in different ways that usually fit into several broad categories. In this collection they started with whistle blowers and leaked documents ("Nuclear Nightmare"), brainstorming among reporters ("Bechtel"), personal observations ("Teamster Madness" and "Boomerang"), tips and rumors ("Panthers"), pursuing a lead from an earlier story ("Citizen Scaife"), a phone call ("Wigwam"), and reading the newspaper ("Hunger Project"). No method seems to ensure a better story than any other. But reporters can always help to "make their own breaks" by being alert to new reports and developments, seeking and maintaining sources, sounding out experts, and producing stories that attract attention. Whistle blowers, for instance, often contact reporters who they feel will give their story the proper treatment. Once the lead is in hand, there are certain techniques and methods that investigative reporters commonly use.

The Investigative Sniff

First, reporters must find out if the lead seems solid. Kate Coleman began by talking to sources to see whether the rumors about violence and corruption among certain Panthers had validity. Suzanne Gordon went to a Hunger Project rally and found that there was no plan for giving food to hungry people. David Weir and Michael Singer traveled to Washington to talk with secretive sources. Sometimes the "sniff" will end the story, and other times it will alter the direction, as in the "Nuclear Nightmare" investigation. The purpose is to feel out a story before the reporter becomes too deeply committed. Of course there are exceptions to every rule. If Weir had not had a magazine assignment before he called old sources on the "Boomerang" story, he might have become discouraged by initial reports that pesticide dumping was no longer a problem.

The Investigative Hypothesis

This useful tool gives shape and direction to a budding investigation. The theory should be grounded in fact and experience and take the story beyond what is presently known to what seems a likelihood. In "Boomerang," for example, the hypothesis was that pesticide dumping was occurring. In Gordon's investigation, she determined that the Hunger Project might be a vehicle to allow Werner Erhard and est to contact powerful people in Washington. Forming a hypothesis allows the reporter to think like a prosecutor and to narrow the focus of the investigation away from irrelevancy. The reporter uses his or her analysis of how the world works to say, "Okay, I think this is probably happening. How do I go about proving it?"

Don't Re-invent the Wheel

At the very start, the reporter needs to find out what's been written or said about the subject under investigation. This means checking the library for newspaper and magazine stories and researching congressional hearings and reports. If someone has already reported on aspects of the story, the focus of the investigation can change or even come to a halt. On the other hand, when there is only a collection of "puff" stories and press handout rewrites, as was the case with the "Bechtel" story, contrary information ensures that the subject will be worthy of further investigation. The important thing is to evaluate carefully all existing information and to avoid duplicating work that someone else has done.

Find the Experts

Many stories involve people or institutions that various experts have studied at length. These experts, whether scientists, analysts, or hobbyists, can provide a valuable shortcut for the reporter. Karen Rothmyer found Wes McCune, an expert on right-wing groups, and not only saved research time but uncovered some new leads as a result. Mark Dowie used the Data Center, a specialized library with an extensive file on the Bechtel Corporation. Doug Foster found a researcher who had followed the U.S. Labor Party for many years. Sometimes the experts may be other reporters or writers, like John Berger in the "Wigwam" story or John Friedman in the "Citizen Scaife" story. Although competitive pressures sometimes rule out cooperation, many reporters are happy to help colleagues once their own work has been published.

Develop a Team

Center stories are typically team stories in which several reporters and researchers work together and divide up the responsibilities. In this collection, only Karen Rothmyer and Doug Foster worked alone. The advantage of the team investigation is illustrated in the "Hunger Project" story, where Suzanne Gordon came to the Center for help. Previously Gordon had done most of her reporting alone, but she saw an advantage in doing an investigative story with others. As part of a team Gordon could benefit from three types of investigations occurring simultaneously. She could take the "front door" approach with Hunger Project officials while Dan Noyes and Lori Lieberman went under cover as volunteers and Arnold Levinson immersed himself in figuring out Werner Erhard's complicated tax-shelter structure. In the "Panther" story, Kate Coleman and Paul Avery provided each other with psychological support as well as investigative help.

One danger of the team approach, as Terry Jacobs and Mark Schapiro experienced in "Boomerang," is that some members may feel that their work is too fragmented from the larger story and thus become isolated. This situation can be avoided if team members compare notes regularly. Taking on powerful people and institutions, or cults and violence-prone groups, is a difficult proposition for the lonely freelancer. It is usually more suitable for a team of reporters.

Document the Story

Following the paper trail of documents is an integral part of most investigations. Numerous public records exist in government offices at the local, state, and federal levels. These pieces of paper help a reporter build the documentation needed to strengthen the story. Documents can become vital when questions of libel arise and proof must be provided to support allegations. A major source for documents from the federal government is the Freedom of Information Act (FOIA), which says that the federal government must either justify the withholding of information requested by citizens or release it. The FOIA puts the burden on the government to justify withholding material rather than on citizens to prove that they need the information. Terry Jacobs made extensive use of the FOIA in the "Boomerang" story to track down lists of products banned or highly regulated by numerous federal agencies. Mark Dowie obtained FOIA documentation on the Bechtel Corporation's dealings with the federal government. The "Wigwam" story was told on national television because of film footage obtained under the FOIA.

When seeking public records, a reporter should study the *U.S. Government Manual* to locate which federal government offices might have had contact with the individual or organization of interest. Thus the "Boomerang" story made use of reports filed with the Securities and Exchange Commission, which regulates corporations, including those companies that manufacture and export pesticides. Karen Rothmyer found helpful information in the 990 tax returns the Internal Revenue Service makes public on all foundations.

Finally, court records are extremely useful in following the paper trail that important people and organizations create. The Tax Court in the "Hunger Project" story provided financial figures on est and Werner Erhard, and the "Boomerang" story benefited from a court case between two pesticide manufacturers arguing over profits.

Develop Sources

A good source can spark the beginning of an investigative story
or strengthen one that is already under way. The anonymous
background source "Barry Steel" caused Michael Singer and David
Weir to focus on nuclear terrorism in "Nuclear Nightmare." Doug
Foster needed to find a source on the Teamster executive board
for "Teamster Madness" since there were few documents to link
the union with the U.S. Labor party. Karen Rothmyer found
background sources who could explain the inner workings of
Richard Mellon Scaife's charitable activities.

Finding a source is a matter of luck, energy, and perception.
In "Boomerang," Mark Schapiro just happened to know, through
a friend, someone associated with the Amvac chemical company.
Suzanne Gordon vigorously pursued sources among former Erhard
associates for her "Hunger Project" story. She found useful
confirmation sources even after her investigation was completed
and she was writing her article. She felt these "rubber stamp" sources
would help strengthen and add confidence to her writing. Doug
Foster used knowledge of the Teamsters gained from books to
identify Harold Gibbons as a possible source. He then succeeded
in persuading Gibbons to become one.

Dealing with sources is a tricky matter; it depends on individual
style. Some sources will be interviewed for direct attribution, others
off-the-record (not for quotation or attribution), and still others
for quotation, but they cannot be identified in the article. The
reporter must figure out how to get the most information and keep
as much of it attributed as possible. Sometimes one source can go
on- and off-the-record for different questions. Other times a reporter
may convince a source to go back on-the-record after initially
agreeing to anonymity.

Perhaps the most difficult source relationships for a reporter are
those with law enforcement officials and with sources who leak
documents. Kate Coleman and Paul Avery had to evaluate carefully
all their background information from the law enforcement source
in the "Panther" story. They avoided talking with the FBI because
they suspected the reliability of that agency's Panther information.
Just as newspapers and reporters vary in credibility, so do law
enforcement agencies. Reporters should use their experience,

knowledge, and caution when they evaluate sources and reasons for sharing information. If possible, they should check with other credible sources to verify a new source's trustworthiness, as Karen Rothmyer did with her first confidential source in "Citizen Scaife."

Observe

Firsthand observation can also start or strengthen an investigation. Doug Foster found the warning signals for "Teamster Madness" in his observations at the Teamsters convention in Las Vegas. Suzanne Gordon saw the Hunger Project in action at a rally.

Sometimes the reporter decides that undercover observations are called for. Dan Noyes and Lori Lieberman volunteered at the Hunger Project. Mark Schapiro tried to apply for a job at Amvac and hung out with the workers. Mark Dowie haunted the bars and cafés around Bechtel Corporation's headquarters. A reporter must exercise great care when deciding how far to mislead people while pursuing a story. Undercover work may ultimately be used to discredit a story. Some critics accuse undercover reporters of encouraging unsavory behavior and influencing events, and thereby creating situations that otherwise would not have occurred. Of late, reporters using undercover or misleading tactics have come under greater pressure from editors and publishers. A *Los Angeles Herald-Examiner* reporter, Merle Wolin, reportedly lost a Pulitzer Prize for a brilliant series of stories she wrote on the working conditions of garment makers because she took a job in a garment factory in order to investigate the story.

Organize Your Files

File systems can vary greatly among reporters. Good organization requires time and supplies that may be beyond the resources of independent freelancers. Still, knowing how to organize files is a useful skill, even if it isn't employed often. One sound method is to keep large "generic" files and then start index cards on all major names, listing the file name and page number or document where the name is mentioned. If a copying machine is handy, duplicate pages can be made and separate files begun on many topics, people,

organizations, and events. A chronology like the one Arnold
Levinson created for the corporate history of est is helpful in some
instances where a series of complicated transactions occur over time.
Sometimes it's useful to compile a file summary that lists the
highlights of each file as it develops. A summary allows you to
glance at and evaluate a file quickly. One basic principle underlies
all filing systems: an unrelenting attention to detail.

Interview

Some reporters have a gift for interviewing; others learn as they
go. Chutzpah helps, as Karen Rothmyer demonstrated in her J.
P. Stevens story for the *Wall Street Journal,* when she went into
the ladies' room to evade officials and interview women workers.
Reporters like Maureen O'Neill in "Wigwam" and Mark Schapiro
in "Boomerang" tried to put their subjects at ease by talking about
themselves and showing concern for their source's life and work.
Doug Foster in "Teamster Madness" tried to meet as many potential
sources as possible in person at the union convention. This personal
contact made it easier for the sources to "open up" to Foster later.
Suzanne Gordon tried to dress attractively and professionally when
she went to interview Hunger Project officials.

Interviewing public relations officials for corporations and other
organizations is generally of limited value. These highly trained
professionals know how to avoid or deflect many questions, as the
"Bechtel" and "Teamster Madness" stories show. But there are
exceptions to the rule. Terry Jacobs obtained some valuable quotes
from the public relations man at Velsicol for the "Boomerang"
story, and Suzanne Gordon obtained the cooperation of the est
PR representative in arranging interviews with top officials there.
Reporters have to be careful, however, of relying on public relations
agents as substitutes for those directly involved in their story.

The final interviews with key figures are a critical step in an
investigation. Sometimes they can make or break a story,
particularly on television, where producers want good "visuals."
Reporters often know 80 percent of the answers to the questions
they will ask. Of course the subject of the interview does not know
this, or at least isn't sure which 20 percent the reporter doesn't

know. The reporter tries to maneuver the subject into telling more than he or she intends. Sometimes a reporter feigns ignorance to seem nonthreatening. Other times the reporter pretends to know more than is the case, bluffing the subject into saying something previously unconfirmed or unknown. Michael Singer did this with the Zimmerman letter in "Nuclear Nightmare." Singer also played this cat-and-mouse game when he interviewed top officials at Los Alamos and the Nevada test site for the "Nuclear Nightmare" story. During key interviews, reporters must be especially careful not to mislead their subjects or misrepresent themselves; the courts have been harsh in libel suits on reporters who have done so.

More often than not in this collection, key subjects refused to be interviewed: Lyndon LaRouche, Bechtel officials, Richard Mellon Scaife, Huey Newton. Of course the reporter can always try to surprise a reluctant subject, as Karen Rothmyer accomplished to great advantage in "Citizen Scaife." Sometimes the ambush interview is all that's available to a tenacious reporter.

Analyze and Organize

Reporters should try to reevaluate or broaden their perspective once in a while. Sometimes documents, interviews, or files will produce hidden veins of information or new leads when the reporter returns to them for a second glance. Analysis like this led Suzanne Gordon to focus her attention on the Hunger Project's contact with people in power in Washington. Karen Rothmyer analyzed documents for patterns in Richard Mellon Scaife's donations, and her story uncovered financial data on the "New Right" as a result. Reporters who wait until the end of the investigation to give their files a thorough review may not discover valuable new leads until it's too late to pursue them.

Writing

Writing is a process of selecting and emphasizing information and therefore is perhaps the most individualistic part of investigative reporting. Each person must find the method that works best. Some reporters try to write the story first and go back to check on the details later. Others need to document their facts as they go along.

One basic approach is to become immersed in the files, then organize an outline of the material, and finally sit down and write the story, referring to the files as little as possible until fact-checking time. In this method the style and organization are paramount. Many reporters try to review books on good writing, such as *The Elements of Style* by Strunk and White or *On Writing Well* by Zinsser before starting. The writing challenge in an investigative article is to weave a story out of material that is heavily laden with factual detail and yet keep within the strict boundaries of what has been proved.

When writing about pesticides or nuclear power, for instance, it is important to minimize the use of technical or bureaucratic terms. Long, confusing quotes from sources often have to be edited slightly, not to change the words or meaning but to cut out the excess. The best approach for any article is to choose simple, direct language. Other rules of thumb: Be prepared to rewrite and reorganize; solicit criticism from friends; and carefully check every fact. In the end, publish only what can be proved.

Most important, reporters have to think about the way the information they are presenting will affect their readers or viewers. They need to explain in a direct fashion why their audience should care about the story. If a story can somehow touch the everyday lives of individuals, it can motivate the public to take corrective action. Such a story may, in fact, make people feel a little bit more in control of their lives.

Fact-Checking and Libel

It is a sobering experience for investigative reporters to sit through a libel trial and see how mundane matters can come under judicial scrutiny. The growth in libel suits makes investigative reporting resemble a sea full of underwater mines. Something can blow up at any moment. But precautions can be taken; learning as much as possible about the law is a first step. *The Associated Press Stylebook and Libel Manual* (Reading, MA: Addison-Wesley, 1982) is a useful introduction. It is equally important to check facts at the end of the writing to make sure that every fact in the article stands up. Of these eight articles, only two were threatened with libel suits—and neither of these was ever filed.

Afterword

The stories in this volume cover a broad range of investigative subjects—an entire industry ("The Boomerang Crime"), a private corporation (Bechtel), the government bureaucracy ("Nuclear Nightmare"), the military establishment ("Operation Wigwam"), a union ("Teamster Madness"), a powerful individual ("Citizen Scaife"), a radical group (Black Panther party), and an offbeat organization (est). Of course, within each investigation many related groups and individuals also came under scrutiny—from the Scripps Institute of Oceanography to the U.S. Labor Party to Werner Erhard's offshore tax-shelter network.

However different they may be, the organizations and individuals exposed in these stories probably could agree on one thing: that they didn't like the stories. Two of the groups—the Panthers and the Hunger Project—threatened to sue for libel. The Defense Nuclear Agency (in "Wigwam") and Bechtel attempted to demonstrate a pattern of errors in the stories. The targets of the other investigations have all let their displeasure be known, in ways ranging from telephone calls and angry letters to publicity efforts aimed at undermining the effects of the original stories.

These responses are to be expected in a society where freedom of speech and freedom of the press are still exercised with vigor. Investigative reporting is by its very nature controversial, both in its techniques and in its results. Muckraking challenges popular assumptions, undermines the status quo, and more or less generally shakes things up. Not surprisingly, these results are often unpopular with individuals in positions of power. They are, nevertheless, the essence of the First Amendment to the Constitution.

These days that amendment is under a state of siege. For over a quarter-century it has coexisted uneasily with a curious bit of legal fallout from the nuclear age—the "born classified" provision of the Atomic Energy Act which reporters Singer and Weir encountered during their "Nuclear Nightmare" investigation. This little-known provision carries with it the potential to render the First Amendment meaningless, because it holds that there is information too dangerous to be free to the public.

But "born classified" is only one of many current threats to the freedom of the press. The growth of secrecy in government in recent decades led to the Freedom of Information Act (FOIA). That act is now under serious assault, however. According to the *Washington Post,* the Justice Department under the Reagan administration has issued guidelines to government agencies to scrutinize the "qualifications" and the intentions of individuals requesting documents. People who frequently use the FOIA have noticed a severe reduction in the quantity and quality of information released by government agencies under Reagan.

While testifying before Congress on the threats to the FOIA in April 1983, New York attorney Floyd Abrams, a leading expert in First Amendment cases, identified a pattern of information-suppressing measures by the Reagan administration. Recent cases included intervention to prevent an American professor from delivering an academic research paper containing unclassified information, the labeling of a Canadian environmental film as "political propaganda," and the refusal of visas to controversial speakers such as the widow of murdered Chilean president Salvador Allende. Abrams charged that "it is almost as if information were in the nature of a potentially disabling, contagious disease, which must be feared, controlled, and ultimately quarantined."

In addition to these government threats to free speech and press, the use of libel as a tool by the powerful to punish or intimidate the press is proliferating. After reviewing a broad spectrum of libel cases, the American Civil Liberties Union late in 1982 adopted a new policy opposing the right to sue for libel in "any case involving an issue of public concern."

ACLU national director Ira Glasser explained in announcing the new policy that "false and reckless speech is undesirable. But even more undesirable are trials to decide which speech should be suppressed. A basic belief of democracy is that if all speech is permitted, the people will be wise enough to sort out the truth. . . . [Libel laws] allow powerful individuals and groups, both in and out of government, to function as private prosecutors 'indicting' their opponents for false and reckless speech. . . . But we believe the First Amendment bars judicial trials of truth or malice of words spoken in the course of public debate over public issues."

The ACLU pointed out that "libel suits place a price on free speech that the speaker or writer often cannot pay." The group documented numerous cases where reporters or citizens were forced to pay huge legal fees and expenses defending "frivolous" libel suits aimed mainly at "suppressing criticism."

In the course of these and other legal actions in recent years, the use of confidential sources by journalists has been repeatedly challenged. As a result, many reporters feel that they cannot print information until they get on-the-record confirmation. As the stories in this collection demonstrate, many important pieces of information can be obtained only by granting sources confidentiality. Their jobs, their friendships, and occasionally even their lives depend on such protection.

Another threat to the free flow of information comes from the increasing concentration of ownership of many of the largest media outlets, especially in the book-publishing industry. A handful of multinational corporations have acquired ownership, leading to charges that books critical of corporate behavior are being suppressed. Author and press critic Ben Bagdikian conducted a major study of the effects of concentrated ownership in books, magazines, newspapers, television, and radio.* His research indicated that not only are individual corporate stories being suppressed, but what is perhaps the most important story of all—the "structural, systematic breakdown of the free enterprise system"—is not being told at all.

The rise of multinational corporations, with their globe-encircling networks of subsidiaries and affiliates and their interlocking directorates with banks and other corporate groupings, has created many challenges for investigative reporters. In today's world, the factory that closes its operations across town may be opening soon in Taiwan; and the new plant next door may be owned by a corporation in West Germany. Meanwhile, air pollutants from American industry are falling as "acid rain" on the plains of Canada; and pesticides that are banned in the United States are shipped overseas by multinational corporations, only to return as residue in the food products we import and eat.

---

* *The Media Monopoly* (Boston: Beacon Press, 1983).

Corporations are not the sole cause of these problems, of course. Nor are they the sole beneficiaries of the new international linkages. Many different kinds of organizations are starting to form global ties, from labor unions to consumer activists to groupings of governments, such as the EEC, OPEC, OECD, or the Group of 77 (Third World nations in the UN). All of these developments demonstrate that today's world is interdependent in a way that was unthinkable even a generation ago, and reporters need to adjust their perspective accordingly.

Other needed changes seem to be coming. Until recently, investigative reporting has been largely the province of men, and women's contributions have often been overlooked. One recent book on modern-day muckrakers contained only twenty-five paragraphs on women's contribution out of 297 pages. Women have been poorly represented in editing as well; a recent survey of American newspapers revealed that over 90 percent of all managing editor jobs are held by men. A 1981 Labor Department survey showed, moreover, that the average weekly salary for women reporters and editors was only 85 percent that of men doing the same jobs. But women are entering the field in increasing numbers, and as they do, they can be expected to bring new perspectives and new priorities for stories, expanding the impact and audience of investigative reporting in the process.

Minority journalists historically have also played very limited roles. Although blacks, Asians, Hispanics, and Native Americans composed 20 percent of the population in 1982, they accounted for only 5.5 percent of all news professionals. A recent Northwestern University survey found that 60 percent of the country's newspapers did not have even one black employee. The American Society of Newspaper Editors reported recently that 20 percent of the editors surveyed feared that hiring minorities would lower the standards of their newspapers. As more minority people take their places in journalism, however, many areas of investigation will be pursued that have previously been overlooked.

Investigative reporting's survival depends not only on the journalists who practice it, but on the audience that demands it as well. The simple truth is that muckraking can sell; it sells magazines, books, and newspapers, and it boosts television ratings.

The CBS newsmagazine *60 Minutes,* which regularly includes investigative stories, is the top-rated television show in America. Indeed, today television has replaced the *McClure's* of yesteryear as the main mass audience vehicle for investigative journalism. No magazine or newspaper can boast of an audience even approaching the 30 to 40 million people who watch *60 Minutes* every Sunday night. Accordingly, reporters at the Center for Investigative Reporting often work with *60 Minutes* or one of its competitor shows, such as ABC-TV's *20/20.* Although they have a huge audience, however, television broadcasts are limited by their emphasis on visual effects at the expense of detailed factual documentation. And, unlike print versions, TV stories come and go quickly, leaving behind no convenient printed record for the audience to use for future action.

With so many competing interests dominating the current American scene, it is sometimes difficult to keep the aggressive practitioners of the First Amendment—the muckrakers—in perspective. After all, how critical is a free flow of information to a society facing the unprecedented threats of possible extinction from nuclear war, global depression, environmental pollution, overpopulation, a coming crisis in agriculture, and growing disparities between rich and poor? Should there not be some new restrictions placed on the press in light of the need to maintain our vital economic health and our essential national security against foreign aggressors?

The answers to these questions are difficult ones, but they will have to be faced in the coming years. While doing so, individuals in positions of power should ponder the collective wisdom of the people who created the Constitution and its first ten amendments two hundred years ago. Nowhere in the Constitution is the right to make a profit mentioned. Similarly, the right to keep secrets does not have a place. Instead, after considering all the factors and freedoms that could contribute to the creation of a genuinely democratic society, the original architects of our system ranked freedom of speech and freedom of the press as foremost in the Bill of Rights. That is why these guarantees are listed not fifth, or tenth, but first among the amendments.

Investigative reporting is the First Amendment in action. As such, it provides a kind of barometer reading of the health of our democratic society. The rise or fall of muckraking in the face of future threats will be one measure by which we can all judge our performance in the hardest job of all—participation in the formation of a truly democratic society. For if there is a common message in the stories in this book, it is that we have not yet succeeded in reaching that goal. And it is our fear that without a strong and vigorously critical press, Americans may ultimately be denied that hope.

Suggested Readings

This bibliography is intended to provide a sampling of materials that should be helpful to investigative reporters. The "Investigative Reference Library" lists inexpensive, easily available publications that help reporters locate information fast. These books and pamphlets complement expensive reference books usually found in libraries: *Where's What, Business Information Sources, Finding Facts,* and *Finding Facts Fast.* Handbooks written by experienced reporters detailing how they practice their profession are listed under "Methods of Investigative Reporters." Included in "The History of Investigative Reporting" are references for original works, anthologies, and all-time muckraking classics. "Recent Investigative Work" offers a selection of the hundreds of books and articles about investigations of various aspects of American life, culture, and politics. Also included is a list of books written by staff members of the Center for Investigative Reporting.

Investigative Reference Library

Arkin, William M. *Research Guide to Current Military and Strategic Affairs.* Washington, DC: Institute for Policy Studies (1901 "Q" Street, N.W., Washington, DC 20009), 1981.   A comprehensive guide to military information sources by a former army intelligence analyst.

"Business Information Sources," rev. Lorna Daniells. Berkeley, CA: University of California Press, 1976.   A wonderful guide to every conceivable source of information on business.

"A Citizen's Guide on How to Use the Freedom of Information Act and the Privacy Act in Requesting Government Documents." Thirteenth Report by the Committee on Government Operations. Washington, DC: U.S. Government Printing Office (Superintendent of Documents, Washington, DC 20402), 1977.   This guide includes texts of the Freedom of Information Act and the Privacy Act and tells how to utilize both in the procurement of government records.

Greenfield, Stanley R., ed. *National Directory of Addresses and Telephone Numbers.* New York: Nicholas Publishing Company, Bantam Books, 1977.   A national phone book, listing numbers alphabetically and by categories, of business, government, media, transportation, etc.

"How to Read a Financial Statement." New York: Merrill Lynch, Pierce, Fenner & Smith, Inc. (One Liberty Plaza, 165 Broadway, New York, NY 10006), 1973.   A guide written for the layperson on how to read annual reports from corporations. Free.

"How to Research Your Local Bank (or Savings and Loan)." Washington, DC: Institute for Local Self-Reliance (1717 18th Street, N.W., Washington, DC 20009), 1976.   Explains common bank terminology and shows where basic information is, how to get it, and what to do with it.

"How to Use a Law Library." San Francisco: People's Law School (558 Capp Street, San Francisco, CA 94110), 1976.   This guide covers uses of a law library and approaches to solving a legal problem through research.

The Investigation of White-Collar Crime: A Manual for Law Enforcement Agencies. Washington, DC: U.S. Government Printing Office (Superintendent of Documents, Washington, DC 20402), 1977.   A description of white-collar crime investigative issues and methods.

Murphy, Harry J. *Where's What—Sources of Information for Federal Investigators.* New York: Warner Books, 1976.   A CIA study now released to the general public which gives information on where to find information from the federal government.

People Before Property. Chicago: The Midwest Academy, Inc. (600 W. Fullerton Avenue, Chicago IL 60614), 1972.   A handbook on tenants' rights, legal procedures, and property law, written for a Massachusetts audience, but valuable to anyone who wants to research property ownership or real estate transactions.

"Raising Hell." San Francisco: Mother Jones (1663 Mission Street, San Francisco, CA 94103), 1978.   A guide to local, state, and federal records and other public sources of information.

Research for Action. Davis, CA: California Institute for Rural Studies (P.O. Box 530, Davis, CA 95616), 1980.   An excellent guidebook to public records research, geared to community activities.

Rivers, William L. *Finding Facts.* Englewood Cliffs, NJ: Prentice-Hall, 1975.   An introduction to pursuing and interpreting facts.

Todd, Alden. *Finding Facts Fast.* New York: William Morrow, 1972.   A handbook for students, political activists, civic leaders, and professionals based on methods used by reference librarians, investigative reporters, and detectives. Out of print.

U.S. Government Manual. Washington, DC: U.S. Government Printing Office (Superintendent of Documents, Washington, DC 20402), updated yearly.   This publication is the official organization handbook of the federal government. It includes the purposes and programs of most government agencies and lists top personnel, as well as how to obtain information and publications from the federal government.

"Using the Freedom of Information Act: A Step by Step Guide." Washington, DC: Center for National Security Studies (122 Maryland Avenue, N.E., Washington, DC 10002), updated frequently.   An excellent guide to the F.O.I.A.

Washington Information Directory, Federal Regulatory Directory, Politics in America. Washington, DC: Congressional Quarterly, Inc. (1414 22nd Street, N.W., Washington, DC 20037), updated frequently.   Useful guides to the federal government.

Methods of Investigative Reporters

Anderson, David, and Peter Benjaminson. *Investigative Reporting.* Bloomington: Indiana University Press, 1976.   A basic guide to the work that focuses on state and local stories.

Anderson, Jack, with James Boyd. *Confessions of a Muckraker.* New York: Random House, 1979.   The story of muckrakers Jack Anderson and Drew Pearson, which tells about some of their investigations, their problems doing investigative reporting, how they found and maintained sources, and the effects their stories had on the public.

Briloff, Abraham J. *Unaccountable Accounting.* New York: Harper and Row, 1972. An outstanding book on concealed accounting tactics.

Gora, Joel M. *The Rights of Reporters.* New York: Avon Books, 1974. An ACLU handbook on the legal rights and problems of reporters.

Hage, George S., Everette E. Dennis, Arnold H. Ismach, and Stephen Hartgen. *New Strategies for Public Affairs Reporting,* 2d ed. Englewood Cliffs, NJ: Prentice-Hall, 1983. A textbook on in-depth reporting with a special section on investigative work.

Investigative Reporters and Editors. *The Reporter's Handbook: An Investigator's Guide to Documents and Techniques.* New York: St. Martin's Press, 1983. A massive guide to public records and investigative techniques.

Manual of Corporate Investigation, rev. ed. Washington, DC: Food and Beverage Trades Department, AFL-CIO, 1981. A manual on how to investigate giant corporations.

Pawlick, Thomas. *Investigative Reporting.* New York: Richards Rosen Press, 1982. A Canadian reporter's guidebook to investigative journalism.

Williams, Paul. *Investigative Reporting and Editing.* Englewood Cliffs, NJ: Prentice-Hall, 1977. A textbook on newspaper investigative reporting.

The History of Investigative Reporting

Anderson, Jack. *The Anderson Papers.* New York: Random House, 1973. Anderson during the Watergate and Nixon years.

Armstrong, David. *A Trumpet to Arms. Alternative Media in America.* Los Angeles: J. P. Tarcher, 1981. The critical culture during the 1960s and 1970s.

Bannister, Robert C. *Ray Stannard Baker: The Mind and Thought of a Progressive.* New Haven: Yale University Press, 1966. Biography of the muckraker who worked for McClure's and later for President Wilson.

Bernstein, Carl, and Robert Woodward. *All the President's Men.* New York: Simon and Schuster, 1974. How Watergate was uncovered.

Chalmers, David Mark. *The Muckrake Years.* Reprint of 1974 ed. Melbourne, FL: Krieger, 1980.

———. *The Social and Political Ideas of the Muckrakers.* New York: Citadel Press, 1964. A study of thirteen muckrakers at the turn of the century.

Downie, Leonard, Jr. *The New Muckrakers.* New York: The New Republic Book Company, 1976; distributed by E. P. Dutton. The new age of muckraking that culminated with Watergate.

Dygert, James H. *The Investigative Journalist.* Englewood Cliffs, NJ: Prentice-Hall, 1976. Brief profiles of modern-day investigative reporters and their stories.

Filler, Louis. *The Muckrakers: Crusaders for American Liberalism.* University Park, PA: Pennsylvania State University Press, 1976. Muckraking at the turn of the century.

Harrison, John M., and Harry H. Stein, eds. *Muckraking: Past, Present and Future.* University Park, PA: Pennsylvania State University Press, 1973. The failures and accomplishments of muckraking from 1900 to the present.

Johnson, Michael L. *The New Journalism.* Lawrence, KS: University of Kansas Press, 1971. Defines and explores the alternative and underground press, with some references to muckrakers of the 1960s.

Kaplan, Justin. *Lincoln Steffens: A Biography.* New York: Simon and Schuster, 1974. The life of the famous muckraker.

Lubars, Walter, and John Wicklein. *Investigative Reporting: The Lessons of Watergate.* Boston: Boston University School of Public Communications, 1975.

Lyon, Peter. *Success Story: The Life and Times of S. S. McClure.* New York: Scribners, 1963. Biography of the muckraking magazine publisher.

Semonche, John E. *Ray Stannard Baker.* Chapel Hill: University of North Carolina Press, 1969. A biography of the early muckraker.

Shapiro, Herbert, ed. *The Muckrakers and American Society.* Lexington, MA: D. C. Heath, 1968. A collection of articles by and about the early muckrakers.

Steffens, Lincoln. *The Autobiography of Lincoln Steffens.* New York: Harcourt, Brace and Company, 1931.

Swados, Harvey. *Years of Conscience: The Muckrakers.* Cleveland: World Publishing, 1970. A collection of muckraking articles from the turn of the century.

Weinberg, Arthur and Lila, eds. *The Muckrakers: The Era in Journalism that Moved America to Reform.* New York: Putnam, Capricorn Books, 1964. An anthology of the most significant articles of 1902–1912.

Wilson, Harold S. *McClure's Magazine and the Muckrakers.* Princeton, NJ: Princeton University Press, 1970.

Winter, Ella, ed. *Joseph Lincoln Steffens.* New York: Harcourt, Brace and Company, 1938. The letters of Lincoln Steffens.

Recent Investigative Work

Bartlett, Donald, and James Steele. *Empire.* New York: W. W. Norton, 1979. The life of Howard Hughes.

Brown, Michael. *Laying Waste: The Poisoning of America by Toxic Chemicals.* New York: Washington Square Press, Pocket Books, 1981. A groundbreaking look at the health problems of Love Canal and other toxic waste dump sites that made them a national issue.

Caro, Robert A. *The Power Broker.* New York: Alfred A. Knopf, 1974. How Robert Moses changed the face of New York through the use of unchecked public agencies.

_____. *The Years of Lyndon Johnson.* New York: Alfred A. Knopf, 1983. LBJ's rise to power with the help of private interests.

Carson, Rachel. *The Silent Spring.* Boston: Houghton Mifflin, 1962. Man's destruction of the environment.

Conway, Mimi. *Rise Gonna Rise: A Portrait of Southern Textile Workers.* New York: Doubleday, 1979. An investigation of work conditions in southern textile mills.

Foley, Lin. *Sexual Shakedown.* New York: Warner Books, 1980. The first book to expose sexual harassment as a major occupational hazard for women.

Frankfort, Ellen, and Frances Kissling. *Rosie: The Investigation of a Wrongful Death.* New York: Dial Press, 1979. The cover-up surrounding the death of the first woman to die of an illegal abortion after the cutoff of federal funds.

Fuller, Chet. *I Hear Them Calling My Name: A Journey Through the New South.* Boston: Houghton Mifflin, 1982. An investigation of poverty in the "New South" that serves as a textbook on undercover reporting.

Hersh, Seymour. *Cover-Up.* New York: Random House, 1972.   The army's secret investigation of the massacre at My Lai 4.

_____. *My Lai 4: A Report on the Massacre and Its Aftermath.* New York: Random House, 1970.   The horror of the Vietnam War which helped turn public opinion against the fighting.

_____. *The Price of Power: Kissinger in Nixon's White House.* New York: Summit Books, 1983.   How Henry Kissinger manipulated power under Richard Nixon.

Howe, Louise Dapp. *Pink Collar Workers: Inside the World of Women's Work.* New York: Avon Books, 1977.   A three-year probe into the working conditions and inequities of "pink-collar" jobs: sales, office work, waitressing, and others.

Lewis, Sasha. *Slave Trade Today: American Exploitation of Illegal Aliens.* Boston: Beacon Press, 1979.   How American interests encourage undocumented workers to migrate to jobs in the United States, where they are denied basic human rights.

Marchetti, Victor, and John D. Marks. *The CIA and the Cult of Intelligence.* New York: Alfred A. Knopf, 1974.   The CIA censored parts of this exposé of intelligence work.

Mendelson, Mary Adelaide. *Tender Loving Greed.* New York: Random House, Vintage Books, 1974.   An exposé of nursing-home scandals that helped start investigations throughout the country.

Mintz, Morton, and Jerry S. Cohen. *America Inc.* New York: Dell, Delta, 1971.

_____. *Power Inc.* New York: Viking Press, 1976.   Who owns and operates wealth in the United States and how that power has been misused.

Mitford, Jessica. *Kind and Usual Punishment: The Prison Business.* New York: Alfred A. Knopf, 1973.   The prison system uncovered.

_____. *Poison Penmanship.* New York: Alfred A. Knopf, 1979.   A collection of Mitford's best investigative articles, with comments about how they were done.

Morgan, Dan. *The Merchants of Grain.* New York: Viking Press, 1979.   The giant companies that sell crops.

Nader Ralph. *Unsafe at Any Speed.* New York: Grossman, 1965.   The famous exposé of the auto industry that launched Naderism.

Reece, Ray. *The Sun Betrayed.* Boston: South End Press, 1979.   Corporate attempts to undermine the development of solar energy.

Scott, Rachel. *Muscle and Blood.* New York: E. P. Dutton, 1974.   How 100,000 workers are killed by their jobs each year.

Stone, I. F. *The Haunted Fifties.* New York: Random House, 1963.   A collection of pieces from Stone's newsletter between 1953 and 1961.

Thompson, Jerry. *My Life in the Klan.* New York: G. P. Putnam's Sons, 1982.   A reporter infiltrates the Klan and reveals its growing threat as a paramilitary organization.

Woodward, Robert, and Scott Armstrong. *The Brethren.* New York: Simon and Schuster, 1979.   Inside the Supreme Court.

Books by Center for Investigative Reporting Staff and Associates

Gordon, Suzanne. *Black Mesa: The Angel of Death.* New York: Harper and Row, John Day, 1973.   The destruction of wilderness areas for energy development.

————. *Lonely in America.* New York: Simon and Schuster, 1976.   How loneliness plagues Americans.

————. *Off Balance: The Real World of Ballet.* New York: Pantheon, 1983.   Exploitation and dependency in the ballet world.

Kaplan, David, ed. *Nuclear California: An Investigative Report.* San Francisco: Greenpeace/Center for Investigative Reporting, 1982.   The nuclear dangers found in California.

Kohn, Howard. *Who Killed Karen Silkwood?* New York: Summit Books, 1981.   An investigation into the famous death and subsequent lawsuit.

Pell, Eve, ed. *Maximum Security: Letters from Prison.* New York: E. P. Dutton, 1972.   A collection of letters describing conditions in California's toughest prisons.

Pell, Eve, with Paul Jacobs and Saul Landau. *To Serve the Devil: Natives & Slaves,* 2 vols. New York: Random House, 1971.   A documentary history of ethnic groups in the United States.

————. *The Big Chill* (working title). Boston: Beacon Press, 1984.   Free speech and censorship since the election of Ronald Reagan.

Rosenberg, Howard. *Atomic Soldiers.* Boston: Beacon Press, 1979.   Why the military exposed hundreds of thousands of soldiers to possible radiation danger during the U.S. atmospheric atomic testing program.

Weir, David, and Mark Schapiro. *Circle of Poison.* San Francisco: Institute for Food and Development Policy, 1981.   Banned pesticides are exported overseas to return in the food we eat.

Index